THE DUBLIN PAPER WAR OF 1786-1788

(Ed.) *A Festschrift for Francis Stuart on his Seventieth Birthday*
(Dolmen Press, 1972)

Sheridan Le Fanu and Victorian Ireland
(Clarendon Press, 1980; 2nd, enlarged edition Lilliput Press, 1991)

(Ed. with A.J. Stead) *James Joyce and Modern Literature*
(Routledge and Kegan Paul, 1982)

*Ascendancy and Tradition
in Anglo-Irish Literary History from 1789 to 1939*
(Clarendon Press, 1985)

The Battle of the Books: Two Decades of Irish Cultural Debate
(Lilliput Press, 1987)

(Ed.) Austin Clarke *Selected Poems*
(Penguin Classics, 1992)

*Dissolute Characters: Irish Literary History
through Balzac, Le Fanu, Yeats and Bowen*
(Manchester University Press, 1993)

POETRY BY HUGH MAXTON

Stones (Figgis, 1970)

The Noise of the Fields (Dolmen, 1976)

Jubilee for Renegades (Dolmen, 1982)

At the Protestant Museum (Dolmen, 1986)

The Puzzle Tree Ascendant (Dedalus, 1988)

*Between:
Selected Poems of Agnes Nemes Nagy Translated into English*
(Corvina and Dedalus, 1988)

The Engraved Passion: New and Selected Poems 1970-1991
(Dedalus, 1991)

FICTION

A Wild Night at the Avondale Hotel
(Cathair Books, 1991)

THE DUBLIN PAPER WAR OF 1786-1788

A BIBLIOGRAPHICAL AND CRITICAL INQUIRY

Including An Account of the Origins of
Protestant Ascendancy and its 'Baptism' in 1792

W. J. Mc CORMACK

IRISH ACADEMIC PRESS

This book was typeset by Koinonia Ltd., Manchester, for
IRISH ACADEMIC PRESS LTD
Kill Lane, Blackrock, Co. Dublin, Ireland.

A catalogue entry for this book
is available from the British Library.

ISBN 0-7165-2505-4

Printed in Ireland by Colour Books Ltd., Dublin

PREFACE

This book is published to mark the bicentenary of the passing in the Irish Parliament of the Catholic Relief Act (1793). Hobart's Act, or '33 Geo III c. 21' as it used to be known familiarly to historians, extended the parliamentary franchise to Catholics, enabled to them to hold civil and military offices from which they had been long excluded, and removed the statutory bar to their taking university degrees. These measures, following on Langrishe's Act of the previous year, constituted important stages in the emancipation of Catholics from the penal code.

Celebration of their bi-centenary on 9 April 1993 is wholly appropriate. But at a time when commemoration has become a virtual industry, it may be appropriate also to consider these events in a more reflective manner than is now customary. For the votes cast in the houses of Commons and Lords were neither liberal gestures nor dramatic symbols; they were the consequence of prolonged debate, initiated beyond the walls of the parliament, expounded and resisted in pamphlet, pulpit and newspaper, subjected to all manner of criticism and analysis varying from philosophical disquisition to personal invective. Nor was the debate exclusively an Irish one—there were British and American dimensions, and (increasingly) a continental context with France as its epicentre.

Some readers will recognise that an exchange of opinion, conducted through the columns of academic journals is herein consolidated. The debate might be likened to that which (implicitly) occurred between R. E. Burns and Maureen Wall thirty years ago on the subject of the Penal Laws. Crudely summarised, Burns sought to show that the code was 'one of the most persistent legislative efforts ever undertaken to change a people' while Wall argued that Irish protestants had made little effort at conversion and were more concerned to maintain the *status quo* of denominational proportions. Summarised in terms of method rather than conclusion, the two offer a different and potentially more illuminating contrast. Burns was keen to stress the importance of philosophical influences—notably of John Locke—while Wall presented empirical evidence from the working lives of Catholic farmers and businessmen, together with

consideration of their neighbourly relations with protestants. Here, in the
backwaters of Irish historical research, we find Theory and Practice locked in
unconscious combat. As Sean Connolly has pointed out, Burns's work has not so
much been refuted as ignored.

The Dublin Paper War (which might have been sub-titled *For This Relief Much
Thanks*) seeks to bring several different kinds of analysis to bear on the pre-
history of the relief acts, with special reference to the evolution of a political
rhetoric, or rhetorics, appropriate to the several contending parties. In its
diversity of method, it stands in contrast to the essentially narrative account
advanced by Thomas Bartlett in *The Fall and Rise of the Irish Nation; the Catholic
Question 1690-1830* (1992) which appeared too late to be absorbed into the
structure of my argument. Essentially, I argue that the great dispute surrounding
Richard Woodward's 1786 pamphlet on *The Present State of the Church of Ireland*
did not see the emergence of a coherent 'protestant ascendancy' ideology, for all
that the term may be found *in a few* of the ninety or so publications constituting
the paper war. Catholic relief, in the early 1790s, was possible partly because no
such ideology had seized the commanding heights of debate, though the 1792
parliamentary exchanges clearly show its rapid development in the face of reform.

If there is one feature of the book requiring emphasis, that should be identified
as its sustained concern with an active theoretical treatment of historical and
critical problems. 'Theory', despite the quotation marks which invisibly distinguish it on the lips of some advocates, is not some exotic mental activity
conducted in an empirical vacuum: on the contrary, it is critical practice
operating from an initial and persistent engagement with the terms and conditions of its own reflexivity. If that sounds abstract, I can only hope that the pages
which follow demonstrate the kind of self-conscious and self-critical activity
which I believe to be a proper exercise of theoretical work in historical research.
Some literary aspects of Irish engagements with Critical Theory are dealt with in
the Introduction. Other particular differences with Bartlett, and with James
Kelly, are aired in the 'Afterword' below and in the notes thereto. These latter
repeatedly focus on the confusion of term and concept in discussing protestant
ascendancy and in no other way complicate the presentation of evidence. Apart
from these features of the 'Afterword', I believe that each chapter of the present
book indicates plainly the approaches adopted therein, and no further explanation
of my procedures is required here.

Other kinds of clarification deserve notice, however. 'All art is a collaboration,'
said John M. Synge. The arts of scholarship demonstrate the truth of this
proposition with especial clarity. In particular, I wish to thank warmly—Charles
Benson, Vincent Kinane and the staff of the Department of Early Printed Books
in the library of Trinity College Dublin; Bridget Dolan and the library staff of the
Royal Irish Academy; Paula Howard and Maire Kennedy of Dublin City Library;
Dr Ray Refaussé of the library, Representative Church Body; Mrs Muriel
McCarthy of Archbishop Marsh's Library; Evan Salhome, librarian in Saint
Patrick's College, Drumcondra; Penny Woods, the Russell Library, Saint

Patrick's College, Maynooth; the staff generally of the National Library of Ireland, the Special Collections room in the library of Queen's University Belfast, the library of the Union Theological College, Belfast, the Boole Library in University College Cork, and the Rare Books room in the University Library, Cambridge.

Naturally, I have greatly benefitted from the published works of several historians who have made the period within which I have focused this inquiry the subject of their own concern. Among these I should name with gratitude Thomas Bartlett, Maurice Bric, James Donnelly, Jacqueline Hill, James Kelly, Gerard O'Brien and Eamon O'Flaherty, while reserving the right to disagree on points— and sometimes principles—of interpretation. It is encouraging to note that in the more recent 'paper war' to which they and I have contributed over the past few years, such disagreements have been conducted with frankness and without rancour. I should like gratefully to specify that, while Dr Kelly and I have been at odds on this topic, we have quietly got on with collaborative work of a different kind in another connection.

Individuals who have informally provided information, guidance or simply help in time of trouble included Maria Bagramian, Trevor Butterworth, Ciaran Brady (repeatedly), Nuala and Louis Cullen, David Dickson, J. B. Lyons, Simon Mc Cormack, Eugene Mallon, and Hilary Pyle. In their case gratitude is extended to cover affable comradeship as well as professional support. Of John Cronin, I would like to say that nobody has done more to keep me on the straight and narrow of private research.

Aspects of the topic have been treated in other publications, notably in the pages of the journal *Eighteenth Century Ireland / Iris an Dá Chultúir* and in the *Field Day Anthology of Irish Writing*. To Ian Ross and Seamus Deane, editors respectively of these, I am grateful for permission to incorporate in amended form some earlier material.

Above all, however, I am happy to acknowledge the example of Mary Pollard, whose sustained dedication to meticulous scholarship has never prevented her from a generous engagement on behalf of humane (and so, too often, unfashionable) values. Her critical support at a much earlier stage of my preparation for this and related work has been matched by a willingness to read a typescript even at the cost of disrupting the projects of her retirement. Aware of the degree to which I fail to meet her standards in bibliographical matters, I should nevertheless distort a vital truth if she were not identified as the pre-eminent influence.

CONTENTS

DO HISTORY AND CRITICISM MEET?

> *Treasure as your granite heart this gem*
> *What I sought was the just truth.*
> AGNES NEMES NAGY

In 1695, Pierre Bayle commenced publication of his *Dictionnaire critique et historique*. Two years before the great work appeared, the compiler, a Huguenot exile, had been removed from a Rotterdam chair of philosophy in consequence of another publication. Despite the vicissitudes of his career, Bayle may claim to have given shape to a distinctive Enlightenment project. Posthumously, he became a leader of European thought in the era leading up to the French Revolution.

Without Bayle, the foundation of the Royal Irish Academy in 1785 would have been unthinkable. Even more locally, we can note the battered sets of his dictionary—usually in English translation—which still turn up in the dispersed libraries of Irish eighteenth-century houses. Yet only a bold commentator would hazard an opinion on Bayle's influence in the 'big house' world of the 'protestant ascendancy'. The history of ideas, as practised in Ireland, has concentrated on ideas of a more recent kind—nationalism, romantic regionalism, even the Irish mind. As a result, the language in which I have summarised the difficulties of assessing Bayle's influence is itself riddled with further difficulties. What do we mean by 'big house' or 'Catholic relief'? Blessed with an Irish rather than Dutch retreat, Bayle would rephrase the questions until they addressed issues not just of meaning but of usage. Thus, he might ask—'What did your ancestors mean when they used the term . . . which ancestors used it and which didn't . . . how can we establish the degree to which one usage differed`in implication from another separated in historical time, or across social class, or whatever?'

Irish historiography is conducted almost exclusively in the English language. That is to say, its normal discourse appears to be identical with that of English or—at a pinch—American commentary in the same professional area. Yet within this 'normal discourse', there are prominent terms which are regarded as special, even unique, to the Irish situation. The intimacy with which an Irish social historian, writing about the nineteenth century, can enunciate notions of *The Big House* is taken to indicate a *higher* degree of normality in his discourse. Yet no one seems to have checked for criteria agreed upon as to how this term is used—a) by historians, b) by their lay contemporaries, and c) by earlier commentators whether lay or professional. Bayle's method, one might interject, would have required a *critique* of one's procedures to figure as one of those procedures.

The Irish scholarly situation is far from unique. A suspicion of philosophising is ever present in the reflections of English historians. As an indication of their attitudes towards German *Begriffsgeschichte* (concept history), Professor John Hexter has coined the term 'begriffstricken'. Ironically, it is precisely the procedures of 'concept history' which may assist us to explore the gap between the normal discourse of Irish historiography and the bewitchingly undefined local terms which distinguish the discourse from that of Hexter, Elton, and the English others. Fortunately, an interdisciplinary spirit is now giving rise to a stricter attention to the methodological issues involved, and both English and American scholars are developing a valuable debate on political concepts and their history. This, together with some encouraging work of a comparative nature, focused on the period under examination in these pages, may yet set an example for labourers in the Irish haggard.[1]

Nor is history and historiography the sole Irish area in which problems of methodology are discernible. Conventional literary criticism in Ireland, or about Irish subjects, breaks down under scrutiny into two contrasting practices. On the one hand, there is a large and growing body of commentary which accepts without question the positive value of literature, even of what it concedes to be literature of the second rank. This maintains a steady flow of expository works, introductions and summaries by which authors from Jonathan Swift to Jennifer Johnston are rendered accessible to the general reader. Figures of the scale of Yeats, Joyce, and Beckett feature in this body of devotional reading, but the studies devoted to them by such commentators are rarely accepted outside Ireland as *significant* criticism. This is perhaps the literary critical equivalent of antiquarianism, where knowledge is preferred before understanding, simple answers valued above complex questions.

On the other hand, there is a contrasting body of critical work which is unconcerned with the issue of value because it is already deeply committed to a professional practice. Joyce's mediaevalism is neither less nor more significant than Yeats's masks or Beckett's boils. Methodologically, this work is often highly sophisticated—and equally demoralised. The influence of Deconstruction may be detected here, though there are other, more strictly professional, pressures at work also. Much of this commentary originates in America, or with teachers and critics who have worked in America. It fits uneasily into the local situation, even when a laying on of hands has been ordained in Oxbridge. It has the effect of re-orienting the study of literature towards such sub-fields or specialised areas as film and the playthings of post-modernist couturiers. It has officially abjured history and, on sight of the historical comment bobbing on the surface (what else?) of post-modernist 'discourse', one is almost relieved by this abjuring.

These are, as I have said, the conventional practices of literary criticism in Ireland. Enthusiasts and cynics may require each other more than they admit, but they also exclude much that is of greater intellectual point. One might point to three practitioners of a different order—Terence Brown, Seamus Deane, and, pre-eminently, Denis Donoghue. Behind each of these, one notes a clearly if not loudly enunciated affiliation. In Donoghue's case, it amounts to a religious conviction, a subscription voluntarily and specifically to Roman Catholicism, and more broadly to the transcendental. Deane's critical and editorial enterprises rarely omit evidence of a political commitment, usually but not always one which is more specific than a commitment to politics as such. Terence Brown's cultural history revolves round an attachment to certain values, notably those of civil rights in areas involving censorship and free expression, sexuality and repression, domestic privacy and so forth, with history serving as a resource of authenticated instances. Each of these figures might be thought of as practicing what Richard Rorty has called 'edifying' philosophies—if the term philosophy can be permitted in what are for the most part still fields of *ad hoc* activity. One may not wish to be edified along Deanean, Brownian or Donoghuist lines, but it makes a change from the district court advocacy of literature's celebrants and the tenured cynicism of deconstructionists.

The edifying characteristic is associated by Rorty with the work of John Dewey, Martin Heidegger, and Ludwig Wittgenstein—an oddly disparate group of thinkers, in my eyes. Yet Rorty is concerned to show that 'the attempt to edify (ourselves or others) may consist in the hermeneutic activity of making connections between our own culture and some exotic culture or historical period, or between our own discipline and another discipline which seems to pursue incommensurable aims in an incommensurable vocabulary.'[2] So far so very good. But there is a quietist strain in Rorty's edification, despite his enlightened comments on the social world in which philosophy takes place. If one were to look for 'edification' theories in twentieth-century thought, surely the work of Theodor Adorno must be considered. I mean in particular his resistance to that abandonment of conceptuality which characterised his prestigious contemporaries, notably Martin Heidegger who is occasionally invoked in Irish debates as a guarantor of a more direct and intimate contact with 'reality'. And so we return to the question of Enlightenment, symbolised here in Bayle's critical dictionary.

The trajectory of Enlightened ideas, from the days of heroism and persecution to those of functionalism and (indeed) lethal mobilisation in the name of an instrumental rationality, provided Adorno with a central and deeply pessimistic theme. In tracing these movements, we are engaged (consciously or otherwise) in following epochal changes in concepts (e.g. reason, causality, etc.) too often thought invariable. Attention to concepts requires the strictest attention to vocabulary, to individual words, and to the grammars and syntaxes in which they operate. In surveying the pre-history of some enlightened Irish legislation of the 1790s, the present book necessarily examines the early stages of one such concept—'protestant ascendancy'—and as a consequence much close reading is involved. Indeed, the discipline of bibliography in something like its professional sense has been recruited to assist more conventional forms of historical and literary research. For too many, bibliography even at the elementary level managed here is an exotic, incommensurable discipline.

The notion of the Anglo-Irish protestant ascendancy—to use a longer formulation than that interrogated in the course of this book—is so familiar as to be virtually transparent. Political pundits, historians, poets, interested laymen—all have utilised the term to indicate (in what has seemed an agreed manner) the top brass in eighteenth-century Ireland. The poet W. B. Yeats has certainly been as influential as any sociologist or professional historian in maintaining the term in use. In the more frequently cited of his several characterisations of the protestant ascendancy, it constituted a necessarily incomplete, but admirably responsible, Irish sub-platoon of European Enlightenment. So much is gratifying—provided that inquiry can sustain Yeats's point. But Yeats also speaks of cruelty and efficiency as characteristics of the protestant ascendancy, achieving in a brief account of the eighteenth-century past a miniature (and reverse-directed) replication of that trajectory from the Republique des Lettres to Auschwitz which Adorno suspected to be an Enlightenment legacy.

To speak of Yeats is to invoke the authority of poetry where heretofore we have pointed merely to the disciplines of historical or philosophical analysis. If Bayle stands for one important aspect of eighteenth-century intellectual activity, then Alexander Gottlieb Baumgarten may stand for another. In the 1750s Baumgarten wrote a long work on notions of the beautiful which gave the literary languages of Europe the term 'aesthetics'. Baumgarten taught Immanuel Kant, and from that fount of German philosophy there flows a gathering tradition of critical activity in which the work of literature is increasingly abstracted into isolated splendour.

It is true that so nimble a dialectician as Ernst Bloch could argue that Baumgarten's initiative actually 'began with a clear contempt for its object.' And 'even if beauty represented perfection in this area, it was not comparable to the value of conceptual cognition and its comprehensive clarity.'[3] Nevertheless, the outflow of this tradition has been the New Criticism, the valorisation of 'the verbal icon', and in general the elaboration of a heightened notion of high literature, embodied in certain formalised genres—lyric poem, novel and, trailing badly, drama. If Edmund Burke's essay *On the Origins of Our Ideas of the Sublime and Beautiful* (1756) strikes one as too psychologically grounded to takes its place in the chronicles of aestheticism, then a close reading of *Reflections on the Revolution in France* (1790) may reveal the arena in which he hypostasised objects of contemplation. Politics turned aesthetic in Burke long before the notion occurred to Walter Benjamin.

As Bloch indicates, the real significance of the aesthetic initiative was the driving an edge between beauty and knowledge: literature, in other words, is denied cognitive power and compensated by elevation into a quasi-transcendental realm of privilege. Much of Adorno's concern with literature was devoted to the recovery of something like such power, in the arts generally, to know the world, with Samuel Beckett providing the unlikely occasion for one of his lengthier endeavours.[4] Adorno and Beckett, however, come together in the wake of Enlightenment's eclipse. Yeats, with his inverted formula of cruelty and responsibility, lies within the protective shadow of an eighteenth century partly of his own invention.

The doctrines of aesthetic privilege have unwittingly given an alibi for these historiographic rewritings. No critic of Yeats has had the temerity to suggest that 'Parnell's Funeral', and the elaborate commentary that surrounds it, should be tested for cognitive accuracy. In particular, the poet's employment of the notion of protestant ascendancy has been approved in Baumgartian and not analysed in Baylean terms. A still inchoate term of social description, descending uncertainly from the eighteenth century, was given the status of a literary icon. Ironically, it was in the decade of Yeats's most trenchant rewriting of the age of Swift, Berkeley, Goldsmith, Burke, Grattan and 'the protestant ascendancy'—the 1930s—that Irish historiography began to undergo a modernisation of attitude and procedure.[5] Until recently, however, the eighteenth century experienced fewer of the benefits of this revolution than later periods. As a consequence, 'the protestant ascendancy' has survived as a seemingly unremarkable element in the discourse of historians, critics, and ordinary human beings.

A Canadian historian of ideas in the eighteenth century has remarked that 'modern scholarship has stressed the phenomenon of public opinion rather than the concept.'[6] The same could be said of Irish practice generally. Yet one cannot investigate the phenomenon of—say—protestant ascendancy (as it allegedly flourished in Swift's day) without formulating some concept of it by which the investigation is carried out. Yet if the historian conscientiously defines such a professional concept how can he ensure that it is at all times distinguishable from the ideological catch-cry (or more) he finally locates in a period much later than Swift's? The concept history of Reinhart Koselleck offers an impressive series of models for emulation, though it is neither possible nor desirable that the problems specific to one culture should simply be treated according to the prescriptions of another—possibly contrastive—culture.[7] At the same time, reliance on the transparent rightness of those seemingly intimate terms of description—'the big house', 'the quality', 'emancipation', 'Home Rule', 'Parnellite'—can decline into thoughtless dependence. With reservations which do not require ritual invocations of the Frankfurt Critical Theorists, we may regard *Begriffsgeschichte* as the latter-day equivalent of Bayle's critical method.

Certainly the German undertaking lies closer to Bayle than does the New English Dictionary (first proposed 1857) which in turn has become today's renowned Oxford English Dictionary. It has been tempting at times to settle arguments about the currency of terms by reference to the latter. But unlike Bayle, the compilers of OED were indiscriminate (or nearly so) in accommodating all words. Here analysis operates upon an etymological rather than critical basis; the compiler remains wholly passive before the evidence though—in practice—he has quietly ignored entire zones of language in making his selections. Of these zones, the intimate vocabulary of Irish social description proves to be one, and that despite the involvment of several Irish researchers in the original preparation of the dictionary.[8] One has to note what certain tools refuse to do before concluding that they *cannot* do these things.

Concentrating on the late eighteenth century and yet implicating Yeats, this essay must give the appearance of dealing in what some philosophers and historians of political thought call 'concept change'. Perhaps so. But, for the moment, it is necessary to consider—first, what distinguishes a casual from a conceptual use of terms; second, the degree to which the term in question (protestant ascendancy) had currency in the 1780s and early 1790s. The evidence suggesting a down-turn in frequency of use, in the first half of the nineteenth century, will have to wait.[9]

But not, I believe, a search for greater certainty and an augmentation of knowledge, for all that historians have grown wary of claiming access to the truth about past events. In this they have been implicitly supported by the genial scepticism of contemporary philosophers. As for professional critics of literature, what have they ever desired above a further refinement of their own sensibilities? It is time to introduce the disciplines to each other, for without some such encounter none of them has a subject.[10]

I should emphasise that the present work is not a Rortyfied version of what I have done before. Far from it. In practice, I have found Saul Kripke's style of philosophising more helpful—and must, in any case, plead that these are instances of heuristic borrowings in the cause of exposing the pretentious complacency of common sense. Ideally, one would wish to practice some form of critique as suggested by Bayle and commended by Adorno. But that smacks of a different pretension, or at least ignores a different set of problems thrown up by the immediate circumstances in which I find myself. One can only work within the specific conditions of one own's upbringing and experience, and strive to ensure that these are not simply accretions but experiments, hazardous extensions of the frontier we share with ignorance.

These conditions are never wholly imposed nor immune to self-reflexion for, as Thomas Mann remarked in the foreword to *Joseph and His Brothers*, 'No one remains quite what he was when he recognizes himself.'[11] A poet far away may posit notions of 'the just truth', and no response can be attempted other than further effort, the confession of failure and error, and further effort.

SOME PHILOSOPHICAL CONSIDERATIONS

I. STATUS QUO ANTE BELLUM

The question of Catholic Relief naturally did not arise, in the first instance, in the establishment from which Catholics were excluded. The earliest stages of the argument in favour of relief are not our concern here. Instead, we shall concentrate on a relatively brief phase in which contending arguments—call them the reformist and conservative, if you like—are so completely engaged with each other that the issue of linguistic usage becomes a battle field in itself. Thus, to understand the pre-history of the Relief Acts of 1792 and 1793, one has to examine how opposition to these proposals (now enjoying an increasing degree of official support in the transformed context of Britain's struggle with revolutionary France) sought to define itself and, in so doing, to establish codes of normative discourse.

Research in this area of political rhetoric has been under way for more than a decade. Commencing with a conference paper delivered in July 1981, an argument has developed challenging the traditional view that a clearly defined social elite known as the protestant ascendancy ruled in Ireland since the victory of King William at the Boyne. Initially, the argument was ignored, discounted and resisted. Then it was—on occasion—confronted. More recently, it has been debated, notably by James Kelly, and something like a consensus offers itself to the original disputant. According to the implicit terms of the consensus, the protestant ascendancy—hero of a thousand theses on the age of Swift and the sagacity of Yeats—is untraceable before the 1780s.

At first glance, the offer is tempting, if only because it would allow one to advance on other, more extensive, inquiries. It would be possible to close down all discussion by agreeing that, while a useful but minor piece of historical revisionism has been accomplished, nothing of major consequence has either been achieved or conceded. Those in favour of the established usage resuming its unruffled procession could argue that an eighteenth-century social elite certainly did exist in Ireland, even if it was not named the protestant ascendancy until some years later. (And even if Yeats would no longer be taken by any historian as a reliable chronicler of its achievements.) The argument has an attractive appearance of common sense to it; after all, we generally believe that things (the planet Neptune, for example, or the quark in physics) existed before they were named or even known. And it is cheerfully conceded here that eighteenth-century Ireland did possess some kind *or kinds* of social elite.

Several considerations advise a closer scrutiny of common sense :

1) Protestant ascendancy did not commence as a historian's term in the professional sense though, at a point yet to be identified, it acquired something of that status. Prior to its acceptance, it would be necessary to agree ground rules for distinguishing between use of the term and the occurrence of the same words in less closely monitored contexts. In particular, such a definition would still be unable, or at least incompletely competent, to distinguish between protestant ascendancy as a quasi-constitutional condition and as a social group, thus to rescue recent commentators from their difficulties.[1]

2) Evidence associated with Sir Boyle Roche and John Giffard gives no support whatever to the view that, in 1782 or 1792, protestant ascendancy was introduced to describe a social group, elite or otherwise. Thus common sense, when it sets up Jonathan Swift as a spokesman for (or from) the protestant ascendancy, is not really back-dating a late-eighteenth-century usage to some relatively adjacent period, for the late usage essentially does not refer to a social group. What common sense is doing is back-dating a usage for which it has yet to produce any date.

3) The same evidence of 1792 etc. has little attachment to landed estate or noble birth or even high station. On the contrary, it is frequently associated with urban and commercial interests, and protestant ascendancy is mocked in contemporary papers for its vulgarity and hypocrisy. To apply glosses borrowed either from Edmund Burke ['a persecuting faction, with a relation of some sort of theological hostility to others'] or from John Philpot Curran ['a little greasy emblem of stall-fed theology'] to Jonathan Swift is hardly to dignify that churchman. More than a discrepancy about dates, more than confusion of principles with social groups, is involved here. There is a quasi-Nietzschean transvaluation at work in the back-dating of protestant ascendancy, by means of which things small and limited, mouldy even, are elevated in a manner which removes all trace of transvaluation.[2]

4) Protestant ascendancy implicates nothing if it does not implicate class, though its impact on class-consciousness may be suffocating rather than supportive. Class is not a physical object, not even an aggregate of human individuals. Class is powerfully altered if the nomination/expression of class is altered. (How incurious the workers were before there were cries of 'What about the workers?') A class (class fraction, unholy alliance or whatever) named or not named is/are two very different 'things'.

5) Acceptance of protestant ascendancy as an unproblematic eighteenth-century elite raises a severe problem of conscience for the historian. What is he or she to do with the protestant ascendancy debates of 1792 and after?

It is not possible to absorb protestant ascendancy's newness in the 1790s, the actual difference inflicted by it then on every other feature of Irish society (the established church, professions, parliamentary rhetoric, the Orange Order, drinking habits, taxation, military discipline) and deny that newness, those changes every time one invokes Jonathan Swift or Francis Hutcheson. Faced with this consequence of common sense historians have had recourse to selectivity in citing the evidence already complained of.

6) And finally, if common sense insists that there was an eighteenth-century elite which was really the protestant ascendancy though the name was delayed in the post, then common sense should promptly supply a receipt for the safe delivery of the item. Yet the terminology of social formations does not refer to things as objects, and the time-table of naming may be more complex, various, reversible, amnesiac, and even incoherent than common sense can tolerate. Is not Samuel Ferguson's apparent ignorance of protestant ascendancy (the social formation he is generally accredited to) except as mnemonic of tap-room loyalism damaging to that argument? And if Ferguson refuses to exemplify what persons wish to find in him, what in fact does lie between 1792 and Yeats's double vision of 1934?

These are objections which deserve consideration, even if the questions raised at the conclusion of the last objection cannot be attended to here and now. Yet it has to be conceded that the urge towards a consensual closing-down of the argument reflects a broader tendency in historiographical debate than the limited focus of the issue of protestant ascendancy would at first suggest.

II. RICHARD RORTY, SAUL KRIPKE, AND GARETH EVANS

Ciaran Brady, introducing a collection of essays significantly titled *Ideology and the Historians*, expresses the belief that

> historical writing is always conducted by means of synecdoche, in the sense that one set of details is selected from the mass of evidence to represent the whole of the phenomenon described. But because such a selection can never be replicated, and because one synecdoche cannot refute another, historical argument can never be 'falsified' in scientific terms.[3]

His more general observations—a) that 'with the exception of those instances where historians have been shown to have misconstrued, misdated or faked their evidence, historical controversies have generally displayed strikingly closed formal patterns;' and b) that 'the inability of the discipline to find the conceptual tools appropriate not for the resolution, but for the analysis, refinement and better comprehension of such disputes is now threatening the very integrity of the craft—'[4] are not directed specifically at professional practice in Ireland, yet strike one as uncomfortably appropriate to the matter in dispute in these pages. It is the search for such conceptual tools as might lead us out of closed formal patterns that introduces Richard Rorty, Saul Kripke and others who concern themselves with questions of language, knowledge, and method. The fiendish technicality of these thinkers should no doubt warn the outsider that he risks misunderstanding their procedures, and there are few examples of the application of such methods to historiographical problems. Yet one assumes that philosophers do fundamentally wish to see their work applied to the solution—or at least, refinement—of specific problems. If the central figures in the philosophy of language construct their models on what strikes the historian as a highly purified basis of a single individual's isolated utterance, there are others—notably Gareth Evans—who acknowledge the social context in which any linguistic performance necessarily is located.

More fashionable today is the philosophical discourse of Richard Rorty who presents the acceptable face of deconstructive postmodernism. His general stance in effect buttresses notions that knowledge is by its nature relative, partial and altering, with endorsements of democratic liberalism. He describes his position as *antirepresentationalism*, which holds that attempts to establish the existence of realities independent of mind/language are pointless. Rorty is thus a pragmatist believing one should rather inquire into the conditions in which it will be possible to explain meaning in terms of what would *justify* an utterance. Language—in the form of nouns, verbs, phases and sentences—does not *represent* some extra-linguistic reality, yet our practice of language can lead us to deal meaningfully with our experience of external realities.

Such realities, of course, can be subdivided into distinct categories between which it is important to avoid confusion. For example, we have already noted that a planet and a social group differ in many essentials. Rorty uses such an example to illustrate what he thinks of as a typically *representationalist* notion—

> that the reality referred to by 'quark' was 'determinate' before the word 'quark' came along (whereas that referred to by, for example, 'foundation grant' only jelled once the relevant social practices emerged.)[5]

Rorty is hostile to terms like 'determinate' and what he calls the 'equally baffling words' employed by realists to gloss it. Historians, in so far as they are concerned with causality, have need of some such concept as 'determinacy'. Yet he cites (with apparent approval) W. V. Quine's parallel hostility to the notion of 'conceptuality' itself as a bluffer's way of glossing what is meant by analysis. (Thus Brady's *desiderata*—improvements in the analysis, refinement and comprehension of historical problems—get short shrift from contemporary philosophers of the language-related school.) It is not surprising that Rorty has taken up themes from the work of Heidegger as broadcast to the Franco-American academy through Jacques Derrida. In the end, while his discussion of how arguments proceed may be valuable, the implications for a productive historical argument are not encouraging.

The examples cited by Rorty deserve a little further attention, even from Irish historians keen to be back in the 1780s settling somebody's hash. The quark is definable as 'a fundamental component of matter' of indeterminable mass, and the moment of its naming can be specified with considerable accuracy. Indeed the source of the name is James Joyce's *Finnegans Wake* (1939). On the other hand, given its nature the quark is as old as matter itself. One can argue that even before that moment people believed in some 'fundamental component of matter'—which they may have called atom, element or even God. The naming of the quark registers a drastic *change* in humanity's belief about fundamental components, even though what is named was both inconceivable and existent before that date. Rorty's 'foundation grant' is presented in contrast to the quark, on the grounds that industrial or corporate foundations have only a very recent history. Yet the item thus named requires no new word, merely the combination of existing words in a form pragmatically distinguishable from—say—the items contributing to 'foundation garment' and 'land grant'. Antirepresentationalism shows how no extra-verbal reality is represented by an extra-real word.

The comic difficulty of keeping grants and garments untangled serves to introduce a further strand of recent linguistic philosophy. Deriving from the work of J. L. Austin, John R. Searle's speech-act theory emphasises the importance of intention and effect in any utterance. Thus I cannot utter a meaningful word 'foundation' without intending something specific, whether it relate to building techniques or corporate finance or another of the fields in which the word has meaning. In relation to the receiver, however, things are more complicated, for while I cannot intend an intention other than an intention I intend, I *can* intend an effect other than the effect effected. Irrespective of the speaker's intention, the hearer of the word 'grant' is already primed (so to speak) to anticipate certain (but perhaps not all) possible fields (grammatical, lexical, technical, colloquial etc.) in which it can meaningfully occur. *Prime facie*, there is no difficulty in applying speech-act theory to historical utterances, except in so far as they are accessible solely in written textual form.

It has proved useful to subject the familiar phrase 'the Big House' to close scrutiny in the light of some of these distinctions. What emerged was the existence of a kind of encounter-zone (or zone of difference) through which the phrase may meaningfully pass from transmitter to receiver but only in accordance with certain tabulatable rules. For example, model conversations of this kind were tested:

1 CIARAN: Is that the road that leads to the Big House?
  AOIFE: It is not. The Big House lies to the west of here.

2 AOIFE: Are you the lady from Abbeyshrule?
  THE HON. ELEANOR CODY: I am. I live in the Big House.

3 SIR JACK SCATTERGOOD: Do you have a Big House in this county?
  LORD CANNY: Egad, yes. Canny Close is the name.[6]

It is obvious to any ear tuned to the idiom of Irish social description that the third model is implausible. This is not a philosophical distinction, of course, yet the reasons why we can reject the third while accepting the first and second models may have philosophical implications of value to the historian. Essentially, 'the Big House' is a phrase which can only be used in a context at least partly external to the social structure implicated. Scattergood and Canny's utterances lack respectively the illocutionary and perlocutionary aspects of justifiable usage. It is not the social class of the speaker which determines whether he/she can use the phrase, but rather the encounter-zone into which it is directed. This zone involves either difference of class between speakers (Model 2), or between the speakers and the social structure alluded to (Model 1).[7]

One further latter-day detail requires consideration before we return to the protestant ascendancy. Within the highly specialised work of the philosophers cited above, much attention has been given to problems involving names, especially proper names. Kripke has advanced and investigated the propositions that names are 'designators'. In *Naming and Necessity*, he proposes that we

> call something a *rigid designator* if in every possible world it designates the same object, a *nonrigid* or *accidental designator* if that is not the case.[8]

Historians will not welcome the addition of all possible worlds to the one they contend with now. But if we accept the existence of an eternal divine being, then 'God' is a rigid designator because in all possible worlds [that in which the earth does not exist, that in which pigs fly, etc] the name 'God' designates that being. Kripke offers examples bearing upon historial writing, as when he shows that the phrase 'U. S. President in 1970' is a non-rigid designator in that Humphrey might have been (though Nixon was) elected. Historians' error—the scandal postulated by Ciaran Brady— has philosophical implication.

The topic has a long history. J. S. Mill believed that proper names denote but do not connote. Early in the present century, Bertrand Russell held that proper names are descriptive, even though this may not be evident at first sight or second. More strictly, he held that the meaning of a proper name was a description (or cluster of descriptions) that speakers associate with the name. Thus the meaning of 'Daniel O'Connell' is the Kerry-born lawyer, achiever of Catholic Emancipation, campaigner for Repeal, etc. But Kripke points out that someone might conceivably have done none of the things we associate with his name. (E.g. O'Connell was not 'the father of bastards'.) Applied to scholarly disputes concerning Old Testament figures—if nobody ever lived in a whale does 'Jonah' name anything?—this objection has implications for a historiography still loosely tied to the biographical method.

Our central concern, however, is not with a named individual but something less clearly delineated. Indeed, one of the arguments advanced by James Kelly proposes a something called by several names—'the protestant interest', 'the protestant ascendancy' etc. Philosophers have ways of treating this matter, but they stick to safe examples like Hesperus/Phospherus. I have argued elsewhere that employment of the word, 'ascendancy', with its previous usage closely linked to astrology and its general currency limited in the extreme, inevitably alters the 'thing' it is said passively to name. Kripke tackles the kernel of the matter when he speaks of the 'baptism' of a thing, the point, moment or process whereby it acquires its name. While noting the ironic aptness of Kripke's metaphor, we could refer to the issue at stake between James Kelly and myself as 'the baptism of protestant ascendancy'. Having acquired a few conceptual tools, we should now return to the arena.

III. REFERENCE, REPRESENTATION AND RHETORIC

The first stage in re-assessing the material which constitutes the debate about the origins of protestant ascendancy in opposition to Catholic relief must be a re-assertion of the textual nature of that material. By this is meant not simply a renewed emphasis on its linguistic basis or even on its practical restriction to printed matter. Elsewhere, it has proved useful to recall what the printed report of parliamentary debate is and is not; with modifications, the passage may be applied to pamphlet and newspaper. Print 'palpably is not'

> a register of non-verbal gesture, a bodily graph of irony, a class calculus of accent and tone, a mirror to absence, indifference and misunderstanding, a reception and an active audience.[9]

To complement this negative listing, we should confirm also that

> Evidence cannot be mistaken for what it is evidence of, and what it is evidence of remains mediately accessible. This mediate access is not a dimunition to be lamented or cheated; on the contrary its rich materiality renders it the stuff of a deeper history.[10]

Having thus re-established confidence in the textual status of historical evidence, let us proceed to apply some of the conceptual tools recently acquired to the real problems which persist. James Kelly has invested much in the utterance of Sir Boyle Roche on 20 February 1782, and in the *Parliamentary Register* covering that period we read:

> I beg leave to observe that the honour and faith of parliament seems to me to be pledged to such Roman Catholics as took the test and declaration under the solemn act of this House, to liberate them so far as is consistent with the Protestants [*sic*] ascendency . . . [11]

In the past I have promptly conceded that the last three words quoted here

should rightly be read 'the Protestant ascendency'. Given the extent to which
James Kelly has seized on what is in fact a far less straightforward invocation, I
now want to qualify that concession. The material evidence for doing so is
uncomplicated.[12] A more fruitful interrogation of the problem should take up the
speech-act theorists' questions about intention and effect. What did Roche intend
with these words? We cannot answer that question with anything like certainty or
precision because the words are appearing for the first time, and the parliamentary reports do not indicate anything—except perhaps indifference, imcompre-
hension, or silence—in the nature of an effect among Roche's auditors. A
meaningful utterance, we should insist, is a two-way process. The absence of this
reciprocity, together with variants and omissions at the typographical level, do
not encourage one to see here anything like the baptismal inauguration of a
proper name. Thus ends our attempt to flesh out the mediational relations
betweeen the evidence (report) and what it is evidence of (Roche's intention).

    With George Ogle's utterances of February 1786, we encounter no typo-
graphical crux but rather an opportunity to apply what Kripke calls 'a rough
statement of a theory' in *Naming and Necessity*:

> An initial 'baptism' takes place. Here the object may be named by ostension
> or the reference of the name may be fixed by a description. When the name
> is 'passed from link to link' the receiver of the name must, I think, intend
> when he learns it to use it with the same reference as the man from whom he
> heard it.[13]

    Now it is very far from established that a 'baptism' occurred when Roche
spoke four years earlier, and it is even further from obvious that anything like a
'link to link' authentification of the same reference can be shown to establish Ogle
as taking up Roche's terminology in any exact sense. Antirepresentalionalists
would of course dismiss all these minute inquiries as time wasted, because for
them there is no confirmed or confirmable existence of a 'reference' beyond
language. As with Roche, the printed record does not encourage one to identify a
perlocutionary aspect to Ogle's utterance; there is no legible response or effect
among his immediate auditors. But for the fact that he himself repeats the phrase
'protestant ascendancy' one is dealing again with a wholly isolated rhetorical item.
The repetition indeed may be seen as confirming the rhetorical—and non-
referring—status of the phrase.

    We come next to December 1786 and the publication of Richard Woodward's
pamphlet, *The Present State of the Church of Ireland: Containing a Description of
it's* [sic] *Precarious Situation; and the Consequent Danger to the Public. Recommended to the Serious Consideration of the Friends of the Protestant Interest. To which
are Subjoined, Some Reflections on the Impracticality of a Proper Commutation for
Tithes; and a General Account of the Origin and Progress of the Insurrections in
Munster*. If, as has been suggested, this lengthy production (running to 128pp in
its first edition) marks the inauguration of protestant ascendancy, we must

remark again the absence of all reference to that concept—or even phrase—from the verbose and accommodating title. The importance of distinguishing between the popularity of the pamphlet and that ascribed (by Kelly) to 'protestant ascendancy' appearing within the text on a number of occasions has already been underscored. On the question of the work's printing history between 18 December 1786 and 6 January 1787 (during which the first six so-called 'editions' appeared), extensive detail is provided below (pp. 50–62). On the question of allusions to protestant ascendancy within *The Present State*, we can once again resume a philosophical analysis.

Passages containing these allusions have been republished in *Eighteenth-Century Ireland* (1989) where interested readers are invited to consult them.[14] While there is little point in re-printing them all here yet again, it may be useful to examine two central examples (labelled 'c' and 'e' in the journal article) at closer range:

> c) The principles contained in a Letter to a Noble Lord in this kingdom, circulated at first in manuscript (at a very critical period, when a Bill in favour of the Roman Catholicks was depending) and afterwards printed, which express the wishes of some of the friends of the Roman Catholicks [sic] interest, and are evidently subversive of the Protestant Ascendency, will justify what has been said, with respect to the necessity of excluding Papists, as much as possible, from Political influence.

> e) In the foregoing Sections it has been placed, I conceive, beyond the reach of doubt, that the Ecclesiastical establishment is an essential part of the Constitution of this Kingdom; that the preservation of it is peculiarily interesting to landed property, as well as to the Protestant ascendency which cements this Country with Great Britain; and that the Church of Ireland would not only be stopped in it's [sic] progress to a complete settlement, by any considerable dimunition of the fund for the support of the Clergy, but would sink rapidly more and more below it's [sic] present very imperfect state, till the consequent progress of Popery had entirely overwhelmed it.[15]

A number of points can be made about these two sentences which constitute the longest (of nine) in which protestant ascendancy is invoked in Woodward's essay of *c.* 30,000 words. In the first, Woodward argues that the principles contained in Edmund Burke's *Letter to a Peer of Ireland* (1782) 'are evidently subversive of the Protestant Ascendancy'. But Burke never used the phrase in this *Letter* (and was later highly scornful of it), so we can conclude that Woodward introduced the phrase to represent whatever (in his view) the *Letter* subverted. Accepting for the moment Woodward's account of the *Letter*, we can identify 'the necessity of excluding papists. . . from Political influence' as that referent (call it *NEP*).

In the second example, things are less heavily veiled, and protestant ascendancy is that which 'cements this Country [Ireland] with Great Britain' (call it

IGB). Now, there is a political view in which these are connected, and it could be stated briefly as *IGB so as to make possible NEP*. But it would absurdly tautological to argue that both of these are represented by the phrase 'protestant ascendancy', for that would lead to the proposition *PA so as to make possible PA*.

This is not to deny that Woodward's argument is powerful, but its power is emotive rather than logical or discursive; and his phrase is successively linked to land, to the notion of an established church, to the exclusion of Catholics, to a constitutional link with Britain etc. Protestant ascendancy cannot be identified fixedly with any one of these, but in each case the reader is presented with an association that affects his security or the stability of the society in which he lives. This would appear to create a situation exactly the reverse of that observed by Mill when he said of proper names that they denote but do not connote. In Woodward's practice, protestant ascendancy is prolific in connotations—sometimes touching on property, sometimes on the franchise, sometimes on constitutional matters—while failing the test for the most elementary kind of denotation. One verdict on his practice in this regard might be expressed in terms of intellectual ineptitude, another in terms of rhetorical dexterity.

When we ask the question—'to what is Woodward referring?'—we can only answer negatively, that on this occasion he does not refer to A or B or C, that this other occasion he does not refer to B or C or D, and on a third he does not refer to C or D or E. And so forth. Kripke's account of how baptism is effected, following a link-to-link transmission, concludes with an observation on faulty communication:

> When the name is 'passed from link to link', the receiver of the name must . . . intend when he learns it to use it with the same reference as the man from whom he heard it. If I hear the name 'Napoleon' and decide it would be a nice name for my pet aardvark, I do not satisfy this condition. Perhaps it is some such failure to keep the reference fixed which accounts for the divergence of present uses of 'Santa Claus' from the alleged original use.[16]

This passage is deeply suggestive of the problems involved in a historical discussion like the present one. If we return to the distinction between illocutionary (intention-related) and perlocutionary (effect-related) aspects of a speech-act, we can see that an intention to use a name in the same way as someone else need not necessarily lead to that effect. Of course, in Woodward's practice of a circulating, undefined 'protestant ascendancy', he is both transmitter and receiver. But the example of Santa Claus underlines the problem involved in various kinds of philological and historical change—a knave is not what a knave used to be, and Europe is now frequently used to denote only a portion of what was meant by the same term thirty years ago. The dynamic of altering reference has to be acknowledged in the case of protestant ascendancy. Kripke's conceit of a baptism has its own limitations. Baptised Algernon, I do not easily become Ernest. But the process of baptism involves *agreement* about names (even prior agreement) for, strictly speaking, sponsors provide these names for the unbaptised infant, and answer the priest's inquiry for such names. Consequently the notion of a single naming of the protestant ascendancy, carried out by a single transmitter, is inadequate. What is utterly lacking in Roche, Ogle, and Woodward, is precisely the dimension of reciprocity.

I am aware that, in so arguing, I may be thought guilty of forgetting the non-textual aspect of even the most rudimentary speech act—that bodily graph of response which may be thought of as nods and winks, raised eyebrows, reverent or embarrassed silence. Doubtless, it is impossible to recover more than the slenderest fraction of any such response. Yet there is an extent to which even the cold ems and ens of the printer's trade can be interpreted more fully. In the first of the two sentences from Woodward's *Present State* examined above, there was reference to 'friends of the Roman Catholicks [sic] interest'. At first glance, it looks as if a possessive apostrophe has been omitted by the compositor, who should have set *Roman Catholics' interest*. Yet the phrase, as it actually is in the final printed text, parallels something noted earlier in connection with Sir Boyle Roche's one sentence of February 1782 as reported in the *Parliamentary Register*: I mean the phrase, 'so far as is consistent with the Protestants [*sic*] ascendency'. Now, we know that this is not the only printed report of Boyle's speech, but only this one contains the paralleling detail:

BOYLE	WOODWARD
the Protestants ascendency	the Roman Catholicks interest

What one can (as it were) hear behind these uncertainly conjuncted nouns is the early stage of an emerging coinage. Such finicking details may not immediately appeal to historians fonder of summarising such texts than scrutinising what particularly constitutes them. But, within a bibliographical approach to the question of protestant ascendancy's role in the paper war, finicking is *de rigueur*. Close examination has, for the moment, served simply to alert the reader to the rough-hewn texture of a few isolated phrases of 1782 and 1786. It is worth checking on the claim made for these utterances of 'protestant ascendancy' before proceeding to analyse the paper war in which they occurred:

> In 1782 Boyle Roche and in 1786 Ogle introduced the term 'protestant ascendancy' into political debate. The two were obviously connected but it was not until Bishop Woodward took them up and synthesised them into a forceful and potent argument centring on the contention that the security of Protestantism in Ireland (Protestant ascendancy) was not compatible with awarding full and equal rights to Catholics or, indeed, to Presbyterians that an explicit ideology of 'Protestant ascendancy' can be said to have been conceived.[17]

There is a good deal of confusion here. At one moment, *The Present State* is seen as an argument against reform of the tithe laws, affecting all denominations; yet here it is presented as resistance to extended civil rights for Catholics (and Presbyterians). There had been earlier minor relaxations of the penal code, notably in 1782, but the Whiteboy background to the paper war cannot be easily transformed into a civil rights campaign, though the emphasis on property in Woodward and other pamphleteers reveals the actual relationship between the question of church establishment and an increasingly ideological concern with 'abstract' rights. Here 1789 is unavoidable, and the crucial struggle on the latter issue arose in the early '90s. That will be the moment—not a pre-revolutionary one—when 'an explicit ideology of "Protestant ascendancy" can be said to have been conceived.' To prevent a deft back-dating of this development, it is necessary to resume a close scrutiny of the publications constituting the paper war. Our objective will be to seek out any 'link by link' transmission of the name of the concept under discussion. Perhaps by the addition of bibliography to linguistic analysis it will be possible to break out of the closed formal pattern in historical argumentation lamented by Ciaran Brady.

THE DUBLIN PAPER WAR OF 1786-1788

I. INTRODUCTORY REMARKS

At first glance, the compilation of a title-list presents few problems. The main issues at stake—tithes, the Whiteboy disturbances, the place of the Church of Ireland in national life—have been widely discussed by historians, in a series of well annotated articles. In addition access to eighteenth-century printed material has been greatly improved by a variety of technical innovations in recent years. Yet there still remain difficulties in setting limits as to what lies inside (or should remain outside) the theatre of this paper war. The sequence of pamphlets in which Barber-Answers-Woodward, and then Ryan-Answers-Barber, by no means exhausts the contexts of Woodward's initiative. For example, arguments about a possible union between Great Britain and Ireland, advanced by John Williams of Oxford, are taken up, discussed, opposed in pamphlets which also bear on questions raised in *The Present State of the Church of Ireland*. Or, to take a different instance, we find that the Welshman, Daniel Thomas, answering Woodward, devotes more time to a defence of the Gaelic language than his lordship had in attacking it. Are these developments external to the dispute, or are they not perceptions of its wider implications? In most instances of this kind, I have taken the inclusive rather than exclusive view. Pamphlets touching on American themes might have been included in greater number, but this would have resulted in a loss of focus at least for the present.

I have omitted William Paley's *Principles of Moral and Political Philosophy* (1st ed. 1785) despite the facts that—a) Woodward himself specified it as a publication prompting him to write; b) it was constantly reprinted not only in London but in a Dublin edition; and c) it had been published originally at the urging of the bishop of Clonfert (John Law). My reasons for this were two-fold: first, discussion of Woodward's reaction to Paley requires a different kind of treatment (see pp. 99–106 below; and, second, so large a work (two vols in some editions) could scarcely be regarded as a pamphlet.

On the other hand, one has to recognise that the issues contended for in the paper war were not confined to pamphlets. Newspapers, magazines and parliamentary reports were also involved, not to mention private correspondence, other

forms of manuscript record, and oral performances such as sermons and
unreported speeches. In this connection, I have taken an exclusive view, only
admitting one or two specially printed reports of individual parliamentary
performances by Henry Grattan, virtually as token specimens of that kind of
material. By the same token, it should be conceded that an examination of non-
printed material *might* affect the conclusions reached here concerned the evolution of specific items of political terminology. The present endeavour has been
focused on the determination of what was the status of these *within the public
debates* conducted, first, in the paper war of 1786-88, and then second, in the
corporation resolutions of 1792.

Some readers might prefer a list alphabetized by authors' names. This
conventional option was rejected for several reasons. First, by no means all of the
items can be attributed to known authors. Second, there are varying degrees of
certainty (hence, of uncertainty also) to which some items can be assigned to
known authors. Third, where pseudonyms seem to be used (cf. no. 5 below) it is
not always clear if the phrase might not (as in the case cited) be better regarded
as part of the pamphlet's title. Finally, however, the purpose of the list was not to
establish or demonstrate authorship, but rather to indicate in as neutral a fashion
as possible the range and extent of the pamphlets published over a stated period.
Title has been regarded as the identifying feature, even if this occasionally
involves the inclusion separately of two titles borne by what is virtually the same
text (e.g. nos. 17 and 44, 76 and 77); any other approach would have resulted in
masking the diverse ways in which material was published.

The choice of titles has, of course, been affected by previous decisions in this
area. The Royal Irish Academy and the library of Trinity College Dublin possess
collections of pamphlets which, in their arrangement, tell one a great deal about
past interpretations as what was thought 'relevant' to this paper war and what was
not. The Halliday collection in the Academy includes many duplicates—see vols
493-543 in particular for the material incorporated here—and is swollen in other
ways which are at times informative. (Occasional manuscript notes of attribution
etc. also occur.) The range of pamphlets catalogued at V i 58-66, in Trinity,
provides in contrast a very concentrated collective image of the dispute, with an
understandable emphasis on contributions by writers associated with the College
at the time. I have augmented these principal sources with titles noted in the
National Library of Ireland, and—to a lesser extent—in some other Irish
libraries. A last-minute visit to the University Library in Cambridge allowed me
to confirm many of my findings, and also to absorb valuable manuscript
annotations on one item which, though it lies outside the confines of the paper
war, is drawn by the annotator into dialogue with the question of political
terminology (see below n. 10 to the Afterword.)

In short I have attempted to compile a list of pamphlets in which the issues
raised (or taken up) in Woodward's *Present State of the Church Ireland* are aired.
Some readers may find it too long, other will note omissions which they will want
to see rectified. No attempt has been made to detail all variants (in the matter of

errata slips etc.), and doubtless instances additional to those recorded here will prove useful in further demonstrating the complexity of the war. Communications from readers of this essay will be welcome.

The classifications (NPA, PA, QPA, etc.), at the end of each item below are explained and utilised in a succeeding chapter (see pp. 86ff). BLACK (followed by a number) indicates that the item in question is listed in R. Collison Black, *A Catalogue of Pamphlets on Economic Subjects Published between 1750 and 1900 and now Housed in Irish Libraries*. Belfast: Queen's University, 1969.

II. AN ALPHABETICAL TITLE-LIST

1 An abridgment of the history of the council of Constance, with an appendix concerning Mr O'Leary in which the absolute dispensing power now claimed by the church of Rome is laid open in a letter of one of the pope's [sic], dated 1712. By the rev Philip Le Fanu. Dublin: printed by W M'Kenzie, 1787. 128pp.   NPA

2 An abstract of the number of protestant and popish families in the several provinces and counties of Ireland taken from the returns made by the hearth money collectors to the hearth money office in the years 1732 and 1733; those being reckon'd protestant and popish families where the heads of families are either protestants or papists; with observations. Dublin: printed by M Rhames for R Gunne, 1736; Dublin: reprinted by W Sleater, 1788. 16pp.   NPA

BLACK 1571.

3 An address to the nobility and gentry of the Church of Ireland as by law established explaining the real causes of the commotions and insurrections in the southern parts of this kingdom respecting tithes, and the real motives and designs of the projectors and abettors of those commotions and insurrections, and containing a candid inquiry into the practicability of substituting any other mode of subsistence and maintenance for the clergy of the church established consistent with the principles of reason and justice in the place of tithes. By a layman. Dublin: printed by Henry Watts, 1786. 112pp. [irregular paging between pp 57 and 73.]   NPA

By Patrick Duigenan.
Also 'The second edition with additions'. 1787. 112pp. A new edition was published in 1808.

4 Advice to the protestant clergy of Ireland in which the present dispositions of the public towards them are considered, the pretended and real causes of these dispositions enquired into, and some measures suggested that seem most necessary and expedient at the present juncture to redress the injuries and secure the rights of the clergy. By a layman of the Church of England. Dublin: printed by P Byrne, 1787. 72pp.   NPA

Signs off (p. 66) Euphranor: an RIA copy carries a two-line and half-erased ms annotation which apparently sought to identify Euphranor. Only the initial G of a Christian name, the final s of a surname, and the phrase 'F T C Dublin' can be made out with any certainty. This just might encourage an attribution to Gabriel Stokes— see also below p. 64. However, the Linen Hall Library attributes this to Richard Graves.

The postscript includes a dialogue (pp. 69-72), in the style of George Berkeley's Minute Philosopher, directed against 'gentlemen White-boys'.

BLACK 1491.

5   The anti-tyther. A memorial and remonstrance of the commonwealth of Virginia against a bill proposed in their provincial assembly, entitled 'A bill establishing a provision for teachers of the Christian religion.' Dublin: printed by J Chambers, 1786. 30pp. Text by James Madison (1751-1836).
                                                                                                       NPA

BLACK 1438

6   A brief and candid vindication of the doctrine and present appropriation of tithes deduced from the principles of reason; their real origin, nature and signification represented, the true reasons assigned why Christ could not (with any degree of consistency) have ordained their payment and use, with many suitable observations on the subject in various lights, meriting the attention equally of all sects. In a letter from a gentleman in Munster to a friend in Dublin. Dublin: printed and to be had at Mr Grierson's, 1787. 68pp.   NPA

BLACK 1497.

7   A brief review of the question whether the Articles of Limerick have been violated? By Arthur Browne.   PA

This title was published in two editions, and the relationship between them remains unclear. They are:

a) Dublin: printed for William M'Kenzie, 1788. 104pp.
b) Dublin: printed by William M'Kenzie, 1788. 100pp.

On the title-page of a), there are decorative initials of the bookseller, and the imprint-date is given in roman letters. The copy inspected also has a list of 5 errata printed on p. [103]. The b) edition, which is re-set and not just a re-issue, gives the imprint date in arabic numbers; no errata list found in copies inspected.

8   A candid review of the most important occurrences that took place in Ireland during the last three years in which is comprised: I) the proceedings of the National Convention assembled in Dublin November 1783 and the succeeding year; II) rise and progress of the bill for effectuating a commercial intercourse between the two nations on permanent and equitable principles; III) his grace of Portland's reason for opposing the twenty propositions sent from the Commons to the Lords of England for their consideration; IV) proceedings of the Irish legislature on the twenty propositions transmitted from England; V) opinion of Mr Fox's ministerial character; VI) the

probable consequences of any proposition in the British parliament to an union with the sister nation; VII) the present state of the press in Ireland considered; in a letter addressed to George Stacpoole esq of Grosvenor Place London. Dublin: printed by P Byrne, 1787. 62pp.   NPA

Black attributes this to John Jackman. (The author signs off with the initials I. J. on p. 61. The Cambridge University Library's copy of the Bradshaw Collection catalogue bears a ms annotation noting that D J O'Donoghue inclined towards attributing it to Isaac Jackman; the latter, however, wrote farces.) Also issued, London: J Bell, 1787. 92pp.

BLACK 1524.

9 The choice of evils, or which is best for the kingdom of Ireland, the commercial propositions or a legislative union with Great Britain? Containing a full answer to the secretary of state's letter to the mayor of Cork; the whole pointing to the original source and secondary causes of those disorders which have for so many years infested the south of Ireland; if the causes be not well understood, the application of remedies is the more precarious. Dublin: printed for Luke White, 1787. 108pp.   NPA

Black tentatively attributes this to 'Campbell, — ?' The QUB copy is annotated on the half-title 'Dr Campbell' and this would imply the authorship of William Campbell (see nos. 18 and 91.) However, the present item is not included in a bound volume of some tracts by Campbell (with mss notes by the author) also preserved in QUB.
    Issued in two states: a) with errata detail printed on p. [108], and b) with a paste-on errata slip attached to this page, the slip incorporating the errata in a) plus one additional correction.

BLACK 1500.

10 A compendious view of revealed religion as delivered in the gospel, with the grounds of the Christian's faith; to which is added a concise and authentic account of the reformation on which important event the civil rights and true happiness of these kingdoms so essentially depend; some occasional observations are interspersed in this little treatise on the pamphlets which have been lately written by the rev Mr Barber, the rev Mr O'Leary, and the rev William Campbell DD. By Isaac Ashe. Dublin: printed by W Sleater, 1787. 132pp.   NPA

The RIA and NLI copies have 9 errata printed on t-p verso; with a lengthy erratum/addendum on p. [132] giving material omitted from p. 72. (Re pointing-hand device on t-p, see no. 86 below.)

11 A congratulatory address to his majesty from the peasantry of Ireland, vulgarly denominated White Boys or Right Boys. Dublin: printed by P Byrne, 1786. 20pp.   NPA

BLACK 1502.

12 Considerations on the political and commercial circumstances of Great-

Britain and Ireland as they are connected with each other, and on the most probable means of effecting a settlement between them tending to promote the interests of both and the advantages of the British empire. Dublin: printed by P Byrne, 1787. 84pp.   NPA

Also issued London: J. Debrett, 1787. 106pp.

BLACK 1504.

13 Considerations on the present disturbances in the province of Munster, their causes, extent, probable consequences and remedies. By Dominick Trant. Dublin: printed by P Byrne, 1787. 78pp.   NPA

Also 'The second edition' 90pp. 'The third edition', 90pp; perhaps in two states, one with folding frontispiece.

BLACK 1563

14 The controversiad, an epistle to a learned friend exhibiting a sketch of the present controversy between Dr Priestley and his opponents, with some allusions to the controversial attacks on the rev C W Hawkins and his wife by Father O'Leary and others. London: printed for the author and sold by Charles Stalker, 1788. 30pp.   NPA

In verse

15 The crisis; or immediate concernments of the British empire addressed to the lord Loftus. By the rev T B Clarke. London printed and Dublin reprinted by W M'Kenzie, 1786. 70pp.   NPA

BLACK 1448.

16 A critical review of the b. of Cloyne's publication, with occasional remarks on the productions of some other writers, particularly those of Trinity College, and on the conduct of the present ministry, addressed to his lordship. By an unbiassed Irishman. Dublin: printed by John Chambers, 1787. 102pp.   QPA

By Edward Sheridan.
    Also 'Second edition to which is added a preface'. Dublin: printed by John Chambers, 1788. 112pp. A new edition was published in 1808 with new material.

BLACK 1505.

17 A defence of the conduct and writings of the rev. Arthur O'Leary, during the late disturbances in Munster: with a full justification of the Irish Catholics, and an account of the risings of the White-boys, written by himself: in answer to the false accusations of Theophilus and the ill-grounded insinuations of the right reverend Doctor Woodward, lord bishop of Cloyne. London: printed for P Keating, 1787. 176pp.   NPA

Printed errata on p. 175. This text is close to, but not identical with, no. 44 below. The 'introduction' to the latter diverges in a number of details, and has an additional final sentence, whereas pp. 10-13 of the present item contains additional matter passim. No full correlation has been attempted. No. 45 indicates (p. 4) that the Dublin edition preceded the London.

18 A defence of the protestant clergy in the south of Ireland in answer to the charges against them contained in the rt hon Henry Grattan's speeches relating to tithes as they are printed and said to have been delivered in the House of Commons, on Thursday the 14th, and Tuesday the 19th of February 1788; with a postscript containing some remarks on his last speech on the re-agitation of tithes, delivered the 11th of April 1788. By Authenticus. Dublin: printed by P Byrne, 1788. 124pp.   NPA

Also issued Dublin printed, London re-printed for J Robson and W Clarke, 1788. 128pp. A ms annotation in a TCD copy attributes the item to Richard Graves.

BLACK 1580.

19 An examination of the bishop of Cloyne's defence of his principles; with observations on some of his lordship's apologists particularly the rev Dr Stock; containing an inquiry into the constitution and effects of our ecclesiastical establishment and also an historical review of the political principles and conduct of presbyterians and episcopals in Great-Britain and Scotland, with a defence of the Church of Scotland from the charge of persecution brought by his lordship's apologist. By William Campbell. Dublin: printed for P Byrne, 1788. 216pp.   QPA

Also Belfast: printed by H Joy sen and jun, 1788. 216pp.

20 A farmer's letter addressed to the gentlemen of landed property in Ireland. Dublin: printed by Robert Bell and Co, 1786. 30pp. NPA

BLACK 1458.

21 A few serious and seasonable observations on some matters that engage now the public attention, in which the subject of tithes, the disturbances in the south and the present state and conduct of the established clergy of Ireland are fairly considered. By a curate. Dublin: printed for the author by B Smith, 1787. 72pp.   NPA

A copy in the RIA carries the inscription 'Geo Fleury' beside the title-page statement of authorship; this might suggest either George Fleury (curate of St Olave's, Waterford) or George Lewis Fleury (d. 1825; archdeacon of Waterford from 1773 until his death) as author.

BLACK 1514.

22 A full display of some late publications on the subject of tithes and the sufferings of the established clergy in the south of Ireland attributed to those dues, with strictures necessary for the further elucidation of that subject. By Candidus. Dublin: printed by W Sleater, 1788. 166pp.   NPA A

Attributed to 'Dr Brown' in a ms note on the copy in the RIA, i.e. Arthur Browne,

MP for the University of Dublin. The copy in the Russell Library, Maynooth, has a paste-on errata slip (14 alterations) on the verso of the t-p.

BLACK 1574.

23 A full report of the speech of the right hon Henry Grattan in the House of Commons on Thursday the 14th of February 1788 in the debate on tithes; taken in shorthand by Mr Franklin. Dublin: printed by P Byrne, 1788. 52pp.   NPA

BLACK 1585.

24 A hint to the established clergy of the kingdom of Ireland in answer to two letters to the right reverend bench by a reformer high in office and which contained a plan for the entire subversion of the ecclesiastical establishment, this hint is recommended to the serious attention of the clergy and laity. By Clericus. Dublin: printed by William M'Kenzie, 1788. 64pp.   NPA

BLACK 1588.

25 Historical remarks on the pope's temporal and deposing power, with some anecdotes of the court of Rome and observations on the oath of allegiance. By a member of the church of Rome. Dublin: printed for William Rainsford, 1788. 68pp.   NPA

26 An impartial discussion of the subject of tithes, containing a paralell [sic] between the tythes paid in England and those in Ireland, a history of the origin thereof, a history of the real causes of the present disturbances, and a plan for the abolition of tithes, addressed to the members of both houses of parliament. By a clergyman of the established church. Dublin: printed by P Byrne, 1786. 48pp.   NPA

BLACK 1465.

27 An inquiry into the justice and policy of an union between Great Britain and Ireland with an answer to the supposed 'practicability' of such a measure, consistent with the welfare of the latter, in reply to the arguments of John Williams, late of Merton College Oxon. Dublin: printed by P Byrne, 1787. 114pp.   NPA

This item answers no. 89 below.

BLACK 1522.

28 The insurrection, or a faithful narrative of the disturbances which lately broke out in the province of Munster, under the denomination of White or Right-boys. Dublin: printed for the author by W Sleater, 1787. 48pp. NPA

BLACK 1523.

29 An irregular ode, as it is to be performed in all the cathedrals in Ireland,

particularly in — Cloyne. Dublin: printed by J Moore, 1787. 20pp.   NPA

In verse. Also issued in a large-paper version, imprint as above.

30 Junius's first letter to Father O'Leary. [1787] 4pp.   NPA

See also no. 71 below The second edition of Junius Alter's Letter to Mr O'Leary ... By the rev T B Clarke. Dublin: printed by William M'Kenzie, 1787. 32pp. This is a new work.

31 A justification of the tenets of the Roman Catholic religion and a refutation of the charges brought against its clergy by the right reverend the lord bishop of Cloyne. By Doctor James Butler. Dublin: printed by P Byrne, 1787. 98, 88pp.   NPA

32 A letter addressed to the public on the subject of tithes and the late outrages in which the propositions and plan of Theophilus in his late address to the lords and commons are amicably discussed. By a friend to equity and moderation. Dublin: printed and sold by R Marchbank, 1787 [recte 1786.] 32pp.   NPA

By Arthur O'Leary. An annotation on a TCD copy (OLS 188 q 49 no. 6) of Woodward's Present State of the Church of Ireland assigns this to O'Leary. Reference to it in Woodward, and in the Dublin Evening Post of 30/1/1787, clearly establishes that it was published before 18 December 1786.

BLACK 1525.

33 A letter from a Munster layman of the established church to his friend in Dublin on the disturbances in the south. Dublin: Luke White, 1787. 30pp. NPA

BLACK 1526.

34 A letter from the most reverend Doctor Butler, titular archbishop of Cashel to the right honourable lord viscount Kenmare. Dublin: printed by P Byrne, 1787. 16pp.   NPA

35 Letter of William O'Driscol, secretary general of the Munster peasantry to Silver Oliver. [Appears as an appendix in item no. 3.]   NPA

36 A letter to Amyas Griffith, late surveyor of the Beau-Walk, Stephen's Green, and formerly inspector general of the Monitor, and of the Polite Conversation of Dodderige and Vanthrump, occasioned by his late scurrilous pamphlet against the bishop of Cloyne, Theophilus, and the dignitaries of the established church, with some observations on the recent conduct of the friar 'of the barbarous sirname'. By Theophilus. Dublin: printed by C Lewis, [1787] 24pp.   NPA

Imprint date supplied as the copy inspected has been cropped with evident loss of text. That Patrick Duigenan was wholly, or even partly, responsible for this item is

40 THE DUBLIN PAPER WAR

questionable, though Griffith responded in a manner which appeared to accept that the same Theophilus was responsible for this and no. 3 above.

37 A letter to the bishop of Cloyne containing a plan of reconciliation and mutual benefit between the clergy and laity. [no imprint] 1787. 12pp.   PA

38 A letter to Dr James Butler of Ireland, occasioned by his late publication intitled A justification of the tenets of the Roman Catholic religion. By Philemon. London printed; Dublin: reprinted by P Byrne, 1787. 26pp. NPA

39 A letter to the rev Doctor O'Leary found on the great road leading from the city of Cork to Cloughnakilty. Dublin: printed by W Sleater, 1787. 30pp.   NPA

The text is a spoof; for use of the name (W O'Driscol) signing off here (p. 30) see nos. 3 and 35. In no. 44, Arthur O'Leary repeatedly suggested that this was the work of 'a certain Reverend Gentleman in the diocese of Cloyne'.

40 A letter to the rev Samuel Barber, minister of the presbyterian congregation of Rathfriland, containing a refutation of certain dangerous doctrines advanced in his Remarks on the bishop of Cloyne's Present state of the Church of Ireland. By the rev Robert Burrowes. Dublin: printed by George Grierson, 1787. 68pp.   NPA A

Black records 'another edition' with the same imprint and date.

BLACK 1499

41 Letters by a farmer originally published in the Belfast Evening Post, with several alterations and additions. Belfast: printed by James Magee, 1787. 138pp.   NPA

Linen Hall Library attributes this to 'J. McCully'.

BLACK 1527.

42 The mirror, or cursory observations on the licentious pamphlets by Theophilus etc wherein the subject of tythes is candidly discussed and the real cause of the late disturbances in the south faithfully developed. By Publicola. Dublin: printed by P Cooney, 1787. 64pp.   NPA

Black attributes this to Thomas Dawson.

BLACK 1506

43 Miscellaneous tracts containing, I) a narrative of the misfortunes of the author, with original letters of pretended friends calculated to deceive and lead him to ruin; II) a letter to Dominick Trant esq relative to his pamphlet against the Munster peasantry and his unfortunate duel with Sir John Colthurst Bt; III) observations on the bishop of Cloyne's pamphlet in which the doctrine of tithes is candidly considered and proved to be oppressive and impolitic, his lordship's fears for the insecurity of the established church are

also demonstrated to be groundless and visionary, much improved from the last edition; IV) extract of Theophilus's letter to the author, his intolerance and cruelty pointed out, as also some of the dreadful effects of bigotry and prejudice dispassionately and candidly treated of in a rejoinder; V) a letter to Daniel Toler esq relative to that unfortunate victim to popular prejudice, the rev Nicholas Sheehy, with an history of the prosecution carried on against him, and the subsequent visitations of providence on those who spilled his blood; in this letter are likewise introduced some observations on the political conspiracies of England, particularly that of Titus Oates. By Amyas Griffith. Dublin: printed for the author by James Mehain, 1788. 264pp. [With a frontispiece portrait of the author.]   NPA A

Also an expanded edition, 'Dublin: printed and sold for the author by W Corbet, B Dornin and J Mehain, 1789.' 294pp.
See also under no. 46 below.

44   Mr O'Leary's defence, containing a vindication of his conduct and writings during the late disturbances in Munster, with a full justification of the Catholics and an account of the risings of the White-boys, in answer to the false accusations of Theophilus and the ill-grounded insinuations of the right reverend Doctor Woodward, lord bishop of Cloyne. [With appendices, including O'Leary's addresses to the Whiteboys.] Dublin: printed by P Byrne, 1787. 178pp.   NPA

Issued in at least two states—a) with 6 errata listed on p. [ii]; and b) with 15 errata listed on the same page.
    Also 'second edition' Dublin: printed by P Byrne, 1787. 176pp with frontispiece. And 'second edition, revised and corrected, to which is annexed A letter from the right rev Doctor Butler, titular archbishop of Cashel to the right hon lord viscount Kenmare concerning the nuncio's letter and the consecration oath of bishops'. Cork: printed by William Flyn, 1787. 152pp.
    Cf. no. 17 above, A defence of the conduct and writings of the rev. Arthur O'Leary (London)

BLACK 1536.

45   Mr O'Leary's letter to the monthly reviewers. Dublin: printed by P Byrne, 1787. 16pp.   NPA

Signs off (p. 15) Cork, July 30, 1787.

BLACK 1537.

46   Observations on the bishop of Cloyne's pamphlet; in which the doctrine of tithes is candidly considered and proved to be oppressive and impolitic; his lordship's arguments for the insecurity of the protestant religion are also demonstrated to be groundless and visionary. By Amyas Griffith. Dublin: printed by T Byrne, 1787. 72pp.   NPA A

Also issued with 5 lines of errata details on p. 72. Also 'Second edition' London: printed for P Keating; Messrs Robinson, Debrett, and Faulder, 1787. 72pp.
    There is a further publication with this title and by the same author. The only

copy inspected (in NLI) has been cropped with loss of what might be an imprint: however, the title-page gives authorship as 'by Amyas Griffith in the year 1787' and this (together with internal evidence) would suggest 1788 as the earliest possible date of publication. Textuallly, this further publication (8opp.) includes material which is not in the edition of the 'Observations' published by T. Byrne but which is included in the Miscellaneous Tracts (q.v.) by the same author. It also includes other, later writings from Miscellaneous Tracts. This second (post Miscellaneous Tracts) edition of Observations is very poorly printed.

BLACK 1518.

47 Observations on the indecent and illiberal strictures against the lord bishop of Cloyne contained in a pamphlet lately published under the title of Mr O'Leary's defence etc. Dublin: printed by W Sleater, 1787. 34pp.   PA

Signs off (p. 34) Detector. This is one of five items which can be attributed to Thomas Elrington, see nos. 57, 63, 78 and 85. See also no. 86 in which he may have had a hand.

BLACK 1534.

48 Observations on the pamphlets published by the bishop of Cloyne, Mr Trant and Theophilus on one side, and on those by Mr O'Leary, Mr Barber, and Doctor Campbell on the other, to which are added remarks on the causes of the late insurrections in Munster, a consideration of the grievances under which the peasantry of Ireland labours, with a proposal of an adequate compensation for tithes. By Daniel Thomas.   NPA A

This title exists in several states and with at least two imprints:
    a) Dublin: printed by P Byrne, 1787. 82pp.
    b) Dublin: printed for the author. At (No. 43) Fishamble-street, 1787. 82pp.
    TCD copy of b) has ms addendum after 'author' reading '& to be had', and a 29-line list of errata is printed on the t-p verso. From this and other evidence, one deduces that the Byrne state came first in time, for it contains the errors listed in the errata details of the other. Both are printed from the same type, with a cancellans t-p in the author's state.

BLACK 1559.

49 Observations on the political influence of the doctrine of the pope's supremacy addressed to the reverend Doctor Butler. By William Hales. Dublin: printed by William M'Kenzie, 1787. xvi, 50, 48pp.   NPA

50 The O'Leariad, translated into English verse and illustrated with notes. Dublin: printed by W Sleater, 1787. 24pp.   NPA

Also another edition, Dublin printed and Cork re-printed by Robert Dobbyn, 1787. 40pp.

51 Plain reasons why the people called Quakers may in conscience and ought in duty to pay tythes. Dublin: printed by W Sleater, 1786. 12pp.   NPA

Signs off (p. 12) J C. On the t-p of no. 88 below, it is claimed that this item was 'said to be written by a prelate of this kingdom'. While this supposition may carry weight, no Irish bishop of the day bore the initials in question, John Cradock of Dublin having died in 1778. Referring (p. 3) to the occasion of his writing, the author mentions 'Some brief and serious Reasons why the People called Quakers do not pay tythes' as a work 'lately put into my hands for my perusal'. No. 88 reprints a work of similar title, said to date from 1768 and certainly in circulation a decade later.

52 The prelateiad, or the rage of the holy bottle, a heroi-tragi-comic poem, written in the time of the late spiritual wars. Dublin: [printed for H Chamberlaine, 1787] 28pp.   NPA

Imprint derived from press advertisments. The only copy inspected survives in large-paper format, with the lower half of the t-p torn off. Text in verse. The RIA Halliday Tracts catalogue records an item of 1789,Temple Spectacles! A Tale, as by the author of The prelateiad: however, this too only survives in fragments.

53 The present state of the Church of Ireland: containing a description of it's [sic] precarious situation; and the consequent danger to the public; recommended to the serious consideration of the friends of the protestant interest; to which are subjoined some reflections on the impracticability of a proper commutation for tithes; and a general account of the origin and progress of the insurrections in Munster. By Richard [Woodward] lord bishop of Cloyne. Dublin: printed by W Sleater, jun. 51, Castle-street, 1787 [recte 1786]. 128pp.   PA

'The second edition with some small additions', 1787 [recte 1786]. 128pp.
'The third edition revised and corrected', 1787 [recte 1786]. 128pp.
'The fourth edition with some small additions, revised and corrected', 1787 [recte 1786]. 128pp.
'The fifth edition with some small additions, revised and corrected', 1787. 128pp.
'The fifth edition to which is added, (from the sixth edition,) an extract from the preface to the London edition', 1787. 140pp.
'The sixth edition', 1787. 124pp.
'The sixth edition, with an extract from the preface to the London edition and many very material additions interspersed and translations of the Latin appendices', 1787. 124pp.
'The sixth edition, with an extract from the preface to the London edition and many very material additions interspersed and translations of the Latin appendices', 1787. 140pp.
'The seventh edition', 1787. 132pp.
'The seventh edition, with many considerable additions' London: reprinted from the Dublin edition, printed for T Cadell in the Strand, 1787. 120pp.
'The eighth edition', 1787. 132pp.
'The ninth edition', 1787. 138pp.
A new edition was published in 1808.

BLACK 1570.

54 A project for a better regulation in collecting the income of the clergy and for the ease and advantage of the laity, particularly the poorer orders. By a beneficed clergyman. Dublin: printed by P Byrne, 1786. 24pp.   NPA

By Luke Godfrey.

BLACK 1457.

55 A proposal for the liquidation of the national debt; the abolition of tythes; and the reform of the church revenue. Third edition. London printed; and Dublin reprinted by P Byrne, 1786. 124pp.   NPA

The work of Sir Francis Blake, this is one of 'some late publications in England, favourable to innovation' referred to by Woodward in the preface to his London edition as prompting him to write. 'When I first read the Title, it reminded me of the representations of St. Ambrose in his carriage drawn by a horse and a Bear.' (p. v)

BLACK 1444.

56 The question considered; have the Articles of Limerick been violated? Being strictures on Mr Browne's Brief review etc. etc. etc.; with observations on Dr Campbell's late publication, and on the illiberality of the monthly reviewers. By the author of A critical review. Dublin: printed by J Chambers, 1788. 40pp.   NPA

By Edward Sheridan.

57 Remarks on a letter lately published, signed Arthur O'Leary, stiled An address to the protestant nobility and gentry of Ireland. By a friend to truth and the publick. Dublin: printed by W Sleater, 1787. 14pp.   NPA

By Thomas Elrington: (see no. 47 above.)

BLACK 1544.

58 Remarks on a pamphlet entitled The present state of the Church of Ireland by Richard, lord bishop of Cloyne. By Samuel Barber. Dublin: printed by P Byrne, 1787. 60pp.   NPA

Also 'The second edition' 46pp. which is a re-set edition and not a re-issue.

59 Remarks on the Justification of the tenets of the papists lately published by Dr James Butler who in the registry of Cashel hath assumed and taken the ecclesiastical rank of Roman Catholic archbishop of Cashel and Emly; herein the whole of that performance is given and the remarks are inserted at the bottom of the page whereby all protestants and all papists of property may be enabled to judge of the true tendency of the controversy excited by the said Dr Butler, and of the danger of their situation; with a preface by the Remarker and an appendix containing extracts from several approved writers of the church of Rome. By A Y U J D, R S & S A S. Dublin: printed by G Perrin, 1787. viii, 84, 70, 44pp.   NPA

By John Erskine.
     This cumbersome work includes the text of Butler's Justification, with extensive commentary added throughout. The TCD Printed Catalogue both assigns under Arthur Young FRS and elsewhere attributes it to his father Arthur Young DD who

had died many years earlier. William Hales alludes to the author as 'Dr. A. Y.' However, the TCD shelf-list assigns it to Erskine, and W. M. Brady concurs in Clerical and Parochial Records of Cork, Cloyne and Ross (Dublin: Thom, 1863.) The elaborate string of initials remains inscrutable.

60   Remarks on the pamphlet of Mr Barber, dissenting minister of Rathfriland. By Edward Ryan. Dublin: printed by P Byrne, 1787. 36pp.   NPA

  BLACK 1548.

61   A reply to the reverend Mr Burrowes's and the reverend Mr Ryan's remarks. By Samuel Barber. Dublin: printed by P Byrne, 1787. 24pp.   NPA

62   A reply to the rev Dr Campbell's Vindication of the principles and character of the presbyterians of Ireland, in which the question is discussed whether our political constitution might be improved by substituting in place of the present ecclesiastical establishment of England and Ireland either the presbyterian or independent model of church polity. By Joseph Stock. Dublin: printed by J Exshaw, 1787. 124, [10]pp.   QPA

63   Reply to the third section of Mr O'Leary's defence [no t.p., 1787] 18pp. NPA

  By Thomas Elrington: (see no. 47 above.) This title appears to exist only in a state conjugate with (i.e. physically attached to) item 76, though the latter was also published separately.

64   A report of the case which some time since depended in the consistorial court of Dublin between the late rev Smyth Loftus, vicar of Coolock, and Peter Callage, one of his parishioners, for substraction of tithes. Dublin: printed for Caleb Jenkin, 1787. 72pp.   NPA

  BLACK 1599.

65   The respective charges given to the grand jury of the county of Armagh at the general assizes held there July 23 1763 by the then going judges of assize, Mr Justice Robinson and Mr Justice Tenison, on occasion of the late commotions in several of the northern counties; published at the particular request of the said grand jury.   NPA

  This title exists in two states, with the t-p details proceeding as follows in each case:
    a) Dublin: reprinted for William Mc Kenzie, 1787. 32pp.
    b) and now reprinted at the desire of several persons of distinction. Dublin: printed for William Mc Kenzie, 1787. 32pp.
    Both states are printed on the same (inferior) paper, and appear to derive from the same type.

66   The rev Mr O'Leary's address to the common people of Ireland; particularly to such of them as are called Whiteboys, revised and corrected by himself. Dublin: printed by P Cooney, 1786. 30pp.   NPA

  BLACK 1474.

67 A review of Doctor Butler's pamphlet entitled A justification of the Roman
    Catholic tenets, in which are a representation of the state of social harmony
    in the kingdom previous to the troubles in Munster, observations on
    ecclesiastical establishments, their propriety vindicated and their practice
    shewn to have prevailed in all nations, antient and modern, some strictures
    on the popish doctrine of indulgences and on the consecration-oath sworn to
    the pope by the Romish bishops, the real origin and motives of the
    inquisition related, and its establishment in Spain, and a demonstration that
    Clement XIV['s] eneyclic [sic] letter cannot be applied to a protestant church
    or state; with an appendix giving an account of the liberties of the Gallican
    church as ascertained by the clergy of France in 1632, and of the bull
    Unigenitus issued by Clement XI in 1713. By a friend to the constitution.
    Dublin: printed and to be had at Mr Grierson's, 1787. 128pp.   PA

    Signs off (p. 107) Clement, Galway April 20th 1787.

68 A review on the bishop of Cloyne's book on the present state of the Church
    of Ireland, addressed to a friend in the city. Dublin: printed by P Byrne,
    1787. 20pp.   NPA

    Signs off (p. 18) Rusticus.

69 A riddle to exercise the genius of an agitating friar: being a description of a
    picture in the cabinet of a monk of the screw wherein the good people of
    Ireland may discover the original cause of the present disturbances and the
    spirit which blows up the coals of the present controversies. [By?] F. O. L.
    Dublin: printed and sold by R Marchbank, 1787. 18pp.   NPA

    In verse. The semblance of an author statement simply inscribes Fr O'Leary's
    initials. The 'monks of the screw' were a convivial club with which O'Leary is herein
    associated in scandalous terms—he wears 'a cork-screw for a crucifix', a detail which
    may derive from p 31 of no. 47 above. The text also uses 'punks' in something like its
    late-twentieth-century sense.

70 The rights of Ireland vindicated in an answer to the secretary of state's letter
    to the mayor of Cork on the subject of Mr Orde's bill presented the 15th of
    August 1785. Dublin: printed for S Watson, 1787. 88pp.   NPA

    BLACK 1546.

71 The second edition of Junius Alter's Letter to Mr O'Leary, with a short
    examination into the first causes of the present lawless spirit of the Irish
    peasantry, and a plan of reform. By the rev T B Clarke. Dublin: printed by
    William M'Kenzie, 1787. 32pp.   NPA

72 Sermon on the state of the distressed curates of the established church
    throughout the kingdom of Ireland, containing among other matter answers
    to some cavils against raising their salaries, respectfully addressed to the
    legislature of that country. By a distressed curate of the above fraternity.
    Drogheda: printed by C Evans, 1787. 58pp.   NPA

A rare if not unique example of a contribution to the paper war originating in a provincial printing-shop.

73 A short account of the doctrines and practices of the church of Rome divested of all controversy and humbly recommended to the perusal of all good Catholics as well as protestants. Dublin: William Watson, 1788. 74pp. **NPA**

NLI and Maynooth attribute this to Daniel Augustus Beaufort.

74 A short display of the principal errors of popery in a letter to a protestant bishop from a popish priest who desired to forsake the communion of the church of Rome. Dublin: printed by W Sleater, 1787. 12pp.   **NPA**

One NLI copy, with a cancellans [A2], has ms annotations identifying the author as 'O'Farrel' and the recipient as Thomas Percy, bishop of Dromore. In a second NLI copy, A2 bears a printed 'advertisement' indicating autumn 1785 as the date of composition, whereas the annotated copy suggests 1783. There were, it thus seems, two issues of this item. For authorship see below, p. 000.

75 A short, plain, civil answer to a long, laboured, and illiberal pamphlet intitled An address to the nobility and gentry of the Church of Ireland. Dublin: printed by P Byrne, 1787. 50pp.   **NPA**

By Luke Godfrey. Signs off (p. 49) A Beneficed Clergyman.

BLACK 1550.

76 A short plea for human nature and common sense in which it is attempted to state a few general principles for the direction of our judgmens [sic] of the Irish Roman Catholics. By a lay protestant. Dublin: printed by P Byrne, 1787. 56pp.   **PA**

Also issued with the typo indicated above corrected. The date of publication is given erroneously as D, MCC, LXXXVII (instead of M, DCC, LXXXVII). This and the next item are essentially the same work, despite the divergent titles and representations of the author.

77 A short plea for human nature and common sense in which it is attempted to state a few general principles for the direction of our judgment of the present state of the Church of Ireland, as described by the lord bishop of Cloyne. By George Grace. Dublin: printed by P Byrne, 1787. 56pp.   **PA**

78 A short refutation of the arguments contained in Doctor Butler's letter to lord Kenmare. By a clergyman. Dublin: printed by W Sleater, 1787. 28pp.
                                                                      NPA

By Thomas Elrington: (see no. 47 above.) Also a 2nd ed., completely reset (18pp.), taking in the errata slip details of the 1st ed. Also issued with item 62 in a single publication, as indicated in the half-title preserved in the Russell Library, Maynooth, copy. (This last item is BLACK 1551.)

79   A short review of the political state of Great-Britain at the commencement of
     the year one thousand seven hundred and eighty-seven. Dublin: printed for
     Colles, Moncrieffe, Wilson, Exshaw, Byrne, White, W Porter, Jones and
     Moore, 1787. 70pp.   NPA

     By N. W. Wraxhall. At least 7 London editions appeared, from one of which this
     Dublin import derives. Also a Dublin 'second edition'. See also The people's answer to
     the court pamphlet entitled A short review of the political state of Great Britain.
     Dublin: printed for Messrs White, Byrne, Moore & Jones, 1787 50pp. (Both of these are
     essentially English works, republished in Dublin; see also under Wraxhall p. 65 below.)

80   Speech of the rt hon Henry Grattan on the re-agitation on the subject of
     tithes, in the House of Commons, Friday April 11, 1788. Dublin: printed for
     W Gilbert, 1788. 32pp.   NPA

     BLACK 1587.

81   Strictures on the bishop of Cloyne's Present state of the Church of Ireland,
     with appendices containing passages alluded to in the bishop's pamphlet.
     London: printed for C Dilly and P Byrne Dublin, 1787. 88pp.   NPA

     Arthur O'Leary (in no. 44, Mr O'Leary's Defence, p. 116) writes that 'strictures on
     the Lord Bishop of Cloyne's publication are sent to the press, by a gentleman of more
     distinguished abilities than I can pretend to.'

     BLACK 1557

82   Strictures on a pamphlet signed Theophilus, explaining the real causes of the
     discontents in every part of this kingdom respecting tithes, and containing
     reasons why tithes ought to be abolished entirely, and the practicability of
     substituting a better mode of subsistence and maintenance for the clergy of
     the church established, consistent with the principles of reason and justice.
     By a Farmer. Dublin: printed for Luke White, 1787. 72pp.   NPA

     BLACK 1556.

83   A survey of the modern state of the church of Rome with additional
     observations on the doctrine of the pope's supremacy addressed to the
     reverend Doctor Butler. By William Hales. Dublin: printed by William
     M'Kenzie, 1788. 226pp.   PA

84   Temperate, unborrowed animadversions on the pamphlet lately published by
     Richard, bishop of Cloyne on the subject of tythes; wherein this writer
     proposes plain radical remedies not only for the evils now complained of, but
     for the abuses introduced into primitive Christianity by ecclesiasticks of all
     denominations; also a cool statement of Mr O'Leary's conduct in which the
     charge of duplicity against that gentleman is honestly done away. By a
     sincere unbiassed protestant. Dublin: printed by J M Davis, 1787. 56pp. PA

     Signs off (p. 56) The UT—T.

     BLACK 1558.

85   To the committee for conducting the free-press. [By Philo-Clericus]. [n.p.,
     1787.] 8pp.   NPA

     By Thomas Elrington: (see no. 47 above.) First published in the Freeman's Journal,
     10 February 1787.

86   To the rev Arthur O'Leary. [no title-page or imprint.] 6, [4], [6]pp.   NPA

     Signs off first (p. 6) Samuel Shaver, and again (p. [6]) A. This item may be the work
     of three different authors, a head-note reading 'The following essays, (two of which
     have already appeared in print) being much sought for, have induced the printer, in
     compliance with the wishes of many of his customers, to publish them in a pamphlet.'
     In physical appearance it resembles no. 85 above which is considered to be the work
     of Thomas Elrington who might be Samuel Shaver. (The baptist John McGowan's
     contemporaneous use of 'The Shaver' as a pseudonym on certain Mullingar printings
     should be regarded as a separate matter.) The use of a pointing-hand device in both
     of these, on the t-p of no. 10, in the postscript to no. 53, and on p 26 of no. 90
     strongly suggests William Sleater Junior as the printer; apart from these, this device
     does not appear (to the best of my recollection) within any other pamphlet
     (advertisements apart) of the paper war.

87   To the reverend doctor James Butler, a titular archbishop. From a friend.
     Dublin: printed by W Sleater, 1787. 16pp.   NPA A

     Signs off (p. 15) A Friend to Toleration upon safe Principles.

     BLACK 1561.

88   Tracts on tithes: I) brief and serious reasons why the people called Quakers
     do not pay tithes, published by said people in 1768; II) plain reasons why the
     people called Quakers may in conscience and ought in duty to pay tithes,
     published in 1786 and said to be written by a prelate of this kingdom; III) a
     vindication of the brief and serious reasons in reply to the last. By J G one of
     the said people. Dublin: rinted [sic] by Robert Jackson, 1786. 76pp.   NPA

     NLI attributes a 19th cent. re-publication of I) to John Gough. For II) see no. 51
     above; see also DNB.

89   An union of England and Ireland proved to be practicable and equally
     beneficial to each kingdom; with supplementary observations relative to the
     absentees of Ireland, pointing out the constitutional means of removing
     complaints arising from that and other causes of present discontent, and
     finally for conciliating the desires of each country: to which is added a
     collateral reply to [Josiah Tucker] the dean of Gloucester's advice to the Irish
     to trade with foreign in preference to the British colonies. By John Williams.
     Dublin: printed by P Byrne, 1787. 56pp.   NPA

     Also London: sold by G Kearsley, 1787. 50pp.

     BLACK 1569.

90   A vindication of the conduct of the clergy who petitioned the House of
     Lords against two bills relative to tithes in the session of parliament held in

1788, with an appendix containing his former answers to certain 'allegations', with additions. By a southern clergyman. Dublin: printed by William Sleater, 1788. 56pp.   NPA

BLACK 1604.

91   A vindication of the principles and character of the presbyterians of Ireland, addressed to the bishop of Cloyne in answer to his book entitled, The present state of the Church of Ireland. By William Campbell. [Dublin:] printed by P Byrne, 1787. 74pp.   PA A

Also 'second edition' [Dublin:] printed by P Byrne, 1787. 74pp.
Also 'The third edition' London: printed for T Evans, 1787. 74pp.
Also 'the fourth edition, with some additions.' Belfast: printed by Henry Joy senr & junr, 1788. 86pp.

92   The whole of the debates in both Houses of Parliament on a bill to prevent tumultuous risings and assemblies and for the more effectual punishment of persons guilty of outrage, riot, and illegal conbination, and of administering unlawful oaths. Dublin: printed by P Cooney, 1787. 120pp.   PA

In publishing the text (but not the title or title page) of this item in Analecta Hibernica (no. 33 1986, pp. 129-198), Gerard O'Brien came close to attributing the work of reporting these debates to John Giffard (see Anal. Hib. p. 134.) However, the collaboration of Giffard as reporter and Cooney as printer seems unlikely. As a parliamentary report, the item might be thought to stand outside the paper war as described in the remarks placed at the head of this list. In connection with the argument over protestant ascendancy, however, it is clearly relevant because it includes Arthur Browne's single sentence—'That there was a faction in the country, (and so there was, and no man would deny it,) hostile to the established church, hostile to the protestant ascendancy, hostile to the acts of settlement, and the titles of their estates.' (ibid. p. 178)

III.   A NOTE ON THE PUBLICATION OF WOODWARD'S *PRESENT STATE*

Contemporaries of Woodward's were evidently impressed by the speed with which further editions of *The Present State of the Church of Ireland* followed on the heels of the first issue of 18 December 1786. The seeming fact of such multiple editions, apparently confirmed by reactions of the day, has been taken up by recent historians without any very close scrutiny of the evidence. The latter may be conveniently considered under three headings— that provided by; a) press advertisements placed by the publisher, Sleater; b) the computerised *Eighteenth-Century Short Title Catalogue* (1990 edition), and c) the collections preserved in major Irish libraries. These last two sources of information overlap, but they do so in a way which assists the analysis of statistics.

a) Sleater's advertising and the *Dublin Evening Post*. As imminent publisher of Woodward's pamphlet, William Sleater Junior first announced it in the *Dublin Evening Post* of Thursday 14 December 1786. This paper was not the sole medium by which the *Present State* was publicised—a parallel campaign can be traced in the *Freeman's Journal*, for example—but there are several reasons which render it particularly suitable for analysis in the present inquiry. Its dating system was clearer than the *Journal*, and as an evening paper it may be thought to have had some closer alignment with the events of a particular day than a paper issued at the commencement of trading. Given the rapid succession of publications in the paper war, these considerations (even if they are partly speculative) deserve attention.

The first advertisement, appearing in the third column of the third page (p. 3:3) of the issue in question, read:

> A PAMPHLET. On Monday, the 18th of December, will be published, by William Sleater, No 51 Castle-street, Price 1s 1d The PRESENT STATE of the CHURCH OF IRELAND; containing a description of its precarious situation, and the consequent danger to the public. Recommended to the serious consideration of the Friends of the Protestant Interest; to which are subjoined some reflections on the impracticability of a proper commutation for TITHES, and a general account of the origin and progress of the INSURRECTIONS in MUNSTER. By RICHARD, lord bishop of CLOYNE.

A similar notice appeared in the *Freeman's Journal* of 12-14 (p. 1:3), and of 14-16 December (p. 1:4). In the *Dublin Evening Post* the campaign continued through 16 December (p. 1:1) but, as no issue of the paper appeared on the day originally announced for publication, the notice 'This day is published . . .' appeared on 19 December (p. 1:4). There is however no reason to suppose that the date of publication was altered from that originally announced.

The next issue of the *Freeman's Journal* (19-21 December) carried an advertisement declaring suavely that 'several gentlemen having been disappointed of the first edition, are respectfully informed, that this day A SECOND EDITION, with some small additions, will be ready.' (p. 1:2). The advertisement was repeated verbatim in the *Journal* of 21-23 December (p. 1:4), with the result that several dates for the day of publication for this 'second edition' can be traced. At one level, these duplications result simply from the publishers' keeping an unaltered notice in the paper for a second (or third) printing, and no real confusion is generated. At another, the proliferation of such duplicate claims of 'this day is published' emphasise the element of immediate, even urgent, demand. These are not, of course, journalistic reports of such demand; on the contrary, they are commercial announcements by the party with most to gain by stimulating it.

On Thursday 21 December the *Dublin Evening Post* carried the next instalment of Sleater's sales campaign, which announced that

> The second edition being out of print soon after it appeared this morning, and having had a most rapid circulation, the public are most respectfully

informed, that on Saturday morning next, a third edition, revised, corrected and improved, will be ready for delivery. (p. 3:3)

This was followed by the description of the pamphlet as given in the original advertisement of 14 December, with the most prominent emphasis (CAPITAL LETTERS) given to such terms as Church of Ireland, tithes, insurrections etc., and a lesser prominence given (by means of italic) to friends of the protestant interest. On Saturday 23 December the (by now) familiar box-ad duly appeared in the *Dublin Evening Post* (p. 2:3) announcing the publication that day of the 'third edition', as previously described, and the title spelled out with the emphasis already detailed. Pre- and post-publication announcements were now pairing each other, and the direct echo of the former in the latter added to the sense of pervasiveness which was Sleater's desired effect.

Exactly a trading week was allowed for the pre-Christmas selling of *The Present State*, commencing on a Monday, concluding on a Saturday evening, with Christmas Eve discounted as a Sunday. In this phase of the advertising campaign, the pamphlet's lengthy title was established as the fundamental 'copy' within the advertisement. The appearance of the ad was made familiar to readers, and while modifications would be introduced later, the campaign had effectively imposed an image of the pamphlet on the newspapers' readers. The ad was big by the standards of others placed to stimulate sales of comparable pamphlets, but not larger than some which advertised books proper. The constancy of the image, and the pairing of its appearances in the press generally, indicate the deliberateness with which Woodward and/or Sleater planned the advertising of their product. The allocation, from the outset, of a budget for regular and extensive advertising further indicates the extent to which either publisher or author (or both together) were willing to invest in preparing the public for a 'best-seller'.

After Christmas, the style of advertising altered in some regards. In the *Dublin Evening Post* of 26 December, Sleater announced his FOURTH EDITION—the edition-numbers now are emphasised, rather than the events narrated—'The rapid and extensive circulation having caused three editions in the space of five days, and a few copies now remaining, the public are respectfully informed' that the next day will see the fourth 'revised and corrected' in print. The day following publication saw the exploitation of this triumph of numbers, the paper's columns declaring that 'four editions, in almost the same number of days, have not been produced since the publication of the Drapier's Letters.' (p. 3:2) Of course the difference in physical scale between Woodward's wordy production and the Drapier's pithy utterances was not alluded to, any more than a difference in political feeling and milieu. Allusion to Swift served to confer a dual aura of commercial success and intellectual respectability on the bishop's efforts.

The paper's editorial harmonising with Sleater and Woodward reached a pitch on Saturday 30 December:

Nothing can be more absurd, that the consternation the clergy have fallen into since the publication of the Bishop of Cloyne's pamphlet. It has totally marred the festivity and pleasure that preside at this season, and if the face be an index of the mind, from the length and sadness of their countenances, one would be inclined to think that they had not eat [sic] a hearty dinner, since Christmas holidays commenced. So clearly has the Lord Bishop proved the dangerous and pernicious state of the mother church, that her sons, the clergy, feel actual trepidation for her existence. (p. 3:2)

If this contained the tiniest flavouring of irony, Sleater was to take no notice. On the same page he announced Woodward's 'fifth edition'—'this day will be produced'—which would suggest a late Saturday afternoon publication, ready for Monday's sales. By now, of course, the opposition was vocal, with the veritable unanimity of the paper and Sleater's cause also coming to a close. On the final page of the same issue of the *Dublin Evening Post*, 'A Friend to Equity and Moderation' (i.e. Arthur O'Leary) responded vigorously to Woodward's pamphlet, alleging that the bishop misrepresented the friar's earlier *Address*. The date of 23 December at the foot of this would suggest that it took longer to get a letter into the newspaper than an edition through the printing-press. One deft stroke of O'Leary's was to note how Woodward, while denying the existence of viable plans for a reformed tithe system, cited one proposed by the dean of Gloucester, that is Josiah Tucker, Woodward's step-father.

It is with this 'fifth edition' that the bibliographer encounters seriously conflicting, even paradoxical, evidence. There are two distinct states of the fifth, one of 128pp, the other of 140pp. While the phenomenon will recur in the lists of the pamphlet's many manifestations, this initial instance is complicated by the claim made for the larger state that it incorporates material from the London edition. (This will not appear for weeks after the alleged publication on 30 December 1786 which quotes from it.) It is possible to argue that Sleater or Woodward were free to quote *in advance* from so prestigious a development as a London edition. But it is more likely that the longer state of the 'fifth edition' only came into existence much later than the advertisement announcing publication of a 'fifth edition'. Indeed, this can be virtually confirmed by consideration of the pamphlet's price: the longer 'fifth' sold at 1s. 7d, that is, the increased price announced for the 'sixth edition'. It would have been ludicrous to have two 'editions' simultaneously available at different prices, and so the longer 'fifth' can be confidently assigned to a post-'sixth' period.

The implications here would include the existence of unsold sheets, rather than extraordinary demand. For, speaking in general, one must note that in none of the nine officially declared 'editions' of his pamphlet did Woodward ever absorb the material which had appeared as a breathless postscript in the first. Methodical revision does not seem to have been attempted, and none of the many states of *The Present State of the Church of Ireland* is fully re-set. Despite the steady advance of edition number, from first to ninth, the printing and publication of Woodward's pamphlet was less than straight forward.

On 2 January 1787, Sleater's advertisement still announced that the 'fifth edition' of *The Present State* 'this day, will be produced.' (p. 1:1) As already noted, the duplication of publication-dates resulted from the mechanical repetition of the ad, but behind the phenomenon lay one of two more significant factors. Either, the repetition resulted from a delay in publication—caused, perhaps, by slower than expected sales. Or, it stemmed from a deliberate policy of placing a strictly inaccurate but effective second ad for an 'edition' already available at the moment it was re-advertised as to be published later. Given the comparative rarity of surviving copies of the fifth, and the illogical basis of its second state *vis à vis* the London edition, we may conclude that the print-run of the first state was short. By print-run we may in fact mean little more than the compilation of a further issue from already existing sheets, with an altered title-page added so as to generate new interest in the publication.

With advertisements for the 'sixth edition', a further shift in advertising emphasis is discernible. In the *Dublin Evening Post* of 4 January, a publication date of the following Saturday was announced (p. 3:4). Delay was now explicitly confirmed. This SIXTH EDITION had 'been delayed by many very material additions interspersed throughout the work, together with the preface to the English edition, and translations to the Latin appendixes, which necessarily raises the price to 1s 7½d.' Though the title-page transcription followed, the phrase THE PROTESTANT INTEREST is now emphasised in capital letters in the centre of the ad, matching the BISHOP of CLOYNE'S PAMPHLET at the top. It was not until the 9 January that Sleater could announce the 'sixth edition' as 'this day is published', though the genuine changes in the text were certainly sufficient to cause delay on this occasion.

Meanwhile, the editorial tone in the *Dublin Evening Post* shifted, for the 'postscript' column in the issue of 6 January had already accused Woodward of alarmism:

> The man who has not traversed Ireland from the North to the South and who would read the Bishop of Cloyne's pamphlet must if he gave credit to it, suppose the nation in a flagrant insurrection. The church at the very brink of annihilation, and the downfal [*sic*] of the constitution at no great distance. A gloomy speculist may brood over his fantastic visions, but he must injure society by imparting them—that is, were there a colour to their face. But pity (a mitre is a shield against contempt) must be the portion of the man, who from the rising of a parcel of the ragged half-starved peasants, could apprehend the ANNIHILATION OF THE CHURCH AND THE OVERTHROW OF THE CONSTITUTION. (p. 3)

If the 'sixth edition' finally came on 9 January, the ad announcing 'this day is published' was repeated on 11 January (p. 1). In the same issue's Postscript column, the editorial 'we' was 'glad to be informed that so able a writer as Mr. O'Leary, has entered the lists against these interested calumniators' (p. 3).

Woodward's 'sixth edition' was still being advertised on 18 January (p. 4), and
then in the subsequent issue (20 January) a 'seventh edition' is announced:

> The confluence of nobility and gentry to town, has occasioned so urgent a
> demand for the celebrated pamphlet on the present state of the Church of
> Ireland, that there is designed to be published on Saturday the 27th instant,
> a SEVENTH EDITION. (p. 3)

Here, with the longest interval between the announcement and the announced
date of publication—one week, Saturday to Saturday—we are nonetheless
engaged in the most politically significant correlation of pamphlet and political
action, meaning by the latter the beginning of the parliamentary session. If an
'edition' could be run off in a day before Christmas, why should this one take a
week at a moment of urgent demand and political consequence? The answer lies
not in mathematical calculations but rather in the recognition of advertisements—
even in the eighteenth century—as a dubious source of factual information. The
advance ad for the 'seventh edition' was repeated on 23 January in which issue of
the *Dublin Evening Post* parlimentary business was reported for the first time in
the new year. The issue of 25 January again saw the 'seventh edition' advertised
in advance, and finally on 27 January 'there was this day published' the long
awaited item. But, turning momentarily to the *Freeman's Journal*, one finds that
the comparable ad does not appear until the issue of 1-3 February, that is, a full
four weeks since the publication of the 'sixth edition'. If publication occurred on
3 rather than 1 February, as seems likely, then Saturday once again proved to be
the preferred day on which to re-launch *The Present State*.

The difference between the advertising campaigns for the sixth and seventh
'editions' on the one hand, and the pre-Christmas 'editions' on the other, relates
principally to a ratio of ads to the specific numbered 'edition'. Before Christmas,
each ad is effectively cancelled or answered by the publication and (alleged) sell-
out of an 'edition'. Commencing with the sixth, a different pattern attaches
numerous ads to a single numbered 'edition', with the curious result that a period
of high activity in parliament and in the press-rooms of rival booksellers is
marked by apparently slower sales of Woodward's pamphlet. Without figures for
the print-runs or sales, these speculations must lead to few reliable conclusions. It
is possible that Sleater printed too many copies of the sixth and seventh, and sales
(though they held up) did not increase to absorb the excess; alternatively, the
presence of counteractive pamphlets may have actually depressed rather than
stimulated sales of Woodward's pamphlet. (A radical further interpretation would
posit a greater interest on the author or publisher's part in strong political
publicity rather than in commercially rewarding sales, with a concomitant
willingness to stock-pile unsold copies of earlier 'editions', either for re-
processing with an altered title-page or simply for storage.)

The seventh was further advertised 'there was this day' published on 30 January
and 1 February. However, by the middle of February publicity had taken a different

form with announcements of support for the bishop among the cathedral clergy in both Christ Church and Saint Patrick's, Dublin. On 13 February 1787, the *Dublin Evening Post* carried a boxed ad announcing the gratitude of the dean and chapter of St Patrick's Cathedral to Woodward, and including notice of the bishop's acknowledgement of same. Similar tribute was paid to Dominick Trant. Sleater took the opportunity to announce an 'eighth edition', for publication nine days later, emphasising how the 'disturbances in the south' were 'at this present crisis, an object in both Houses of Parliament'. (p. 3) Unfortunately, the next day saw Trant mortally wound Sir John Colthurst in a duel arising from allegations made in Trant's *Considerations*. Undeterred, the cathedral clergy repeated their advertisment of gratitude to their champions in the issue of 15 February, and Sleater's advance notice of the 'eighth edition' was also repeated not only in that issue but in the following one (17 February). On 20 February, the cathedral clergy's ad again appeared, augmented by a similar tribute from Christ Church, Dublin. Likewise Sleater's advance notice was repeated—making a total of four successive announcements of the 'eighth edition'. The ratio of ads to publication of a further 'edition' had now greatly altered since the pre-Christmas phase of the campaign. Moreover, though announced for the 22 February, this 'eighth edition' did not appear before 3 March and probably not before 6 March. The combination of these two different kinds of evidence would strongly suggest that the booksellers were not shifting the remaining stock—however large or small—as quickly as Sleater had expected. Advertising now was directed towards the generation of sales of the lingering seventh 'edition' rather than the advance promotion of an eighth. The existence of a London edition at this point may help to explain the sluggishness of the current Dublin edition's sales.

The advertisments announcing availability of the eighth—'this evening will be published' (3 February, p. 3) and 'this day was published' (6 February, p.1)— adopted a new strategy. Lengthy parrying with Arthur O'Leary's response, quibbles over quotation or misquotation, and sundry other details were summarised in a paragraph attached to the citation of the pamphlet's title. As with Patrick Duigenan's *Address to the Nobility and Gentry of the Church of Ireland*, published the previous autumn, Fr O'Leary was singled out as the preferred antagonist, not so much in tribute to his talents as a controversialist but because protestant opinion might be expected to fall in behind one locked in combat with a Capuchin. In parliament, John Philpot Curran complained that Woodward's publication had been 'industriously circulated' through 'a number of editions'. (See *Freeman's Journal* 20-22 February 1787, p. 2.) Pamphlets by liberal members of the Church of Ireland deplored Woodward's extremism, and generally there was no shortage of opponents with whom the bishop might be advertised to good effect. Having been placed in the tradition of Swift, then supported by the cathedral clergy of the day, Woodward at last was set up in a straightforward contest with the Catholic champion. In these details, as in the altering ratio of ads per new 'edition', one sees Sleater's advertising campaign adjusting to the fluctuations of the paper war.

In all of this we find little or no evidence suggesting that the protestant ascendancy had been rapidly adopted as a conservative rallying-cry or concept. The transfer of emphasis within Sleater's advertisement on details in Woodward's title might be interpreted as indicating some altered view of what the paper war was about—not TITHES or MUNSTER but the PROTESTANT INTEREST. Yet this last phrase had been current for decades, and could not have been confused with the other. It was at the time Sleater encountered difficulties with the 'eighth edition' that secondary commentary from the conservative camp began to emerge. We will see in due course how Thomas Elrington, under various signatures, buttressed Woodward's position and did so through William Sleater's printing press. In two of five publications, he repeated Woodward's use of protestant ascendancy but added no distinctive endorsement of his own. A solo performance by Arthur Browne in the House of Commons, in which he is reported as paraphrasing and approving Woodward's contention with respect to the protestant ascendancy, was duly noted in the press (*Freeman's Journal*, 20-22 February 1787, p. 4), but it was also ridiculed by Edward Sheridan in a later pamphlet.

In the *Dublin Evening Press* of 10 March 1787, a different perspective can traced. A northern presbyterian addressed himself to the duke of Rutland, then lord lieutenant of Ireland, and declared that he and his fellow-presbyterians thought that

> it is not the most effectual method to prevent a Popish ascendancy, to discourage and mal-treat a very large majority of Protestant subjects, or that a party comparatively small should think themselves entitled to treat as aliens many thousands of steady and faithful citizens, who would sacrifice life and property, to maintain a REAL PROTESTANT ASCENDANCY in this kingdom. (p. 2)

Within the *Dublin Evening Post*'s coverage of the paper war, this scathing response to Woodward constitutes the nearest thing to an adoption of protestant ascendancy. It should not be overlooked that Sleater, as the person responsible for promoting Woodward's publication on a grand scale, does not appear to have noticed a new concept or catchy phrase, worthy of emphasis or even citation in his many advertisments. Hostile commentators on Woodward's performance did not ignore these details of bibliographical uncertainty. The author of *An Irregular Ode*, for example, mischevously added to his doggerel footnotes in which the bishop of Cloyne ('Dickey C') bemoans the progress of sales:

> See my book, you may get it at Sleater's, indeed you may get some of them in every shop, and a few still of the *first* edition; be careful to ask for the *first*, and they will bring you a parcel out of the back-room or ware-house. (p. 12)

And again:

> The eighth edition of my admired pamphlet advertised, and yet no address;

not even a deputation from the Commons, no vote of thanks; but sure some
of my brothers will move it in our own house. (p. 17)

These comments only make sense if stocks of the first edition (18 December
1786) could be plausibly claimed as still extant when the eighth was advertised
(13 February 1787). In addition, high political responses—mention of the work in
an address from the throne, or even a parliamentary vote of thanks—were
explicitly related to the *advertising* of a work, not to its intrinsic merit. This, of
course, was a satirical commentator deflating appearances, but the presupposition
upon which he operated was that the claims of publishers are highly suspect. The
satirical perspective should not be allowed to exclude the undeniable impact of
Woodward's pamphlet, nor the extent to which it penetrated the market, the
paper war, and public opinion generally. In May 1787, and again in August, the
Dublin Evening Post referred to 'the war of pamphlets'. *The Present State of the
Church of Ireland* was central to the war—central rather than initiating. References to it abound, but one or two of these hint at *gratis* distribution or *industrious*
circulation. It is noticeable that advertisements for the 'eighth edition' after its
appearance, and for the ninth generally, did not appear with anything like the
frequency noted in connection with earlier 'editions'. By the time the eighth was
available, the political aim of the campaign—protection of tithes—had been
largely achieved in parliament, and sales could be allowed to look after themselves. It is true that, in the ninth edition, Woodward adds some new material
looking back over the campaign and replying to critics. But this was in the nature
of a mopping-up operation, and not a crusade deserving numerous ads in the
Dublin Evening Post.

Finally, such notes as grace *An Irregular Ode* can alert us to distinguish
between the assumption of sales announced so as to achieve those sales, on the
one hand, and verifiable statistics on the other. A similar distinction should be
made at the ideological level. Just as the success of the pamphlet on the market
has been confused with adoption of a particular ideological term within that
publication, so the occurrence of protestant ascendancy within Woodward's text
has been fused with a later usage. This in turn has been made the more difficult
to detect by the manner in which commercial publicity for *The Present State of the
Church of Ireland* has been accepted as objective historical evidence. In order to
examine this latter point more fully, we must turn to examine surviving copies of
the pamphlet in all their suggestive abundance.

b) *The Eighteenth-Century Short Title Catalogue* is principally based upon
collections preserved in the British Isles and the north American continent.
While some anomalies and gaps can be detected, the data-base nonetheless
provides details of a large number of copies from which reasonably reliable
generalisations may be deduced. In the case of Woodward's pamphlet, the ESTC
recognises twelve title-page variants and lists locations where specimen copies
may be found. These twelve range fruitfully through the *nine* officially declared

on the title-pages, including one non-Dublin edition, and produce the following table:

[First edition]	128pp.	20 copies verified
Second edition	128pp.	5 copies verified
Third edition	128pp.	4 copies verified
Fourth edition	128pp.	5 copies verified
Fifth edition (a)	128pp.	2 copies verified
Fifth edition (b)	140pp.	1 copy verified
Sixth edition (a)	124pp.	8 copies verified
Sixth edition (b)	140pp.	4 copies verified
Seventh edition (a) (London)	120pp.	21 copies verified
Seventh edition (b)	132pp.	9 copies verified
Eighth edition	132pp.	3 copies verified
Ninth edition	138pp.	4 copies verified

These figures are no substitution for a professional collation of all known variants of Woodward's pamphlet as distributed in 1786-7, but they are sufficiently striking to establish a few basic points. From 86 copies of nine so-called editions registered in the edition of ESTC consulted—it is up-dated from time to time— we find that twenty (23.8%) are relatively uncomplicated samples of the first issue of 18 December 1786, and a further twenty-one (25%) carry a London imprint, one of two 'seventh' editions. This tally for two 'editions' amounts to just about half of the copies verified for all variants in ESTC. The importance of the first edition needs no emphasis, and the London edition (genuinely a re-set text and so entitled to be called an edition) was designed to serve the same purpose in the imperial as distinct from provincial capital.

Beyond these two, the (b) version of the 'seventh'—following on the wake of the high profile London edition—survives in appreciable numbers, with the preceding 'sixth' (a) accounting for nearly as many as the 'seventh' (b). The existence of a 'fifth' in a state citing the London edition demonstrates the extent to which British publication influenced (apparently in retrospect) the presentation of Dublin 'editions'. Six (a) and Seven (a & b) cluster round the important transfer of the book to London, and together account for 38 copies (or just under half of the total registered in ESTC) Here again is further evidence that the production of *The Present State of the Church of Ireland* was calculated—initially, to maximise an immediate Dublin market just before Christmas 1786, and then, to repeat the exercise in London at the end of the following month. (The element of calculation cannot yet be exactly measured in terms either of deliberate planning or of retrospective damage limitation.) Other 'editions' amount to strategic re-issues, accommodating a small amount of new material and some re-setting, but with the title-pages adjusted to suggest a massive prior demand and a sustained further demand for copies. 'Strategy' in this context may be regarded as accommodating both a political desire to issue a seemingly fresh version of a crucial text and a commercial need to shift existing stock of the same title.

c) A census of copies of *The Present State* held by the major Irish libraries throws up further statistics, not to be identified with the ESTC tally, bearing upon the question of the pamphlet's renowned multiplicity of 'editions':

National Library of Ireland (14 copies)

5 of the first edition
1 (incomplete) of the 'fifth edition'
2 of the 'sixth edition' (124pp)
1 of the 'sixth edition' (140pp)
4 of the 'seventh edition' (132pp)
1 of the 'eighth edition'.

Royal Irish Academy, Dublin (9 copies)

1 of the first edition
1 of the 'second edition'
2 of the 'third edition'
1 of the 'fourth edition'
1 of the 'sixth edition' (124pp)
1 of the 'seventh edition' (120pp London)
1 of the 'seventh edition' (132pp)
1 of the 'eighth edition'
1 of the 'ninth edition'.

Trinity College, Dublin (6 copies)

2 of the first edition
1 of the 'second edition'
1 of the 'third edition'
2 of the 'ninth edition'

Russell Library, St Patrick's College, Maynooth (5 copies)

2 of the first edition
1 of the 'second edition'
1 of the 'third edition'
1 of the 'sixth edition' (124pp)

Queen's University, Belfast (5 copies)

1 of the first edition
1 of the 'fifth edition' (128pp)
1 of the 'seventh edition' (120pp London)
1 of the 'eighth edition'
1 of the 'ninth edition'.

Union Theological College, Belfast (3 copies)

1 of the first edition
1 of the 'seventh edition' (132pp)
1 of the 'eighth edition'

Boole Library, University College, Cork (3 copies)

1 of the 'sixth edition' (124pp)
1 of the 'seventh edition' (124pp London)
1 of the 'eighth edition'

Linen Hall Library Belfast (3 copies)

1 of the 'sixth edition' (140pp)
1 of the 'seventh edition' (120pp London)
1 of the 'seventh edition' (132pp)

Marsh's Library, Dublin (2 copies)

1 of the 'fifth edition' (128pp)
1 of the 'ninth edition'

Dublin City Library (2 copies)

1 of the 'fifth edition' (140pp)
1 of the 'ninth edition'

The presence of two first editions in the Russell Library faciliated a rapid, and almost random, comparison. The two were discovered to differ in a fashion which showed correction of a complex misprint on p. 12 (cf the 4th line up) in one copy.

Some comment on the 'fifth', 'sixth' and 'seventh' edition copies in the NLI is in order. As the 'fifth' only includes matter up to p. 112, it is not possible here and now to identify it further as an (a) or (b) variant, as defined above with reference to the ESTC statistics. It will be obvious, from these figures generally, that the 'fifth edition' is by far the rarest, a fact not insignificant in that this (in its 'a' state) was the last 'edition' advertised in Dublin prior to the launching of the 'editions' which included an extract from the preface to the London edition.

Each of the three NLI copies of the 'sixth' is distinct. With one copy amounting to 140pp. and two with 124pp. each, it would seem clear that both variants (a) and (b) are present. However, the 124pp. copies themselves are far from identical: one has an edition-statement reading 'The sixth edition. With an extract from the preface to the London edition, and many very material additions interspersed and translations of the Latin appendices.' The other is simply stated to be 'The sixth edition', with no further description following. The NLI copies reveal another relationship between these differing instances of the 'sixth edition'. The example of that with the longer edition-statement carries on the index page (p. 124) certain deletions in ink. These deletions have been effected on the index page of the other. We can thus establish that at least three distinct states of the 'sixth edition' are identifiable.

From examination of a small number of copies of 6(a) and 7(b), it is possible to hazard a good guess at the printing history linking the two. At the bottom of p. 4 of the former, the half-word INTRO- appears as a catchword. However, though the INTRODUCTION does duly commence on the page numbered 5, there intervene eight pages (numbered i-viii) of the 'Extract from the preface to the London edition' with the last page of the entire pamphlet being p. [124]. In 7(b) these interruptive eight pages are accommodated into the main pagination sequence, thus allowing the former p. [124] to become p. [132]. It is clear then that, in part at least, the 'seventh edition' has been effected by a change of page-numbering in the 'sixth', and that the 'sixth' was created by inserting new material into sheets from some earlier state (possibly the 'fifth' for this would account for the scarcity of surviving examples in the last instance.) Far from edition succeeeding sold-out edition, the printing history of *The Present State* must be regarded as possessing at least one phase in which an 'edition' absorbed unsold quantities of its predecessor.

IV. ANNOTATED COPIES OF THE PRESENT STATE

NLI possesses a copy of the seventh (b) 'edition' of Woodward's pamphlet with extensive annotations in the hand of John Barter Bennett. These are mainly concerned to identify individuals referred to but not named in Woodward's text, and to supply some additional information together with the names of persons whom Bennett consulted. Naturally, the copy has been most useful to historians of the period, and has been frequently quoted. As an illustration of how the general argument of *The Present State* was received at the time it is less revealing.

The Department of Early Printed Books and Special Collections, in the Library of TCD, has recently acquired a disbound, annotated copy of the first edition of Woodward's pamphlet, the title-page bearing the ms. inscription 'From the Author'. Two sets of annotations occur, one in eighteenth-century ink, the other in pencil. Many of the notes amount to little more than single words or phrases acting as a summary of the paragraph beside which they appear. However, four of the ink annotations are of more interest. One, on p. 105, identifies 'O'Leary' as the author of the anonymous *A Letter Addressed to the Public* (no. 32 above): not only does this add a further item to the list of Arthur O'Leary's contributions to the paper war, it also confirms that the *Letter* (dated 1787) was in circulation prior to 18 December 1786.

The other three annotations of significance are attached to sentences where the term 'the protestant ascendancy' occurs:

on p. 17 The Protestants [*sic*] Title in Danger

on p. 20 The Pope's Legate's Letter annuling Oath of Allegiance

on p. 21 Inefficacy of Oath of Allegiance on Papists.

While these do not add greatly to our understanding of contemporary responses to Woodward's argument, they suggest no particular attention was paid by one reader to the occurrence of the tic-phrase 'the protestant ascendancy'. J. B. Bennett, annotating the copy now in the NLI, left all invocations of protestant ascendancy without comment.

The QUB copy of the 'ninth edition' bears 15 marginal marks including just one attached to a passage invoking protestant ascendancy. ('I need not tell the Protestant proprietor . . .' etc. p. 31.)

Both copies of the pamphlet held by Marsh's Library contain annotations. The 'fifth' has marginal bar-lines and/or underlinings on fifteen pages, but apart from that marking the passage (p. 53) relating to the Irish language these do not strike me as distinctive: none relates to the innovations of protestant ascendancy. The 'ninth edition' is signed on the title page by Thomas Davis (1818-1845), but there are no further annotations.

Sir John Gilbert's elegantly bound copy of the 'ninth' in the Dublin City Library carries the inscription 'From the author' on the fly-leaf.

V. A NOTE ON SOME AUTHORS AND PUBLISHERS

The identifiable authors contributing to the paper war were

ASHE, Isaac (d. 1834) appointed vicar choral in Armagh cathedral in 1782. A graduate of Trinity College Dublin (1771). No. 10.

BARBER, Samuel (1738?-1811), presbyterian minister at Rathfriland, Co Dublin, from 1763 to his death; colonel of volunteers, 1782; favoured extensive reform; imprisoned in 1798. Nos. 58, 61.

BEAUFORT, Daniel Augustus (1739-1821), geographer; vicar of Collon, Co Louth from 1790 to his death; related by marriage to the Edgeworth family. No. 73.

BLAKE, Sir Francis (1737-1818), English political writer. No. 55.

BROWN OR BROWNE, Arthur (1756?-1805), born in New England of Irish parentage; educated at Harvard and Trinity College Dublin; became regius professor of Law in TCD in 1785; MP for Dublin University from 1783 until the Union. Nos. 7, 22.

BURROWES, Robert (c.1758-1841), a Fellow (1782) of Trinity College and a founding member of the Royal Irish Academy: he was dean of Cork from 1819 till his death. No. 40.

BUTLER, James (1742-1791), Catholic archbishop of Cashel from 1771 until his death. A descendant of Viscount Mountgarret, Butler was reckoned a very wealthy and well-connected man. Nos. 31, 34.

CAMPBELL, William (d. 1805) Born in Newry, Co Down; presbyterian minister in Armagh from 1764 to 1789 and in Clonmel, Co Tipperary, from 1789 to death. Nos. 9?, 19, 92.

CLARKE, Thomas Brooke (born Dublin 1756 or 1757, son of Nathaniel Clarke, merchant) educated TCD; was librarian and chaplain-in-ordinary to the Prince of Wales. He later took part in the paper war centred on the Union debates of 1799 etc. Nos. 15, 30, 71.

DAWSON, Thomas (writer on agricultural and industrial topics since the 1750s, consistently signing himself Publicola) No. 42.

DUIGENAN, Patrick (1735-1816), Fellow of TCD, ecclesiastical politician; elected MP for Old Leighlin in 1790. It may be significant that, when the Irish House of Commons resumed business early in 1787, a writ to fill the Old Leighlin seat was moved by Thomas Conolly, Woodward's parliamentary patron. Duigenan was accused of place-seeking by opponents in the paper war of 1786-7. After his election he became a virulent critic of Henry Grattan's political conduct. Nos. 3, 36?

ELRINGTON, Thomas (1760-1835), Fellow (1781) and Provost (1811-1820) of TCD; bishop of Limerick from 1820 to 1822, and of Ferns and Leighlin from 1822 to his death; a formidable if narrow intellect. Nos. 47, 57, 63, 78, 86.

ERSKINE, John, dean of Cork died 1795.   No. 57.

FARRAL, the rev. Charles; possibly the same man as the O'Farrel referred to in the NLI annotated copy. Farral published *Philoneika; or, an answer to Mr [Arthur] O'Leary's remarks on . . . Wesley* (Dublin: Hillary, 1780) on the t-p of which he is described as having preached in St Michan's Dublin in March 1779. The author describes himself (p. [iii]) as 'having lately renounced the errors of that church which Mr O'Leary has undertaken to patronise by apologies.'   No. 74.

FLEURY, George (or Fleury, George Lewis; d. 1825). Both of these were clergymen in the diocese of Waterford, George Fleury being curate of St Olave's from 1784 onwards, George Lewis Fleury being archdeacon of Waterford from 1773 until his death. No. 21.

GODFREY, Luke (d. 1799), rector of Kenmare, County Cork. A graduate (1763) of Glasgow University.   Nos. 54, 75.

GOUGH, John (1721-1791) Born in Kendal, Westmoreland; master of the Friends' School in Dublin from 1752 to 1774, afterwards at Lisburn, Co Antrim. Author of a *History of the People Called Quakers*.   No. 88 (initials of author only).

GRACE, George. Is this the George Grace who subsequently became proprietor of the *Clonmel Herald*?   No. 76, 77.

GRAVES, Richard (1763-1829), dean of Ardagh from 1813 to his death.   Nos. 4?, 18.

GRIFFITH, Amyas (1746-1801), journalist and poetaster.   Nos. 43, 46.

HALES, William (1747-1831) chronologist; fellow of TCD 1768; rector of Killeshandra, Co Cavan from 1788 until his death; prolific writer.   Nos. 49, 83.

JACKMAN, John   No. 8.

LE FANU, Philip (fl. 1790), clergyman of the Church of Ireland; of the same Huguenot family as the novelist Joseph Sheridan Le Fanu.   No. 1.

MADISON, James (1751-1836). Later 4th president of the United States of America, Madison wrote the *Memorial and Remonstrance* in June 1785; it circulated anonymously in broadside form. Its republication in Dublin almost certainly occurred without his knowledge.   No. 5.

MC CULLY, J., possibly a resident of Ballyherbert, Co. Down.   No. 41.

O'LEARY, Arthur (1729-1802), Capuchin friar who worked in France as a chaplain before returning to Cork. Prolific pamphleteer and controversialist. Noted also as a wit and bon viveur.   Nos. *17*, 32, *44*, *45*, *66*.

RYAN, Edward (d. 1819), prebendary of St Patrick's, Dublin, from 1790 to his death.
                                                                             No. 60.

SHERIDAN, Edward (d. 1829). A medical doctor, and relative of the Catholic bishop Patrick Joseph Plunkett (1738-1827), he was prosecuted in 1811 as a member of the Catholic Committee.   Nos. 16, 56.

STOCK, Joseph (1740-1813), Fellow of TCD, 1763; bishop of Killala from 1798 to 1810 and of Waterford and Kilmore from 1810 until his death. Remembered for his balanced account of the French invasion of Connacht in 1798 and for scholarly works.   No. 62.

STOKES, Gabriel (1731-1806), sometime fellow of Trinity College, Dublin; father of Whitley Stokes (1763-1845, United Irishman and professor of medicine); translator of

Euripides and author of at least one anonymous defence of tithes, *A Letter to the Right Honourable J — n L — d A — y* (1773).   No. 4?

THOMAS, Daniel (Welsh-born medical doctor) Also wrote *An essay on the yellow fever of western India* (Dublin: Porter, 1797)   No. 48.

TRANT, Dominick (barrister and MP for Kilkenny, 1776-1783) In the year he entered parliament he married (as his second wife) Eleanor FitzGibbon, daughter of the future earl of Clare. Also wrote *Observations on the late proceedings in the parliament of Ireland on the question of a regency for that kingdom* (Dublin: Sleater, 1789)   No. 13.

WILLIAMS, John   No. 89.

WOODWARD, Richard (1726-1794), step-son of Josiah Tucker (1712-1799, economist and dean of Gloucester); educated at Wadham Colege, Oxford; befriended by Thomas Conolly whom he met on the continent, he came to Ireland under Conolly's patronage; dean of Clogher from 1764 to 1781; bishop of Cloyne from 1781 until his death; wrote on philantropic topics; subsequent to *The Present State* published *A Charge Delivered to the Clergy of the Diocese of Cloyne, at the Ordinary Visitation, on the 3rd of July 179* (Cork: Edwards, 1793).   No. 53.

WRAXALL, Sir Nathaniel William (1751-1831) Indian administrator and English memoirist. (Perhaps Wraxall's pamphlet should not be listed as it originated outside Ireland. However, as discussion of the war has focused on the allegedly wide adoption of protestant ascendancy, it seemed right to include at least one example of a London publication reprinted in Dublin, surveying the political scene in 1787, and omitting all reference to the matter. Negative evidence is no less evidence than positive.)   No. 79.

The above list of thirty-five authors accounts for fifty-five of the ninety-two pamphlets/titles which have been taken as constituting the paper war. Though the attributions to Farral, Fleury, Graves and Stokes can hardly be regarded as certain, if one bears in mind that a number of other items (e.g. Grattan's speeches or the charges of named judges) can be attributed also, then a figure of 60% or more can be established for pamphlets where the author is now known.

Of the ninety-two items listed and analysed here, three Dublin bookseller-publishers were responsible for well over half. Patrick Byrne, who dominated the trade, issued almost one third of the titles— 28 items—viz. 4, 8, 11, 12, 13, 18, 19, 23, 26, 27, 31, 34, 38, 44, 45, 54, 55, 58, 60, 61, 68, 75, 76, 77, 79*, 81, 89, 91. This includes one item* where he collaborated with several other publishers. Byrne's range was comprehensive: he not only made available to the public arguments from all sides of the debate—established church, Catholic and presbyterian—he was also willing to publish specific replies to publications issuing under his own name.

This commercial ecumenism stands in contrast to the attitude of William Sleater Junior, whose imprint distinguishes the second largest number of items, 17 in all—viz. nos. 2, 10, 22, 28, 39, 47, 50, 51, 53, 57, 63, 74, 78, 85, 86, 87, 90. Sleater's involvement begins with Woodward's *Present State*, includes all of Elrington's contributions, one of Arthur Browne's, the item by Isaac Ashe, the item possibly by the convert Farral/O'Farrel, and the re-published abstract of denominational statistics. The remainder is anonymous or pseudonymous work.

Nowhere is Sleater's record marked by pro-Catholic or dissenter feeling.

One observable minor event of the paper war is young Sleater's removal from his premises in Castle Street down to the New Buildings in Dame Street. This is effected by St Patrick's Day 1787, and the alteration of address—there was an overlapping period when both were used on title-pages—serves to establish a chronology of publication in some instances. All but the last of the nine Dublin 'editions' of Woodward's *Present State* carry the earlier address.

The third notable publisher was William M'Kenzie, though with only nine items to his credit he trails a poor third after Byrne and Sleater. His publications were nos. 1, 7, 15, 24, 30, 49, 65, 71, 83, and his authors included Arthur Browne (one item), Thomas Brook Clarke (three items), William Hales (two items), and Philip Le Fanu (one item). It is clear from the imprint on Clarke's first title-page that M'Kenzie acquired this author via London and effected a Dublin reprint: two other reprints insert re-publications of strategic archival (no. 65) or historical matter (no. 1) into the debate. The only pseudonymous author publishing through M'Kenzie was 'Clericus' (no. 24) who seems to have had confidential access to (if he was not one of) the higher clergy of the Church of Ireland. All of M'Kenzie's known authors in the paper-war were members of the established church and supporters broadly of Woodward's position.

Notes follow on some other participating booksellers, printers and publishers. (Strictly speaking the term publisher should not be used of the Dublin book-trade in the eighteenth century as the activity had not been separated from that of printer or of bookseller.)

ROBERT BELL issued a re-print of *The Whole Works of Sir James Ware* in 1759, patched together from earlier editions. A vigorous advocate of the Irish book trade's rights, he emigrated to America in 1767: consequently the imprint of R Bell on no. 20 above should be treated with caution.

HANNAH CHAMBERLAINE may claim the distinction of being the only woman known to have participated in the paper war.

JOHN CHAMBERS was regarded with suspicion by the authorities, and subsequently became a United Irishman. Given the exotic and anonymous origins of *The anti-tyther*, it may be regarded as Chambers's own personal, if indirect, contribution to the pamphlet war.

PETER COONEY also printed *The Sixth Edition, Much Improved, Being a More Minute and Particular Account of that Arch-Imposter Charles Price . . .* (1786)

J. M. DAVIS is listed in the *Dublin Directory* as a printer and pawn-broker; his activities in the former connection were conducted on a very small scale.

JOHN EXSHAW published the *English Registry* etc in Dublin.

GEORGE GRIERSON (II) was King's Printer, and so licensed to print the bible etc.

CALEB JENKIN specialised in literary reprints.

CHRISTOPHER LEWIS appears to have commenced business in 1786; his name appears very infrequently on title-pages and usually with other booksellers.

R. MARCHBANK published both Arthur O'Leary and a verse satire on that author.

JAMES MEHAIN participated in the issuing of a *Description of Killarney* in 1776 and a House of Lords appeal in 1788. He later published one work of considerable cultural significance *Memoirs of the Life and Writings of the Late Charles O'Conor of Belnagare* [1796] by the rev. Charles O'Conor. In 1791, he published a pamphlet touching on one of the participants in the paper war—*A Narrative of the Misunderstanding between the Rev. Arthur O'Leary and the Rev. Mr Hussey.*

GEORGE PERRIN was printer to the Society for Promoting English Protestant Schools in Ireland.

BRETT SMITH was based at 34, Bridge Street.

SAMUEL WATSON launched the *Gentleman's and Citizen's Almanac* in 1733.

HENRY WATTS was a law-bookseller who in 1783 had published two editions of Patrick Duigenan's anonymous *The Alarm; or An Address to the Nobility, Gentry, and Clergy of the Church of Ireland.*

VI. THE WAR ELSEWHERE AND QUESTIONS OF METHOD

The larger concentration of the war within the book trade of the capital reflects the concern of the participants to influence parliamentary opinion specifically, rather than the wider public which might be reached through booksellers in Cork (near the Whiteboy disturbances) or Belfast (the centre of dissent). Only William Campbell appears to have taken the trouble to publish in the northern metropolis. And yet it is important, even at this early stage, thoughtfully to cross the city limits of Dublin to consider the implications of publication occurring elsewhere.

Naturally, London looms largest. Woodward's preface to the London edition of *The Present State* will be examined in due course; for the moment that edition represents one relationship between the two capitals and, of course, between parliaments (the Irish and British.) These relations were undergoing shifts and strains in the wake of the 1782 constitutional adjustment, and the book trade was no more immune to these pressures than any other commercial operation. Both Woodward and O'Leary have their work re-published in the imperial capital. From the title-list above, the total number of items (12) which appear in a London guise at first looks substantial. The author of no. 27 provides insight into the attitudes and practice of a major Dublin bookseller with regard to English copyright—see pp. i-ii—but on the whole the cross channel business lacks lustre. An exception might be declared in the case of no. 81 where Patrick Byrne's name in the joint-imprint does not suppress one's suspicion that the initiative in printing this elegant pamphlet lay with other parties.

Byrne is also implicated in most of the few titles which implicate Belfast, the exception being no. 41. The absence of Dublin from Byrne's imprint on the 1st and 2nd 'editions' of William Campbell's *Vindication of ... the Presbyterians* (no. 91), should be read in the emerging context of the 4th 'edition'—Belfast: printed by Henry Joy senr & junr. The 1st edition of Campbell's other contribution to the paper war is unique in that it is 'printed for' Byrne; given that another state with Belfast specified as the place of publication declares it 'printed by H Joy sen and jun', we can hazard a guess that Byrne acted in a secondary role on that occasion also. It may be that the author was dissatisfied with the Dublin bookseller—cf. the several states of no. 48—but it is more likely that Campbell was concentrating his forces within the stronghold of dissent rather close to the seat of parliament.

Despite Munster's role in the disturbances leading to the publication of Woodward's pamphlet, not to mention the southern residence of several prominent contributors to the war—Butler, Erskine, Godfrey, O'Leary, and Woodward himself—Cork features on just two title-pages. In both cases, Arthur O'Leary is central. The 'second edition, revised and corrected' of *Mr O'Leary's Defence* (no. 44) is apparently straightforward, with William Flyn following after the Dublin edition printed by Byrne. Though no. 50 casts O'Leary as victim rather than author, and despite the Cork reprint's citation of Robert Dobbyn as printer, Flyn seems to have been implicated here also. A note by John Barter Bennett on his copy of the Dublin *O'Leariad* can only be interpreted as unmasking the Cork imprint as an imposture at least in part:

> Mr O'Leary was always reputed to turn his Writings to the best Acct. Miss Flyn told me that her Father offer'd Mr O'Leary 200 Copies for one of the first of his Pamphlets which [illegible] be printed in Dublin, to reprint from here [i.e. in Cork], which Mr O'Leary declin'd, therefore on the Pamphlets being brought to Cork Mr Flyn printed this Edition to vex Mr O'Leary. The Dublin Edition was 2/2. Mr Flyn's 1/7.[2]

Robert Dobbyn was no convenient invention; he is credited with the 2nd (Cork) edition of Arthur Browne's *Thoughts on the Present State of the College of Dublin* (1782) which had been originally issued in Dublin without a printer's name. Though the evidence for 1786-8 is slight, it would seem that provincial printer-booksellers lacked the cash to pay authors of O'Leary's standing; authors in turn scorned barter, and the result for *The O'Leariad* was the unique provincial re-publication of a title originating in William Sleater's new printing-house down on Dame-street, a few hundred yards from the Irish parliament.

Thus the only truly provincial publication is no. 72 which, by styling itself a sermon, achieves a double distinction in 'the spiritual wars' of 1786-8. Charles Evans of Drogheda can certainly be confirmed as a printer and newspaper publisher. Identity of authorship for the *Sermon* which he issued in 1787 remains to be established. But attribution in these terms is not always the most urgently needed datum of empirical research. The economic distress of curates can be readily assessed against the tithe income of their superiors, and yet leave room for an interpretation (e.g. of the *Sermon*'s pathos) which takes account of landlords' interest in limiting any groundswell of sympathy for the established church.

But if Evans is transparent as an imprint, what are we to make of those cases where seemingly dual-editions of the same title emanate above versions of the same imprint? Returning to Dublin, we find that William M'Kenzie (as his name is usually given) appears to have a hand in two states of both no. 7 and no. 65, featuring in each instance not only as printer but also as one for whom the work has been printed. In the case of no. 65, the same type was used, so straight-forward piracy can be ruled out—unless of course M'Kenzie printed neither state. Charles Benson has warned against taking title-page details wholly at face value, and our examination of Sleater's advertising campaign serves to confirm the prejudicial nature of what might be naively taken as 'fact'. This is not to cast doubt on the existence of Charles Evans or the actuality of Richard Woodward's fears. Simltaneously, we need more factual information about press-room practice and a broader interpretative methodology in which concepts such as property and labour might ultimately be readmitted to the historical debate. Bur, for the moment, what one is encountering is the complexity of seemingly raw empirical evidence, a complexity inscrutable within its own terms.

Sherlock Holmes is famous for the taunting re-assurance offered to his colleagues—'you know my methods.' Insufficient attention has been paid to the multiplicity of techniques implied here; and if historians are prepared to concede that events may have many causes, perhaps it is timely to suggest that interpretation can only emerge from a similarly diverse plurality of interpretive visions and revisions. Empirical data necessarily have their place, but these do not determine the range of conceptual tools brought to bear on any single problem. For example, pseudonymous descriptions such as 'a layman of the Church of England' (cf no.4) or 'the anti-tyther' (no. 5) are no less loaded than a bishop's specified name and title (no. 53). Interest, that increasingly compromising term, may suggest that a plethora of pseudonyms (cf. Thomas Elrington's in nos. 47, 57, 63, 78, 85; cf also nos. 86 and 69) is not simply a matter of disguise but is deployed so as to resist the ideological pressure of numbers per se, of that free trade in opinion which we will encounter in some writers of the mid-1780s whom Woodward acknowledged as prompting him to write.

The paper war dates itself from late 1786. Perhaps this is an empirical chimaera which a deeper concern with methodology and conceptualisation might refine. Yet refinement often and admirably demands an attention to irreducible crudities, and by this paradox is the dialectical relationship of method and interpretation inaugurated. Consider the initials which bring to an end the *Plain Reasons why the People Called Quakers ... Ought in Duty to Pay Tythes* (no. 51). Do these—JC—signify the Christian (James, Jasper, John, or what have you) and surname of some individual publishing in 1786? Or, if we were to attend closely to the suggestion that a bishop wrote this text, then a Christian name followed by the name of an episcopal see (Cashel, Clogher, Cloyne etc.) might be detected. Yet it seems that no single interpretation of the initials in 1786 can be sustained in these terms. Might it be possible therefore to shift the question into another area, that of inquiry why Quakers should be implicated in a paper war so trenchantly defined in terms of the establishment's confrontation with Catholicism, and Dissent's resentment of that monopoly? For, if John Cradock (died 1778) was author of an anti-Quaker text not published before 1786, then responsibility for its appearance must be sought elsewhere. Authorship, in such circumstances, is displaced by less traceable powers. In the case of the Drogheda *Sermon*, it may be significant that the TCD copy derives from nearby Collon Library; that is to say, authorship could, in theory, be pursued and established as a local phenomenon. But the real significance of the Drogheda publication and the anti-Quaker tract probably lies in their tangential relationship to the declared major issues of the paper war. Distressed curates offended the self-image of establishment, and introduced the dangerous topic of genteel poverty. Quakers had often been in trouble with state and church, with tithes and pacifism to the foreground of previous disputes. But their unsought role, as a minority vulnerable to the anxious and deflected attentions of an established minority, now momentarily symbolises a Catholic majority which still lacks political definition. In due course, relief and emancipation will acquire conceptual precision and power, but for the present one senses through the anomaly of the Drogheda *Sermon* the paper war's untidy frontier with the past, with undeclared issues (including economic ones), with impersonal patronage and systematic manipulation. Thus a bibliographer's fussing over a brace of initials raises fundamental issues as to whether the war had any determinate beginning, and whether it is possible to isolate one concept without implicating other unintended ones.

THE DEBATE SURROUNDING
WOODWARD'S *PRESENT STATE*
WITH SPECIAL REFERENCE TO PROTESTANT ASCENDANCY

I. FOUR CLERICAL CONTENDERS

Strictly speaking, we cannot locate Richard Woodward's publication of 18 December 1786 at the start of the paper war. Earlier salvos had been fired, and the bishop's own acknowledgment of Patrick Duigenan's *Address to the Nobility and Gentry of Ireland* as a precursor indicates a line of succession and possibly a degree of consultation.[1] Duigenan in turn had been replying to *A Project for the Better Regulation in Collecting the Income of the Clergy*, now known to be the work of Luke Godfrey, rector of Kenmare. Thus the so-called hardline publications of late 1786 should be seen as responses to more charitable discussions of the peasant's condition under existing tithe laws. It is true of course that *The Present State of the Church of Ireland* turned a skirmish into a battle, and that the paper war can be structured round Woodward's pamphlet, responses to it, and responses in turn to these.

The overall body of work published can then be divided into three parts, aligned to the three major denominational divisions of Irish Christianity—the presbyterians, the Roman Catholics, and the Church of Ireland establishment of which Woodward himself was a prelate. Yet if this tripartite division suggests a tightly structured debate, the topics covered ranged far and wide, to touch on the decline of the Irish language, poverty, papal authority, smuggling, the Treaty of Limerick, legislation in the United States of America, sumptuary excess etc. Woodward himself, as James Kelly has usefully observed, never re-enters the fray save to amend the successive 'editions' of *The Present State*.[2]

Our interest in the paper war can be more closely focused than this survey of its main features would suggest. According to one view, the concept of protestant ascendancy is therein debated, adopted and developed. Naturally, the three parties to the dispute cannot be expected to treat the notion in the same manner. Members of the established church might embrace it, while those beyond the establishment might legitimately be said to have adopted at least the terminology *if they specifically used it* in resisting Woodward's argument. Kelly is confident on the point of the term's adoption. Discussing the situation in 1787, he writes of 'what conservative Protestants now termed "the Protestant ascendancy".'[3] Elsewhere he specifies who these conservatives were

Irish Protestants regarded the Church of Ireland as one of the pillars of their 'ascendancy'. That, after all, was the contention of Woodward, Duigenan, Hales, Ryan and others in the mid-1780s.[4]

In this connection, the implication has been made that one resisting this conclusion has declined to scrutinise the evidence establishing that 'a respectable number of the Protestant pamphleteers who contributed to the public debate on the Rightboys in 1787 and 1788 justified their hardline position by referring to the need to uphold "the Protestant ascendancy".'[5] On another occasion, Kelly names Robert Burrowes, Edward Ryan, and Joseph Stock as the three principal articulators of the establishment position.[6] In addition to Richard Woodward, whose employment of 'protestant ascendancy' has been gauged already, we now have the names of four ordained ministers of the Church of Ireland on whose behalf it is claimed that they employed a concept of protestant ascendancy.

While taking this group of conservative spokemen first, we should recall the extent of the debate to which they contributed. In all it generated over ninety publications, not counting re-prints, 'second editions' and varying states. Duigenan's *Address to the Nobility and Gentry* had appeared in October or November of 1786, and the absence of protestant ascendancy from its vocabulary deserves comment on two counts. First, insofar as Duigenan precedes Woodward, the absence is unremarkable and does not damage the case in favour of the bishop as populariser of the concept. Second, insofar as Duigenan follows on George Ogle's parliamentary outburst of February 1786, the absence is damaging to the case which relies on Woodward's popularising something already in 'the public domain'. Given that Woodward acknowledges Duigenan explicitly, the *Address* cannot be honestly advanced as evidence of Duigenan's 'contention' that the Church of Ireland was a pillar of 'ascendancy'. If we turn to the 'second edition' of the *Address*, which incorporates a date-line of 3 April 1787—some fourteen weeks after Woodward's first appearance—nothing has changed. The type has been reset at least in part, and eight pages of preliminaries added, permitting the correction of 'Booksellors' from the first. An errata list on p. [viii]—not without error itself—serves as well for the 'first edition' as the 'second'. Thus, where we find Duigenan writing prior to Woodward and then amending after the publication of *The Present State*, there is equally no trace of protestant ascendancy.[7]

Duigenan, it might be argued, is an exceptional case, not least in the violence of his language and the early point at which he engaged the enemy. The trio of conservatives (I have reservations about the term, but let it pass for now) preferred by Kelly entered the controversy relatively late in the day. Woodward, it will be remembered, had launched the 'first edition' of *The Present State* on 18 December 1786. Various replies issued from the booksellers in the following weeks, but it was not until 6 March 1787 (at the earliest) that Ryan appeared in print, not so much in defence of Woodward as in attack upon a presbyterian respondent, Samuel Barber.[8] One feature of Woodward's pamphlet is reverse-mirrored in Ryan's: where the bishop looked back to Duigenan as a precursor,

Ryan specifies Burrowes as another writer who shall take up the cause. Here, in two instances, one finds the linking of contributors to the conservative side of the debate enacted within the pamphlets themselves. Nothing conspiratorial is alleged in this observation; on the contrary, one sees a public linking by one commentator to the work of another. However, with respect to James Kelly's citing of Ryan as a contender on behalf of protestant ascendancy, one has to report that—as in the cases of Duigenan and the Pseudo-Theophilus—no trace of the term can be found in *Remarks on the Pamphlet of Mr Barber*, Ryan's sole contribution to the paper war.[9]

We come then to the rev Robert Burrowes, whom Ryan had obligingly introduced in his concluding paragraph. Both address themselves to Barber, a feature which might suggest that it was the vigour of the dissenter's response to Woodward, rather than Woodward's own case, which drew them into print. Whereas Ryan had wholly failed to pick up a concept of protestant ascendancy from the prelate, Burrowes was prepared to do a little better. On three occasions, he makes the effort, but lapses into an earlier terminology in the end. Consider these passages:

i) Is it *Quixoticism* in the Protestant Dissenter, to uphold the establishment of the Church of Ireland, against the ascendancy of the church of Rome?

ii) Is it not highly probable, that on the first favourable opportunity, a Popish ascendancy would annul the [land] grants and avenge the usurpation [of estates]?

iii) The Roman Catholics are indebted for your compassionate and irritating history of their oppressions, and your support of their title to that religious ascendency, you would never think of granting them.

iv) Could any means be worse devised to promote the Protestant interest, with liberality of sentiment and harmony among all religions, than to confine each to a separate district?[10]

Subjected to analysis, the first of these sentences displays the noun 'ascendancy' in contradistiction from 'establishment', an usage hardly compatible with anything we found in Richard Woodward's nine sentences on a similar topic. The second and third of Burrowes's sentences, however, suggest that this 'Popish ascendancy' is a thing of the future, while the fourth employs 'the Protestant interest' in a manner which gives one no cause to suspect the coincident existence of a 'protestant ascendancy'. In Kripkean terms, no 'link by link' transmission of name with a constant reference has been achieved between Woodward and Burrowes. Indeed, Burrowes quite simply gives no evidence of its 'popularity' whether in the 'public domain' or elsewhere.

William Hales was slow to come in aid of his fellow contenders on behalf of protestant ascendancy, and when he did he too manifested no knowledge of the term's existence. His contribution was first advertised in the *Dublin Evening Post*

on 8 February 1787—'speedily will be published, An address to the rev. Dr
Butler . . . by Wm Hales'.[11] But the same paper on 1 March announced that 'the
domestic anxiety and distress in which Dr Hales has been involved for some time
past will, he hopes, plead his excuse with Doctor Butler and the Public, for
delaying the publication of his Address etc for a few weeks longer. T. College
February 4.'[12] In the event, the address (now re-named *Observations on the . . .
Pope's Supremacy* was published on 24 April, and with such irregular pagination
as would indicate an interrupted or rushed job in the printing-house. Whatever
the delay and distress, protestant ascendancy puts in no appearance in Hales's
lengthy production, though it is now over four months since the *Present State*
first appeared.

Hales published a second pamphlet in 1788, *A Survey of the Modern State of
the Church of Rome*, in which he displays a close knowledge of pamphlets
published in the new United States of America. By this time, he was no longer a
Fellow of Trinity College, but had taken up residence as rector of Killeshandra in
County Cavan. Historians of the College have commended his industry in post-
academic life, while suggesting that rural seclusion affected the quality of his
work. Yet the *Survey* constitutes perhaps the longest contribution to the paper
war, and contains a close approximation to the concept of protestant ascendancy
said to be a key element in the political thinking of conservative protestants,
though the term 'had been in popular currency for but a few years.'[13] The
occasion arises in the latter half of the book where Hales quotes James Butler of
Cashel in dealing with the historical allegiances of Irish Catholics and the
circumstances

> which led them 'to persevere in their fidelity to the Family to which *they
> thought* the power of the Crown annexed' in opposition to the Protestant
> Government, Religion, and Ascendancy here . . .'[14]

If we turn to Joseph Stock, the last of the four clerical contenders on behalf of
protestant ascendancy identified by James Kelly, we have at last the satisfaction
of finding the complete phrase incorporated into the pamphlet dispute ignited by
Woodward in December 1786. Stock's *Reply to the Rev Dr Campbell* was
advertised in the *Freeman's Journal* of 31 May—2 June 1787, and its publication
can be assigned to a date in late May at the earliest. It cites the 'eighth edition' of
The Present State which appeared on 1 March. Of the nine sentences in
Woodward, Stock chooses to quote one *verbatim*—'I need not tell the Protestant
proprietor of land . . . that the security of his title depends very much, if not
entirely, on the Protestant ascendency; or that the preservation of that ascendency
depends entirely on an indissoluble connexion between the sister kingdoms.'[15]
This was not quite the last of the matter, for a few pages later Stock appears to
quote William Campbell whom he is officially refuting—'Don't be afraid, on the
deposing of your [i.e. Woodward's] church, that Presbyterians will not be in
readiness to make a proffer of their own, for the maintenance of government and

the protestant ascendancy.'[16] This passage led to confusion when Campbell in turn replied with *An Examination of the Bishop of Cloyne's Defence . . . with Observations on . . . Dr Stock* in January 1788. But for the moment we note that, in the work of the four contenders for protestant ascendancy published in 1787, one finds the term occurring only twice, in each case lodged in quotations from a) Woodward himself, and b) Campbell (in Stock) sardonically quoting Woodward back at his lordship.

We have then a negative report to file, in relation to the four clerical writers identified by James Kelly as a group particularly vocal in articulation of protestant ascendancy which (he claims) had, by 1788, 'become a key concept in the political thinking of conservative Protestants.' Nowhere in the pamphlets which they issued in the course of the paper war does one find an author using the term protestant ascendancy, *in propria persona*, not in even one of them.

II. DOMINICK TRANT AND THOMAS ELRINGTON

So far we have considered the response of pamphleteers pre-selected on the basis of their alleged advocacy of protestant ascendancy, and it may be time to examine the contributions of other figures, still concentrating within the ambit of Richard Woodward's thinking. Among lay writers attached to the Church of Ireland, Dominick Trant had the distinction of provoking a duel and killing his man, all on the strength of his defence of the ecclesiastical establishment in *Considerations on the Present Disturbances in . . . Munster*. We can fix the date of publication as 30 January 1787, though the author's subsequent apology for printing errors (and his alterations to the text in the second edition) indicate that he might usefully have delayed at least a day or two into February. According to Maurice Bric,[17] Trant was financially supported by Woodward; in any case he argued a case in relation to tithes so offensive to some of the gentry, that Sir John Conway Colthurst challenged the author to a duel on 12 February, the day that the second edition was due from the press. Sir John subsequently died, and (in one variant state at least) the third edition of Trant's pamphlet bore an engraved frontispiece depicting the duellists.

Trant was one of the few laymen to attach his name to a pamphlet issued in the paper war. His work was one of a small number—always excepting Woodward's—which ran to more than one edition. That he touched on sensitive issues can hardly be doubted, and his association with Woodward confirms one's suspicion that the linking of names in certain publications—Theophilus in Woodward, Burrowes in Ryan etc—was only one aspect of a pattern of collaboration within the conservative camp. Yet for all his centrality to the debate ignited by Woodward's *Present State of the Church of Ireland* and its inscription of protestant ascendancy, Trant nowhere employs the term in the three editions of *Considerations*.[18]

Thomas Elrington, however, is another matter. Though his name appears on none of the publications constituting the paper war, he can be proven to be the author of at least four and probably five. Issued between 10 February and 24 March 1787, these are:

To the Committee for Conducting the Free-Press By Philo-Clericus.

A Short Refutation of the Arguments Contained in Doctor Butler's Letter to Lord Kenmare By a Clergyman.

Remarks on a Letter Lately Published signed Arthur O'Leary, Stiled 'An Address to the Protestant Nobility and Gentry of Ireland' By a Friend to Truth and the Publick. [Signed Verax.]

Observations on the Indecent and Illiberal Strictures aginst the Lord Bishop of Cloyne Contained in a Pamphlet Lately Published under the Title of Mr O'Leary's Defence etc. [Signed Detector]

Reply to the Third Section of Mr O'Leary's Defence.

In one sense, the highly pseudonymous writer made no secret of his common authorship, for the last named item was printed with and was inseparable from the second, though the second also had an independent existence of its own and ran to a second edition. Other hints of sequels and so forth can be found in the texts themselves. The imprint, in all cases where one is present, is that of William Sleater who had been the publisher of Woodward's own *Present State* in December 1786 and who continued to issue further 'editions' of it. In two of the five—the *Observations* which names Woodward in its title and in *To the Committee* which attacks James Butler—Elrington employs the notion of protestant ascendancy or something like it. The instances are instructive:

Observations

The Bishop's object is to support the Protestant Ascendency, as inseparably interwoven with the very spirit of the Constitution. . .
[Quoting Woodward] 'but it may be suggested that the terms of the Oath might *in future* be extended to comprehend the entire Constitution, and the Protestant Ascendency would be secure . . .'
Upon the whole, the Bishop of Cloyne argues that the Protestant Ascendency ought to be preserved inviolably, and that this cannot be done, if too much Influence be allowed to Dissenters, who from Interest, Inclination, or conscientious motives, may meditate an Innovation . . .
When Presbyterianism obtained a temporary Ascendency in Great Britain, the Church was the first object of it's [sic] fury and resentment . . .
[Woodward] exactly and fairly stated . . . that it was inconsistent with the support of the Protestant Ascendency, that the whole of the Constitution should be entrusted to Presbyterians or that too much Political Influence should be afforded to Roman Catholics.

To the Committee

should Protestantism lose its present ascendancy, we would . . . find . . . that Mr Butler . . . would not be altogether so moderate . . . [19]

When Elrington invokes 'the Protestant Ascendency' he does so either by directly quoting Woodward or by explicitly paraphrasing those passages in *The Present State* where the bishop had introduced the phrase. When he uses the noun 'ascendency' without the familiar adjective, he implicates (as Woodward had done) the applicability of the notion in Great Britain or Scotland. There can be no doubt that Elrington followed Woodward in this usage, and their sharing the services of Sleater the bookseller may well have facilitated them. Nevertheless, there are discernible limits to Elrington's adoption of the term. First, he does not so much take it into his own idiom as cite its existence in Woodward's. Second, he only employs it in two of his five pamphlets. (Indeed, strictly, it only occurs in *Observations*.) Nevertheless, his role in the subsequent propagation of a conservative protestant ideology will be a notable one.

III. THE PRESBYTERIAN RESPONSE

In dealing with contributors to the paper war, we may find it useful to distinguish between those who plainly attach their names to their publications (like Hales or Woodward himself) and those (like Elrington and Duigenan) who prefer anonymity or pseudonymity. There was of course a tradition of respectable pamphleteers who did not sign their names on their productions but, in the case of a writer so prolix in sobriquets as Elrington, one can detect an intent to suggest a larger number of participants than was actually supporting his position. No such strategem can be observed among the dissenting contributors to the war, who were notably Samuel Barber, William Campbell and Amyas Griffith.

The first of these to respond to Woodward was Barber, presbyterian minister at Rathfriland, County Down. While the bishop's immediate concern was Munster, the implications of his defence of the establishment had profound implications in Ulster where dissenters constituted a very large proportion of the population. Before his elevation to Cloyne in 1781, Woodward had been dean of Clogher for seventeen years; several writers commented on his experience of northern conditions. Through Ulster, the argument between the established church and its rivals reached into Scottish history and so 'the present disturbances in the province of Munster' became a microcosm of larger concerns both contemporary and historical.

Barber wrote two pamphlets, the first in direct response to Woodward, and the second replying to the contributions of Burrowes and Ryan which we have already analysed. *Remarks on a Pamphlet entitled The Present State of the Church of Ireland* cites the 'sixth edition' of Woodward's pamphlet which reached the public on 6 January 1787. It was in fact the first issue of the work to appear in the

new year, and carried 'an extract from the preface to the London edition'. Barber
signs off with the date-line 26 January 1787, and by this means we can measure
the lapse of time between Woodward's first appearance and the first presbyterian
response. He taxes the bishop with failing to quote the bible in his own support—
'not a text of scripture, not even an allusion to one, appears in the whole
performance'—and proceeds to enunciate some frankly modern opinions. Religion, he declares is 'a personal matter between God and every man's conscience',
while tithes are discussed wholly without reference to the bible or the clergy; they
are a 'discouragement to agriculture'. Adam Smith features several times as an
authority on economic and social questions. Discussing ecclesiastical history,
Barber hints at evidence in the Church of Ireland of tory resistance to the
accession of George I, but crowns his performance with an uncanny glance into
the future:

> A century hence when some of our posterity shall read your celebrated
> Pamphlet, and learn from it that tithes were at this time paid by the whole
> people to the eight [sic] part, they will immediately conclude that the
> Presbyterians were a conquered people, or they never would have submitted
> to such a disgraceful situation as to be the helotes of the Episcopalians; worse
> than Helotes; for the Lacademonians never encreased their servitude,
> whereas that of the Presbyterians keeps pace with their industry . . . They
> assisted in conquering the Roman Catholicks, and were reduced to the same
> servitude.[20]

Barber's pamphlet ran to a second edition, re-paged and at least in part re-set.
The date-line of 26 January is retained and the text remains unaltered. Stung by
the comments of Burrowes and Ryan, the presbyterian ventured a second time
into print. Considerably shorter than its predecessor, the *Reply* is unusual among
follow-up contributions in maintaining the calm tone of the first and in
dismissing the critics without loss of temper. To Burrowes, Barber observes
'about a third of your book is taken up in raising terrible spectres from premises
invented in your own brain', but in repeating his preference for the establishment
of Catholicism in Canada to the establishment of episcopalian protestantism in
Ireland—if establishment there must be—he worked on an anxiety more than
merely personal or local.[21] The situation across the Atlantic, both in Canada and
in the newly independent United States, constituted one of the larger contexts in
which the conservative Irish churchmen of 1787 should be considered. Finally,
let it be recorded that Barber makes no reference to notions of ascendancy,
whether protestant, popish or presbyterian.

Amyas Griffith was a controversialist very different from Barber. Though he
championed dissent he was personally a member of the Church of Ireland who
claimed an archbishop among his relatives. The most authoritative historian of
the Irish book trade has recently described him as a 'flamboyant and dubious
character'.[22] In the 1770s, his anonymous gossip column written for the *Monitor*

newspaper had resulted not only in a court action but in the introduction of a Stamp Act by which government effectively censored such publications. Yet his *Observations on the Bishop of Cloyne's Pamphlet* deserves attention not only for its contents but also its sentimental style. The paper war did not throw up a literary genius, and one reads in vain to find anything approaching the talents of a Swift or Burke. Nevertheless, attention to style is advisable, even if most of the pamphlets fall into the categories of either—a) earnest argumentation unalloyed, or b) ditto, with occasional sarcasm. Griffith's sentimentalism, which attempts an identification of the writer's feelings with those of the poor, may seem bogus to those informed of his career in other quarters. Laurence Sterne was no saint, and yet his sentimental style came to represent an extension of the psychological resourcefulness of the English language.

Griffith's manner does not deter him from openly mocking Woodward's play upon the fears of his readers:

> How alarming must these words sound to all who love their country,—'the moment is critical, *it is decisive of the Protestant interest.*' But when we come to enquire what it is that renders it critical and decisive, all our fears vanish like a vapour:
> 'This is the crisis, and the crisis now!
> The Sow hath pigg'd, and pigged hath the Sow.'[23]

Nothing is more difficult to calibrate than the anxiety of those whose feelings, motives, interests, and attitudes we tend to discount. While Barber and Griffith accuse establishment spokesmen of conjuring spectres and exaggerating dangers, they fail to provide any means of gauging the actuality or mere display which these expressions may be. Perhaps it is this distance between them which explains—in two further instances—the absence of protestant ascendancy from their vocabulary.

But the most formidable champion of the dissenters in 1787 was undoubtedly William Campbell. A native of Newry, County Down, educated at Glasgow University, and for some time resident in France, he brought to the controversy both intellect, vigour, and confidence. In *A Vindication of the . . . Presbyterians*, he went further than Barber in discussing the relationship between the establishment of a denomination and the allegiance it commands in the population, to propose (not wholly in earnest, perhaps) that a nervous episcopal establishment might be replaced by one still protestant in character:

> And if, in the course of things, it should appear eligible to the wisdom of parliament to change the ecclesiastical Establishment, don't be afraid that the protestant ascendancy, or the stability of government would be in danger from the want of another national church. For, if a national Church be essential to the civil constitution, the Presbyterians might disappoint your anxious fears for the safety of the State; and as they so far outnumber your Church, they would give a greater strength to the constitution.[24]

Here, beyond question, is—*ipsissima verba*—'the protestant ascendancy' appearing in the text of an antagonist to Woodward. Yet, on closer examination, the passage displays less evidence of the adoption by Campbell of Woodward's phrase than of sardonic mimicry. However that may be judged now, it was this perhaps unguarded passage in *A Vindication* which allowed Joseph Stock to mount a counterattack upon the presbyterians. Stock's *Reply* has already been analysed, because it forms part of the Trinity-connected body of writing in which the adoption of protestant ascendancy was allegedly traceable. It is now time to consider Campbell's second contribution to the paper war, *An Examination of the Bishop of Cloyne's Defence* (1788), which replied also to what the author termed Woodward's 'apologists'—including Stock.

This lengthy performance dates itself (p. 208) to 25 January 1788; thus its publication comes more than thirteen months after the first edition of Woodward's *Present State*. A contorted starting point for the argument is set up when Campbell complains that Woodward, in the prefatory matter of his 'third edition', did not quote from Campbell (as claimed) but from Stock's paraphrase of Campbell. This is substantially true, and the demonstration of it is used to cast Stock as 'his lordship's apologist'. The phrases, borrowed from Stock and attributed to Campbell, include this in relation to the presbyterians—'to make a proffer of their own, for the maintenance of Government, and the Protestant ascendancy'.[25] Campbell complains bitterly that these words will not be found in his *Vindication*, his overall purpose being to minimise the impression given that presbyterians were eager to take on the role of an established church, in the event of episcopacy collapsing into nervous exhaustion. On three further occasions, he quotes from Stock to underline the point, and on each he is careful to employ quotation marks indicating precisely what is his own terminology and what is that of the established clergy with whom he contends:

> We are told [Stock p. 24] 'another pretence for expecting the final ascendancy of Presbyterianism in these kingdoms may deserve more attention—its model is better suited perhaps to the temper of our people, and to the genius of our civil constitution.' To have argued with clearness, it was necesary to explain Presbyterianism, and what is meant by the final *ascendency* of it...
> Dr Stock tells us, that to make a proffer of *their* own church, for the maintenance of 'Government, and the Protestant ascendancy—is a fear, which the *alacrity* of the sect considered, I dare say not one of us churchmen even entertained.'

And again quoting Stock:

> 'another pretence for expecting the final ascendency of Presbyterianisn in these kingdoms . . .'[26]

Convoluted though the argument is, Campbell's concern to resist the term protestant ascendancy, to reinscribe it exclusively as that of his opponents, manifests itself. It is true that the problem was partly of his own making, in that he had written in *A Vindication* that 'as Presbyterians would maintain the Protestant ascendancy, and as they out number your church [i.e. Woodward's] so very far, they ought to form the ecclesiastical establishment . . .'[27] What Campbell discovered was precisely that elusive dimension of printed discourse alluded to earlier in this essay—the unwritten and unmeasurable degree to which irony, tone of voice, a nod and a wink, can be misjudged on either side of an exchange. Seeing how his words had been turned by Stock, Campbell in his second pamphlet was attentive to quotation marks and to the business of re-placing the notion of protestant ascendancy where it belongs—back among those pamphleteers of the Church of Ireland who chose to use it. His own gloss on Stock's phrase 'the final ascendancy' is 'or general prevalence', by means of which he hopes also to allay fears that presbyterianism seriously contemplated a move towards establishing itself as the established church.[28] As with Elrington, in the one pamphlet of his which utilised the noun 'ascendancy', Campbell deployed it as often in a Scottish or British historical context as he did in a contemporary and Irish one. What one finds in the paper war is a modest proliferation of the noun 'ascendancy' (for the most part previously used in astrological contexts), with 'protestant ascendancy' occurring as a specialised sub-division in this modest proliferation.

The dissenters' response to Woodward's pamphlet, in the work of Barber, Campbell and their churchman-ally Griffith, is for the most part confident, even ebullient. Only in Campbell does the notion of protestant ascendancy appear, first as a mocking echo and ironical paralleling of Woodward's own phraseology, and then in a cumbersome, and not wholly good-tempered, exercise in resistance to its insinuation into his own phraseology. It may be argued that the latter represents a triumph for the 'neo-logism' which is said to have 'achieved respectability and currency remarkably quickly'.[29] Yet it is important to distinguish between '[the] protestant ascendancy' as actual words—*ipsissima verba*—occurring in a text following upon Woodward's (e.g. Campbell's first) and those words used by an author writing *in propria persona*—Elrington's *Observations* is the nearest thing to this so far discovered. We have still to find one contributor to the paper war in whose discourse the phrase has been naturalised.

IV. THE CATHOLIC ARGUMENT, BEFORE AND AFTER WOODWARD

The claim that protestant ascendancy had achieved ideological force by the time of, or during, the paper war can only validly stand if it can be shown that opponents of those espousing the cause of protestant ascendancy have acknowledged the currency of the term and used it themselves in debate. First of all, this requires the specification not only of the *ipsissima verba* (protestant ascendancy) but of a writer employing them *in propria persona*. Second, it is necessary in order to demonstrate the success of protestant ascendancy as an an *ideological* force to show that it has been imposed upon a discourse other than that propagating it, for only thus can it be shown to have altered modes of thought. In the case of the dissenters, we have seen how William Campbell came very close to endorsing the notion, but that his comments in *A Vindication* (1787) were couched in sardonic or ironic tones, while in *An Examination* (1788) he was careful to establish (with ostentatiously placed quotation marks) a cordon sanitaire between himself and users of the phrase. The dissenters were, at one level, fellow-protestants of Woodward's episcopalians; that is to say, they already had a perfect right to the first half of the phrase. The case of the Roman Catholics was wholly different.

Different also was the timetable in which the most publicly renowned of the Catholic spokesmen operated. Fr Arthur O'Leary (1729-1802), a Capuchin friar who had served his church in France in a manner which nonetheless gained the respect of the British authorities, was a popular spokesman for Irish Catholicism and an experienced controversialist long before the paper war began. In 1771 he had returned to Cork from the continent, and his public career included exchanges with John Wesley and interventions into debates concerning Catholic communities in America. His wit and polished manners enhanced his status as one who defended his people and yet urged on them a full and unqualified loyalty to the Hanoverian regime. O'Leary's earliest contribution to the controversy under analysis here, *The Rev Mr O'Leary's Address to the Common People of Ireland*, should be read also as part of another sequence of publications— O'Leary's own—which Patrick Duigenan (signing himself Theophilus) was anxious to cut short: hence the vehemence of language displayed in *An Address to the Nobility and Gentry*, the very title of which seeks to answer O'Leary by commanding a more elevated audience. Duigenan's intemperate and highly personal form of invective—he referred pointedly to 'the Fryar *with the barbarous Sirname*'—should be decoded not as the opening shot of the paper war as defined here but as an exercise in provocation directed at a cultivated opponent who had held the field for some time.[30]

O'Leary's second contribution to the debate struck contemporaries as arriving a trifle date. John Barter Bennett, annotating his copy of Duigenan's *Address*, calculated that it had 'appeared about Octr or Novr 1786 & O'Leary's not till about the February following.'[31] There may even be some evidence that efforts had to be made further to provoke him into a response to Duigenan and Woodward, for the suspect *Letter to the Rev. Arthur O'Leary* intervenes between the earliest editions of *The Present State of the Church of Ireland* and *Mr O'Leary's Defence*. The latter, unlike Woodward's publication, was not extensively advertised in the press, and O'Leary's plan appears to have revolved round his travelling personally to Dublin and his established reputation with parliamentarians and administrators. Certainly, the *Defence* opens with mocking comments on pamphlet controversy as if that were a business which the writer held in no high regard:

The murmurs of the lower orders against proctors and tithe-canters induced the authors of several publications .. to wish for some other mode of supporting the clergy . . . This plan . . . made Theophilus *mad*, and the Bishop of Cloyne *somewhat* angry. The alarm bell was rung by Theophilus, and the presses began to teem with the Bishop's pamphlets.[32]

The Dublin and London versions of what is basically the same text (cf. nos. 17 and 44 above) indicate in their difference the care O'Leary took in addressing two separate audiences. His testimony to the energy with which Woodward's *Present State* was disseminated is particularly valuable. Though he deplored the bishop's 'passive silence . . . for the space of fifteen months' during which Whiteboy outrages had disturbed the diocese of Cloyne, he noted also how Woodward had been 'intent upon collecting materials for a pamphlet, to surprise the public on the eve of the meeting of Parliament.'[33] O'Leary drew attention to the London edition of the *Present State*, commenting that 'the Lord Bishop of Cloyne's pamphlet has been read at St. James's, and his Majesty must entertain an extraordinary opinion of the Dissenters and Catholics of Ireland.'[34] Yet he chose to cite the 'fifth edition', this being the state least easily located now among surviving copies of the work. Whatever the reason for the relatively late appearance of *Mr O'Leary's Defence*, or for its choice of Woodward's fifth edition, O'Leary presents himself as a combatant ready to meet his opponents in the open: 'The senate of the nation is now assembled. The Lord Bishop of Cloyne and Counsellor Trant are in Dublin, and I am here to meet them.'[35]

Both in the *Address* of 1786 and the *Defence* of the following year, O'Leary made some play upon the term 'interest'. To his co-religionists, he advised that 'it is more your interest than you imagine, that the Protestant clergy of this country should be maintained in their rights.'[36] Some protestant readers undoubtedly found O'Leary's unimpeachable loyalty almost as irritating as his oft repeated witticism about Purgatory—that you could go further and speed worse. But his turning of the protestant interest into an argument to which loyal Catholics should subscribe illustrated a potential shift of emphasis or implication within the common usage of 'interest'. The *Defence* opened with the lofty announcement that 'whoever attempts to give an account of public transactions should be above the reach and power of hope and fear, and all kinds of INTEREST.'[37] This had its *ad hominem* dimension, for clerical defenders of the tithe system were clearly self-interested parties to the dispute. But O'Leary also penetrated to the centre of Woodward's title-page, with its italic emphasis upon *The Protestant Interest*, and in doing so he demonstrated an intersection between personal advantage and constitutional principle at the point where these share the noun, interest. Earlier, it had been possible to uphold the protestant interest in the name of security (as we would say nowadays.) But in the light of a more sensitive moral concern with personal affairs (itself not unconnected with changes in Established Church attitudes recommended by John Wesley), interest was becoming too frank, too revealing a term for continued incorporation in the

formulations of constitutional orators. While O'Leary nowhere adopts or acknowledges the terminology of protestant ascendancy—even in his *Letter to the
Monthly Reviewers* which he signed off as late as 30 July 1787 when the paper war
was virtually over—he does in a sense expose the vacancy into which it might in
time conveniently drop.

This familiarity, even intimacy, of O'Leary's with the tonalities of Church of
Ireland rhetoric is traceable at other levels. Basically, O'Leary argued that
Catholics had long demonstrated their loyalty, and that liberal-minded
protestants were happy to concede the rightness of measures to relax the penal
code. The ease with he was able to instance personal friends and acquaintances
among such protestants doubtless contributed further to the irritation of
protestants less benignly disposed towards concession. On several occasions, he
goes far towards identifying the author of articles appearing under the pseudonymous description 'A Dublin Shopkeeper', referring to him as 'a protestant
gentleman, an acquaintance of mine' or, more specifically as a 'Protestant
gentleman, who is married to the daughter of a clergyman in the diocese of
Cloyne'.[38] O'Leary knew that diocese well, for he been given certain responsibili-
ties therein when the Catholic bishop was infirm and the Whiteboys were causing
trouble. Such links with liberal protestants underscore a telling point when he
complains mockingly that 'the Bishop of Cloyne' [i. e. Woodward] 'must be a
stranger to the passions of the heart, of which *interest* has so strong a hold.'[39] This
latter jibe related to Woodward's apparent callousness in leaving his daughters at
risk in Cloyne while he himself travelled to Dublin declaring the diocese to be in
a state of insurrection. O'Leary's argument—that Whiteboyism was a declining
phenomenon at the time of the paper war, and that self-interest motivated some
at least of the contributors—was rendered the more offensive for its locating
domestic detail alongside political and constitutional opportunism. At the level of
verbal nuance and of linguistics generally, his pamphlets may have been all too
effective, even to the point of rendering less evident his repeated declarations of
loyalty, fellow-feeling, and common sense. His own humble origins exacerbated
the offence in the eyes of some readers, notably Patrick Duigenan whose
background was not wholly dissimilar.

The other champion of Catholicism in the paper war was James Butler (1742-
1791), Catholic archbishop of Cashel and Emly, author of *A Letter . . . to Lord
Viscount Kenmare* and *A Justification of the Tenets of the Roman Catholic Religion*
(both 1787). Butler himself claimed in the second of these pamphlets that the first
had been published without his consent, its having entered the printed domain
through (apparently unauthorised) publication in *Finn's Leinster Journal* in
January 1787. Kenmare's significance in all of this is based upon his status as a
Catholic nobleman who had acted as a forward scout on behalf of Catholics keen
to improve relations with the authorities; in this connection he had been the
recipient of Edmund Burke's letter in 1782. All of these figures—Burke,
Kenmare, Butler himself—underline the manner in which Irish Catholicism had
preserved its social dignity and found advocates willing to commend its historical

connection with nobility, ancient family, and something better than mere respectability. Butler himself was distantly related to the Ormonde family though—as befitted a Catholic—his titled ancestor was merely viscount Mountgarret, a supporter of James II in 1689. Nevertheless, 'according to the standards of the time the Archbishop was a very wealthy man.'[40] His social position assisted cordial relations with his opposite number in Cashel's other palace—Charles Agar—of whom it is said that he shared Butler's misgivings on the subject of *The Present State* and its impact upon inter-denominational relations.

Despite his social graces, Butler did not succeed in besting Richard Woodward. In part, he was caught up in an argument concerning the consecration oath taken by Catholic bishops and the alternative interpretations of its bearing upon their allegiance to the pope and to temporal authority. This was an area in which hardline protestants could cite other, hardline Catholic positions to the effect that papal allegiance overrode all other claims on a bishop's actions. Butler himself might argue a course of loyalty to the crown, but traditionalist, Counter-Reformationist texts did nothing to prove his position universally accepted throughout the church of Rome. Here again language lay at the heart of the dispute, and pernickedy translations of Latin phrases run throughout the attacks on Butler and the counter-responses provoked by these. But a further linguistic aspect of Butler's original argument contributed to his discomfort. On the topic of suffregans and titular bishops etc, 'I have been obliged,' he wrote,

> to employ those epithets, and names of description, usually known in the country. Because, otherwise, without devising new names I could by no means describe them, and the inventing of a vocabulary of that sort might breed a distraction in my readers' minds, that would possibly be not very agreeable.[41]

The conservative attitude towards language is exquisitely caught on its own poinard here. Resistant to innovation in terminology, and fearful of misleading or evasive euphemisms, Butler sticks to a set of 'names of description' which concede the subordinate existence of his church's dignitaries. At the same time, he is anxious to demonstrate their full commitment to the political order which has established a different church whose bishops are not titular merely.

A paradox thus emerges. While neither of the Catholic clerical spokesmen in the paper war adopt (even passingly) the terminology of protestant ascendancy, each in his own way reveals a level of linguistic susceptibility to such a 'neologism'. While the dissenters utterly reject episcopal establishment, the tithe system, and all that goes therewith, Campbell can go so far—but no further—as to recite 'the protestant ascendancy' in scorning the pretensions of the phrase. Each party indicates in distinctive fashion that the language of inter-denominational debate might be ready for the subsequent incorporation of a concept like that of protestant ascendancy.

Observers and participants at the time could not have been expected to anticipate the events of 1792, nor even finely to analyse the linguistic evidence of the paper war. William Ogilvie, husband of Emily duchess of Leinster and step-father of Lord Edward Fitzgerald, felt in February 1787 that 'the Roman Catholic Party [were] acting on Very Extensive Plans of Ambition.' An MP loosely attached to the parliamentary following of Thomas Conolly (Richard Woodward's patron), Ogilvie was far from being a protestant 'out-and-outer'; indeed by the end of the session he had distanced himself from such affairs.[42] The Catholic cause was always liable to exaggeration by foes of one degree or another, and the beacons of liberal protestantism to eclipse by brighter conflagrations. No fully comprehensive view of politics and its implications for the future was available in 1787—or ever. Even the scale of the paper war—let alone its minute verbal innovations—could not have been measured accurately at the time.

V. SOME STATISTICS

It is then useful to take stock of the situation. We have demonstrated that *neither* the Trinity-based conservatives (as identified by James Kelly) *nor* the leading figures among the presbyterians *nor* the spokesmen for Catholicism absorbed protestant ascendancy into their vocabulary, even to the point of employing it once—whether pedantically or colloquially—*in propria persona*. Who then were the contenders for the notion proffered in Woodward's *Present State*—apart of course from the bishop himself? What proportion of the debate did they control or influence? These questions might be temporarily posed in statistical terms, and an interim summary reported.

Of the ninety-two pamphlets taken here to constitute the paper war of 1786 to 1788, 77 belong to the classification, NPA, in the list given above (pp. 33–50). This signifies that no 'protestant ascendancy' citation can be found therein, though it should be noted that 6 of the 77 do employ the single word 'ascendancy' in a manner which will be noted in due course. In the same classification, PA (11 items) signifies that a citation of 'protestant ascendancy' *is* present, and QPA (4 items) signifies that 'protestant ascendancy' is present but within quotation marks (which may include more material than the two words but which also generally refer back to Woodward's *Present State*.) This is undoubtedly a crude method of assessing the extent to which protestant ascendancy had been current at the time of the paper war, but it is necessitated by the unsubstantiated claims made for its presence in the works of Burrowes, Hales, and Stock.[43] The following statistics emerge:

NPA	77	(inc. 6 'ascendancy' citations)
PA	11	(nos. 7, 37, 47, 53, 67, 76, 77, 83, 84, 91, 92)
QPA	4	(nos. 16, 19, 62, 90)
Total	92	

These figures can hardly give much comfort to those who wish to sustain the argument that protestant ascendancy possessed popular currency and achieved conceptual rigour by the end of the paper war. A closer examination of the PA category above will further dampen their ardour. Nos. 76 and 77 being the same text issued under two divergent titles, only one of them can be cited as evidence of proliferation, resulting in a tally of 10 rather than 11 in the PA category. Nor it cannot be assumed that all the pamphlets in this category *adopt* the terminology; on the contrary some can be shown to be deeply hostile to it, not just on ideological, but on linguistic or stylistic grounds. Indeed, if we bring together the maximum number of items which employ—however slightly, slightingly or by way of quotation—the term protestant ascendancy, the total (14) amounts to 15% of the publications constituting the paper war.

At first glance, 15% might seem an impressive proportion of pamphleteers converted to the new term, but the number of texts thus affected gives no sense of the slight degree within such pamphlets to which the term is adopted. Moreover, this total includes Woodward's own *Present State of the Church of Ireland*, which can hardly be held to extend the currency of the phrase which it is allegedly popularising at the same time, though it is noteworthy that no other contributor approaches the 'frequency' with which his lordship used the term, and the 15% of *publications* grossly flatters any measurement of the phrase's adoption within a publication. The total also includes two items (of Elrington's five) which invoke the magical term as Woodward's, the two (hostile) pamphlets by William Campbell already examined, and that of Stock with which Campbell took such exception. The parliamentary report (no. 92) does not properly feature in the war of pamphlets, and so will be set aside here as already adequately treated in the discussion of oral performance. Thus, six items are eliminated from our search for those pamphlets which might exemplify the adoption of protestant ascendancy so easily assumed by James Kelly.

Let us briefly survey the remaining seven. These are

7. A brief review of the question whether the Articles of Limerick have been violated? By Arthur Browne. Dublin: M'Kenzie, 1788. 104pp.

16. A critical review of the b. of Cloyne's publication, with occasional remarks on the productions of some other writers, particularly those of Trinity College, and on the conduct of the present ministry, addressed to his lordship. By an unbiassed Irishman [i.e. Edward Sheridan]. Dublin: Chambers, 1787. 102pp.

37. A letter to the bishop of Cloyne containing a plan of reconciliation and mutual benefit between the clergy and laity. [Signed Moderator] [n. t.] 1787. 12pp.

67. A review of Doctor Butler's pamphlet . . . By a friend to the constitution [signing as Clement.] Dublin: Grierson, 1787. 128pp.

76. (i.e. also 77) A short plea for human nature and common sense . . . By George Grace. Dublin: Byrne, 1787. 56pp.

83. A survey of the modern state of the church of Rome . . . By William Hales. Dublin: M'Kenzie, 1788. 226pp.

84. Temperate, unborrowed animadversions on a pamphlet late published by Richard,

bishop of Cloyne . . . By a sincere unbiassed protestant [signing as the UT — T]. Dublin: Davis, 56pp.

VI. WHO *WERE* THE PROCLAIMERS OF PROTESTANT ASCENDANCY IN 1787-8?

It will be clear that that the works and authors listed immediately above constitute a very mixed group indeed. Browne, an MP for the University, was fervently loyal to Woodward. Sheridan, a medical doctor, was one of his shrewdest critics. Both Moderator and Grace had hard things to say of his lordship, while Hales only managed to invoke protestant ascendancy in a phrase already glanced at—'the Protestant Government, Religion, and Ascendancy'. The sincere unbiassed protestant (of no. 84 who also signed himself 'The UT——T') should not be confused with the unbiassed Irishman (of no. 16), though both opposed Woodward's arguments. Thus, of the seven items left for examination, one (no. 83) is already shown to include no strict citation of protestant ascendancy. As Edward Sheridan deserves attention in a later chapter, we shall now transcribe at length the relevant passages from the remaining five items.

BROWNE
Self interest must have compelled them [his forebears] to lament the laws [resulting in diminished value of lands etc.], which self-preservation enjoined. To preserve their estates, they consented to load them with this incumbrance. It never could have been their interest to consent to laws tending to weaken and impoverish the kingdom at large, if they had not known that kingdom to be divided against itself, and apprehended danger to their titles, to their religion, and to the Protestant ascendancy. If they had these apprehensions, they were justifiable on principles of self-defence. If they were even mistaken, and misled by groundless fears, who can censure a conduct conformed to the persuasions of their own minds? What have our own eyes beheld in later days! As soon as men were persuaded, that the firm establishment of the House of Hanover on the throne, and long experience of its mild and gentle rule, had extinguished the hopes of its enemies, and converted hatred to friendship, as soon as they conceived that the laws might be relaxed without danger to the Protestant interest, and the settlement of property,—they seized with avidity the earliest occasion; With returning safety, relaxation dawned, and every Protestant, who had monied or landed interest, loudly avowed his hopes of reciprocal advantage; of benefit to himself, linked with privilege to the Catholick.[44]

Now this is an instance, the first we have come upon, of the phrase protestant ascendancy naturalised into the idiom of a writer other than Woodward himself. It is a late instance, and it is (within the pamphlet) an isolated instance, but protestant ascendancy has here at last found an independent advocate.

MODERATOR

I must exceedingly regret that your lorship did not rather chuse to come forward with some plan of reformation, instead of sending forth a violent publication, which, from the boldness of its assertions and the clearness of its inferences, may unhappily lay the foundation of distrust between the protestant, the catholic, and the presbyterian . . .

Dispell, then, my lord, these fears and apprehensions with which you seem so heavily oppressed for the protestant ascendancy, which, you may rely upon, will be perfectly safe, whilst the law and the constitution remain.[45]

In this instance, one can see that the protestant ascendancy functions in the prose as a reference back to Woodward's own utterance. Unlike Browne, Moderator has declined to naturalise or accommodate the phrase, and this refusal is linked to the psychological difference between them—between apprehension and fear. This analysis is confirmed by reference to Browne whose entire historical argument is founded on notions of insecurity and change, with protestant ascendancy acting as the third item in a rhetorical triad (cf. Hales above) inducing confidence.

CLEMENT

Yet this extraordinary coincidence of doctrine between two such discordant sects [i.e. Catholics and presbyterians] can be reconciled only on a similitude of enmity to the *Protestant* ascendancy, which inspires both . . .

. . . such has been the influence and extravagant excess of this *truly christian virtue* and *equitable right* of all men, that whoever hazarded a word in *exclusive* support of the Protestant accendancy [sic] of late . . . was reproached with the epithets of *unchristian, prejudiced*, and *bigotted*.[46]

Here is another instance where protestant ascendancy appears to have achieved idiomatic status. It is not so late an occurrence as that found in Browne's *Brief Review*, being dated by the author himself as 20 April 1787. Again, in contrast to Browne, Clement provides more than one citation—he provides two. The second of these, however, testifies not to acceptance of the term but, on the contrary, to the resistance offered against those who 'hazarded' use of it.

GRACE

I should not have dwelt so long on this objection but the Right Reverend Author takes it in the same way himself p. 25 of the Present State where he tells us how much 'the security of the Protestant Proprietor of land depends on the Protestant ascendency.' . . .

In Ireland the Roman Catholic Religion was displaced by Power, and the truth of the Gospel was not assented by logic or Divinity, but left to be defended by Constables, Informers, and Hangmen. And the Protestant ascendency was secured by referring the purity of its worship and belief to punishments and incapacities.

One man has been found rash enough to venture on the world a system of reasoning and authorities, that afford his enemies all the room they could wish for, to exhibit him as an object of danger, distrust, and detestation . . .

In all the modern distractions of Britain, and in every contest for its crown, a considerable body of the people was easily brought to join that side, from which they expected to obtain a religious ascendency. But a brighter ray of liberality and benevolence had diffused itself amongst us. . .[47]

In the four paragraphs relevant to our inquiry, Grace first quotes directly from Woodward's *Present State* without endorsing such terminology, proceeds then to link protestant ascendancy to coercion of the most comprehensive kind, excoriates Woodward in a sentence more memorable for its passion than its style, and finally makes a general use of the single word 'ascendancy' in discussing the religious history of Great Britain. Nothing here suggests a conservative protestant giving currency to a concept of protestant ascendancy.

THE UT——T

[Commenting on the 7th paragraph of Section I in *The Present State of the Church of Ireland*] We observe and admit, that the Ascendancy of Protestantism in Ireland, is most undeniably the *sine qua non* of national Happiness, and that a Connection with Britain seems at present the *sine qua non* of that Ascendancy; but we humbly ask his L — p is it certain that Britain would seriously fall out with us, for our having *middling, humble, and exemplary* Clergy?

[On 2nd and 3rd paragraphs of Section VI] Here his L —p holds out Fears to the Presbyterians, in case of the Established Church's losing the Tenths [i.e. tithes], and consequently losing the Protestant *Ascendancy* . . . Here again his L — p holds out prophetic Terrors as to the Protestant Ascendancy, etc in Ireland; but these Terrors seem rather Visionary, and are also obviated by the System of Commutation [of tithes] herein proposed . . .[48]

Again we find here two examples of the term protestant ascendancy (and two variants) incorporated into the writer's idiom, though it is also abundantly clear that he writes with Woodward's text in front of him and writes to rebut the conclusions which Woodward reached. These examples meet Kripke's requirements as to a 'link by link' transmission of a name, though their extreme isolation in the *c*.1.6 million words under under examination should temper celebrations of this achievement. If this represents a successful imposition of an ideological concept on the UT——T, a highly questionable proposition still, there is no possibility whatever of classifying the writer with those 'conservative protestants' who are alleged to have adopted protestant ascendancy at this time or earlier.

Indeed, of the five residual witnesses under examination, only the American-born Browne could be so classified.

Browne is undoubtedly a figure of some interest, and Edward Sheridan's *Critical Review* will be shown to pin-point the American's exceptional status as a proponent of protestant ascendancy. For the moment we might conclude by noting the extraordinary inwardness, even solipsism of the psychology underlying his argument. Writing of earlier generations of protestants in Ireland, he declares, 'If they had these apprehensions, they were justifiable on principles of self-defence. If they were even mistaken, and misled by groundless fears, *who can censure a conduct conformed to the persuasions of their own minds[?]*'[49] Later in the passage quoted, the referant of the pronoun 'they' becomes uncertain; first it has denoted protestant forebears, then 'men' generally, and in the near present 'they seized with avidity' is a phrase in which the verb leans closer to identifying 'they' with the aggressive Catholics rather than the concessive protestants. All of this is of a piece with the larger evidence of apprehension lying behind the intermittent citations of protestant ascendancy, apprehension which sceptics were unable to measure.

In short, those who positively endorsed protestant ascendancy in 1786-88 are a) Woodward himself, b) Elrington in two of his five contributions, c) Browne in one of his two contributions (and very briefly in the House of Commons), and d) Clement of Galway of whom nothing more is known. Apart from these, one finds in the many hundreds of thousands of words analysed only a paltry scattering of isolated half-phrases. These findings have their value, but a broader field of interpretation will ensure that they are not relegated merely to the role of counter-statistics in a local dispute.

SOME INTELLECTUAL CONTEXTS
LOCAL, AMERICAN, AND BRITISH
IMPLICATING EVEN JAMES MADISON AND WILLIAM PALEY

The paper war, like most wars, can be seen as a conflict of parties none of which could claim to have possessed any external objective point of reference. Each relied on the existence of another or others as the justification of its position. At the same time, the Establishment itself persisted in defending the notion of 'interest'—through invocations of 'the protestant interest'—for all that the latter term was increasingly recognised as one admitting the partisan, even the subjective, dimension of the issues at stake. Indeed a major feature of the war was the tacit acknowledgement that all arguments were arguments of self-interest, however 'self' might be defined. Woodward certainly presented little in the way of an intellectual justification of the status quo, while Butler (who recruited the term 'justification') found that his position was compromised by earlier statements from the Catholic camp. Nevertheless, an examination of the vast body of material constituting the paper war might still throw up valuable evidence as to what—hypothetically at least—might have been regarded as an intellectual case. This in turn may turn up unexpected evidence of a broader context in which these Irish events occurred, evidence involving—however passively—a future president of the United States.

In this connection the contribution of Edward Sheridan takes on additional significance in the eyes of the cultural historian. *A Critical View of the B. of Cloyne's Publication* has been variously assigned to Charles Brennan and to Edward Sheridan, with the consensus of opinion accepting the latter attribution. It is one of two pamphlets appearing under the signature of 'an unbiassed Irishman', both printed by John Chambers, who put his name to just one other item in the controversy, the *Anti-Tyther* of 1786. As the latter can be shown to be a re-print of a major American text from the last phase of the War of Independence, Sheridan is further rendered interesting as a contributor to the paper war.

It could be argued that the title-page of Chambers's first contribution names 'Anti-Tyther' as the pseudonymous author of the work. The ambiguity as to whether the phrase indicates an author or is simply part of the title may have been deliberate on Chambers's part, for the author was in fact James Madison (1751-1836), a leading member of the American revolutionary intelligentzia and later fourth president of the United States. The text, familiarly known as the *Memorial and Remonstrance*, laid down a firm basis for the separation of church and state in the new republic, and did so on arguments accepting that man's duty to God preceded his social and political obligations. Published anonymously, and circulated initially in broadside form, the *Memorial* was written in June 1785. A 1786 reprint by Isaiah Thomas, effected in Worcester, Massachusetts, gave Madison's name as author, yet as late as 1789 the text continuted to circulate in what was still an anonymous form. The text provided by Chambers is almost *verbatim* that now preserved in Madison's papers. However, the footnotes citing or alluding to the American declaration of Rights (1776), which appear throughout the Dublin edition, were probably provided by Chambers himself, with a view to underlining the quasi-constitutional status of the document he was introducing into the local dispute.[1]

Chambers later distinguished himself as a founder member of the United Irishmen in Dublin and served on their Executive Directory. He was disenfranchised in 1798, and spent some years in gaol before reaching New York in 1805 by way of France. His political commitment, and the dexterity with which he drew attention to analogies between Irish and American versions of the church-state phenomenon, combine to suggest a figure of considerable intellectual courage and ability. Through Chambers and Edward Sheridan, a slender line of connection between the debates of 1786-7 and those larger contentions of the next decade may be established.[2]

Behind the celebrity of Woodward's pamphlet, the unbiassed Irishman detected a combination of forces within the Church of Ireland. These began, in his view, with 'the unparalleled slanders, falsehoods, and invectives of the spurious Theophilus' which were in turn adopted by

> the Bishop of Cloyne, by the dean and Chapter of St. Patrick's, by the dean and Chapter of Christ's [*sic*] Church, by Trinity College; for so the many publications issuing from that Lyceum testify . . .[3]

But he proceeded immediately to suggest a more widespread system of propagation:

> these slanders are supported by numbers of the established clergy in many other parts of the kingdom: the most exceptional pamphlets being distributed gratis with uncommon assiduity by churchmen, and by persons deriving under churchmen, as looking up to them.[4]

The idea that items in the pamphlet war were given away free is nowhere else echoed, yet it is consistent with an analysis of certain publications which indicate a very lavish multiplication of 'editions' and successive issues. The phrase—'as looking up to them'—mimes Woodward's own contemptuous remark about Catholics and their 'superstitious veneration of Priests to whom they look up for absolutions'.[5] The unbiassed Irishmen is relentlessly attentive to language throughout his *Critical Review*; near the close, he observes that 'language is so often abused in this unhappy country, that we may readily distinguish between the title and the nature of a thing; between its apparent and real tendency.'[6] He does not confine himself, however, to general statements. On the contrary, addressing Woodward directly, he declares:

> Some of your lordship's expressions are very general, very equivocal and very incoherent. For instance, 'to watch over, and extend the Protestant interest,' are expressions which often carried along with them, in this unhappy island, an idea of the rankest oppression and injustice . . .[7]

And elsewhere, rejecting Woodward's argument:

> This my lord, requires proof, and the words established religion and establishment should, but have not been defined with accuracy and precision. The loose manner in which your lordship has wielded these big words, would make them applicable to the most extensive assertion of tyranny.[8]

This last point will be made again by Edmund Burke in the next decade, in a prognosis of protestant ascendancy. Sheridan in 1787 has only one truck with the term—he quotes it direct from Woodward, passes over it, and returns to the matter of verbal obscurity:

> 'by raising in the like proportion the number and influence of the Romish Priests, Etc. with the animation of hope and foreign assistance overturn the Protestant ascendancy.' The expressions, 'the raising in the like proportion the number and influence of the Romish Priests,' are not clear to me.[9]

Yet he was alert both to the slight degree protestant ascendancy had been taken up and to the influence of rhetorical language upon young minds. In the first connection, he declared that 'Mr Brown stood up the formidable advocate of the Bishop of Cloyne's pamphlet; but to the honour of our House of Commons he stood alone.' In the second, and referring to 'a certain patriotic country member', he added:

> He received early in life the unjust and absurd ideas annexed to the words, *popery, slavery, Protestant interest, glorious revolution.*[10]

In the *Critical Review*, Sheridan revealed himself to be acutely aware of the importance of language, and particularly of key conceptual elements presented in terse phrases. His critique of Woodward returns again and again to matters of verbal obscurity. Yet, apart from one quotation (itself the subject of complaint on grounds of obscurity), he nowhere refers to, nor resorts to, the term ascendancy or protestant ascendancy. His second publication, *The Question Considered* (1788), is directed against Arthur Browne, for the question in question was that raised by the university MP concerning the Articles of Limerick. Here too protestant ascendancy is absent, though Sheridan notes that 'Mr. Browne seems to have quitted the scorching meridian in which he formerly stood', taking up a subject 'different from that which gave rise to the late contests, and upon which Mr. Browne entered with so much warmth.'[11]

Sheridan regarded Browne's second publication as belonging virtually to a different debate from that initiated by Woodward, the topic now being historical rather than one urgently bearing upon the politics of the morrow. Several pages were devoted to a discussion of the science of history. Though he got bogged down in questions about the early Christian church, Sheridan did commence this discussion with definitions of history which he extended into a defence of his own critical procedures:

> History, like all other sciences, consists in general comprehensive notions resulting from a comparison of numerous particular facts. In making this comparison, facts may be brought together according to their natural relations, and the result will be Science; or they may be forced into unnatural connections by an arbitrary process of fancy, and the consequence will be error . . .
>
> Doctor Campbell seems astonished that I should think myself qualified to *write what I call a Critical Review*. He has not shewn the incongruity between the title and the work.[12]

As in the *Critical Review* itself, Sheridan was here concerned to defend— however late in the day it might have been—an Enlightenment view of language in which some kind of correspondence between the title and the nature of a thing was essential. It was perhaps the tragedy of Ireland that late-seventeenth and eighteenth-century Enlightenment views would acquire political force only in a decade to be dominated by the French Revolution. The debates of 1786-8 underline the point by being incapable of making it.

Among aspects of the debate deserving note as intellectual concerns is discussion of the Gaelic language, which is variously considered as a factor in the pastoral life of the churches, as a barrier between the political administration and a great proportion of the people, and as a cultural phenomenon in its own right. Woodward had declared that 'it should be the object of Government . . . to take measures to bring it into entire disuse.'[13] He was not without supporters, but the lengthiest discussion of the matter poured scorn on the Englishman's attitude to a language he did not understand. This was the work of Daniel Thomas, a Welshman evidently resident in Ireland who had also travelled in America: 'What! should a language confessedly derived from one of the first tongues which subsisted amongst polished nations, be abolished, merely to make room for

another compounded of all the barbarous dialects which imperfectly communi-
cated the thoughts of savages to each other.'[14]

Among Woodward's defenders, one of the more thoughtful was the author of
A Few Serious and Seasonable Observations who signed himself 'A Curate'. In
some respects, he shared many of prejudices mocked by Daniel Thomas,
declaring even more unambiguously than the bishop that 'the Irish language
should, if possible, be abolished; for as long as it is spoken universally among the
people, so long unavoidably they must be barbarians.' Yet there is evidence to
suggest that the author of this pamphlet was not the simple forthright bigot we
might suppose from these remarks. There is a Swiftian tone to his acknowledgment of possible retributions to be wreaked on him by his superiors, and a
sustained (if one-sided) concern for the state of polite learning in Ireland:

> It is also an universal subject of complaint, that men of real desert are scarce
> ever rewarded in our church, and that blockheads, with the fashionable
> accomplishments, are raised high above their heads. Then the people
> commonly point out some instances to prove all this. That their complaints
> are wholly imaginary, I am not so bold as to assert; and if I should,
> experience might possibly give me the lie. However I should not enter
> particularly into a subject so nice as this, lest I should give offence to some of
> my superiors, which I will endeavour always to avoid . . . The various church
> preferments should be considered as so many rewards offered to diligence,
> literature, and virtue; and I hope they often are so in fact. If these were
> lessened or destroyed, then so many inducements to industry, learning, and
> piety would be diminished or removed. The elegant University of Ireland,
> the great support of the protestant religion, so famed for its admirable system
> of education, would then be sensibly injured . . . Literature then would daily
> decline, and a nation without literature is a nation of barbarians.[15]

Behind the biblical and evangelical gestures of its opening pages the *Few
Serious and Seasonable Observations* reveals itself to be a thoughtful, grave, yet at
times mischievous, statement of a conservative position. It is overtly hostile to
Catholics on political grounds, and ignorant of the existence of literature in
Gaelic. Like Grace's *Short Plea*, it looks for better men to fill clerical posts, less
worldly men. Yet it is also more attentive to Woodward's writings prior to *The
Present State*, especially commending his pamphlet on smuggling.[16] As it happens,
it makes no allusion to the bishop's pet phrase about protestant ascendancy but,
as we have seen, this feature places it in no minority among the publications of
the paper war. Whoever the 'curate' was, he exploited the occasion of the war to
voice his own disquiet about the quality of men advanced in the ranks of the
clergy and to point out implications for the educational and cultural life of the
country. The remarks concerning Trinity College at first seem to be wholly
commending but, as with the treatment of 'fashionable accomplishments', an
ironic note may be discernible.

It may be timely to begin a consideration of the wider contexts in which the exchange of opinions on tithes, establishments, and civil rights occurred, for the dispute had implications beyond its official concerns. The paper war of 1786-88 involved a number of very young Dublin intellectuals, especially on the Establishment side. Richard Graves was twenty-three, and Thomas Elrington twenty-six, when *The Present State of the Church of Ireland* appeared just before Christmas in 1786. A third contributor, Robert Burrowes, was still in his twenties when Lord Charlemont invited him to contribute a preface to the first *Transactions* of the Royal Irish Academy, founded in 1785.[17] All three had been very recently incorporated as (junior) fellows of Trinity College. Their participation, together with that of older men such as Hales and Stock, gives some degree of justification to Edward Sheridan's pin-pointing of the College as a centre of hardline protestant attitudes during the controversy aroused by Woodward's publication. Nevertheless, one should not accept Sheridan as a wholly reliable guide. The provost of the day, John Hely-Hutchinson, was no die-hard defender of Irish protestant exclusivism: on the contrary, he had been at the top of Edmurd Burke's Dublin visiting-list in October 1786.[18] Though Elrington (who later succeeded to the provostship) was to prove his staying power as a doughty champion of the Establishment, the other two fellows (Burrowes and Graves) may have experienced some pressure to participate in the pamphlet campaign. Certainly neither of them sustained a career as controversialist.

Despite the scorn heaped on him by Samuel Barber, Burrowes deserves a little more attention. His preface to the Academy *Transactions* did cite the division of Irish society into 'two classes of inhabitants entirely dissimilar in their inclination and habits, and afterwards more widely separated by a difference in religion' as a reason for the late foundation in the country of an institution such as the Academy.[19] This was a line of thought pursued later by Irish conservatives in the columns of the *Dublin University Magazine* (founded 1833). The young fogies of 1787 constituted, not so much a praetorian guard for the Establishment of their day, but an avant-garde of reaction—so to speak—not fully taken up for at least a generation. The ice-cap reaction which set in after 1798, and the failure to deliver Catholic Emancipation with the Union, had the paradoxical effect of quelling the articulation of conservative *thought* until, with O'Connell's success in 1829, the need arose once more. It is significant that, at the time of the municipal and parliamentary debates on protestant ascendancy in 1792, Burrowes was completing his impressive *Observations on the Course of Science Taught at Present in Trinity College Dublin, with Some Improvements Suggested Therein.*

It would be wrong, then, to equate fogyism with lack of talent, at least for the period under discussion. To the same volume of Academy *Transactions* Burrowes also contributed a critique of the style of Samuel Johnson, remarkable for its independence of thought and its attention to verbal obscurity. Though Burrowes was clearly alert to questions of linguistic innovation, he saw no reason to comment in this connection when he came to support the author of *The Present State*. Arthur Browne, Woodward's promptest disciple, also contributed to the proceedings of the RIA, his field being the classics. He was about thirty years of age when the paper war began, and one may discern in Edward Sheridan's portrayal of him some bitter amusement at the young man's zeal. Hales (1747-1831), Stock (1740-1813), and especially Woodward (1726-1794) were older men. Stock later distinguished himself after the French invasion of Connacht by writing an account of events remarkable for its lack of partisan feeling. Hales withdrew into scholarly work of the most absorbing kind. Daniel Thomas, the cheeky pan-Celticist of 1787, became by 1792 a scourge to all 'direct and consequential atheists', as the sub-title to his *Answer on Their Own Principles* described them. Meanwhile Woodward continued to administer his diocese of Cloyne, publishing a *Charge* to his clergy in 1793, an annotated copy of which will provide some further evidence of his lordship's contribution to linguistic innovation.

That general topic has preoccupied us principally in its local features. If nothing else, we have established that the noun 'ascendancy' underwent a remarkable extension of usage in the last quarter of the eighteenth century. This extension would undoubtedly be revealed as far greater than that examined in the preceding pages if the examination were to range beyond the confines of a single pamphlet war conducted almost exclusively within the political arena of the Irish capital. Yet, for all that ascendancy strikes us as having a distinct period tonality, there is no reason to doubt its antiquity or, at least, that of its cognates. Thomas Blount's *Glossographia*, first published in 1656, includes the following entry:

> Ascendant (*ascendens*) or *Horoscope*, is the point of the Ecliptick, arising at some determinate moment of the natural day; in which the Infant is conceived or born . . . which is the scope to be aimed at; for the condition of the whole life is believed to depend on that moment; and therefore that moment and point of the Ecliptick, is to be prepared and established as the principal scope level'd at in Astrological consideration.[20]

The semantic origins of ascendancy in the terminology of astrological prediction can be confirmed from a dozen other sources, ranging from general dictionaries to specialist manuals and including a growing literature of less respectful commentary (as in the plays of William Congreve and the fiction of William Godwin.) Yet the process should not be written off simply as the extension of an arcane term into wider usage, nor even as the secularisation of a term previously locked into what might be regarded as a sub-code of sacred writing. These aspects of the process are significant, but in addition one should note the emergence of the *abstract* noun 'ascendancy' where earlier and more technical usage had employed a strictly definable set of relations. The triumph of modern chemistry over alchemy, and the scotching of astrological plans by the mathematical calaculations of astronomers, constitutes a strand of general scientific advance in the late seventeenth- and early-eighteenth centuries which was still resisted in certain quarters. The apparently incompatible interests of modern giants like Isaac Newton and Robert Boyle—in what we would now probably term both magic and science—persisted in the language and in social practice well into the latter half of the eighteenth century. And it might be added that Yeats, who reinforced the political concept of protestant ascendancy, was also an adept in the magical arts. Michel Foucault's history of a drastic rupture in epistemological presupposition, shifting from the valoration of resemblance to that of difference, does not exclude the likelihood that such a break did not occur in a single event, nor even in a series of autonomous but simultaneous events. The appeal of Swedenborgianism and homeopathy—to take two symptomatic examples from the realms of spirit and body respectively—was sustained well into the Victorian era. Each of these was structured upon a notion of *correspondence* which itself incorporated an overlap of magical and scientific methodologies. It is no accident that the doctrine of correspondence should resurface in the poetic practice of a Baudelaire and the history-making of a Yeats, for modernism involves the working out of certain delayed consequences in the epistemological revolutions indicated by Foucault.[21]

If the Irish paper war of 1786-88 constitutes one provincial instance of a broader linguistic development, there is no difficulty in identifying certain specific publications which prompted Richard Woodward to action. While early issues of *The Present State of the Church of Ireland* were content to instance Patrick Duigenan's *Address to the Nobility and Gentry* as a precursor on the same behalf, the preface inserted in the London edition pointed to 'some late publications in England, favourable to innovation' as evidence of a dangerous trend in contemporary thought on ecclesiastical income and church-state relations. The first of these—Rayner's *Cases at Large Concerning Tithes* (3 vols, 1783)—simply reported the project of an English nobleman for reform in this area. The second, unnamed, is characterised as a pamphlet focused on the county of Northumberland, thought pernicious for its marginality. These preliminary flourishes then lead Woodward into a far longer account of a more formidable opponent, William Paley, whose *Principles of Moral and Political Philosophy* had been first published in 1785. It can hardly be held that the list of innovating projectors was either comprehensive or intellectually intimidating: its sequence was designed simply to reach the specific climax of an attack upon the far from original philosopher, Paley.

Nevertheless, what Woodward had to say about Paley is less revealing of the issues implicit in the paper war than what Paley had to say almost two years earlier:

> Throughout the political disputes that have within these few years taken place in Great Britain, in her sister kingdom, and in her foreign dependencies, it was impossible not to observe, in the language of party, in the resolutions of popular meetings, in debate, in conversations, in the general strain of those fugitive and diurnal addresses to the public, which such occasions call forth, the prevalency of those ideas of civil authority which are displayed in the works of Mr Locke.[22]

Britain under the Georges conducted its civil and legal business within a framework sanctioned in Locke's political treatises. That Britain had been challenged, in the name of essentially Lockean principles, by American colonists and Irish whigs, indicated a need or at least capacity for reform disturbing to supporters of the regime. Paley's instancing of both America and Ireland further revealed the extent of what might have been termed a crisis. Indeed, one Dublin-published item in the paper war of 1786-88—T. B. Clarke's *The Crisis; Or Immediate Concernments of the British Empire* (1786)—had appeared anonymously a year earlier (1785) in London. Disturbances in Munster were seen as part of a wider pattern, and the diagnosis of American-style revolt was applicable closer to home. Amyas Griffith's disrespectful response to Woodward's pamphlet—

This is the crisis, and the crisis now!
The sow hath pigged, and pigged hath the Sow.[23]

not only mocks (and so confirms) the widespread fear felt by the conservative element but unconsciously indicates the extent to which language played a part in generating a sense of crisis. The echoing repetitions of Griffith's doggerel re-enact the multiple invocations of 'protestant ascendancy' in Woodward's *Present State* while also suggesting their purely sonar quality, their existence merely as sound effects. Yet the noun 'ascendancy', occasionally preferred by Woodward to earlier concepts such as 'interest' or to more familiar terms such as 'dominion' or 'control', is apt to the sense of crisis. In the words of the seventeenth-century *Glossographia* there was now in 1786 a moment upon which 'the condition of the whole life is believed to depend.' The life in question is no longer that of an infant but rather of a collective entity whose definition is indeed precisely that which requires determination. Modifying Blount's words, one might proceed to complete the translation of sevententh-century astrology into late-eighteenth-century controversy, thus—'And therefore that moment and point of the Eclipitick is to be prepared and established as the principal scope level'd at in political consideration.'

There is therefore more than simple urgency in such phrases as 'the *Church of Ireland is, at the present moment, in imminent danger of Subversion,*' and 'the Moment is critical; *it is decisive of the Protestant interest.*'[24] Woodward is not concerned to show that the situation of the Church could have been better, had certain measures been adopted in the past. The sense of crisis does not relate to the circumstances of the moment but to its essential character. Indeed a concept of 'the moment', symbolising if you like, new apprehensions of time is as much under scrutiny as anything else. Ascendancy, with its inherent implications of determining moment and crucial conjunction of portents, signs, and forces, will aptly encapsulate this permanent urgency though (ironically) by the time the political concept is adopted those inherited nuances of a strictly temporary conjunction will have been largely forgotten. For what we have said of Woodward's use of protestant ascendancy in 1786, in relation to crisis, will be all the more apt to the circumstances of 1792 when the phrase is conceptualised.

Among the pamphleteers of 1786-88, Thomas Dawson is near-unique in two respects—his commitment to Irish industrial development and his analysis of a magical dimension in Woodward's thinking. Doubtless, the latter was in part designed as vigorous polemic directed against political opponents. But as it anticipated a central image in Edmund Burke's satirical conceptualisation of protestant ascendancy in 1792, Dawson's phrasing deserves attention. Variously presenting Woodward and his supporters as a 'scribbling Junto' and 'these amazing Soothsayers', he commented that 'in an aera pregnant with extraordinary events, it is really astonishing that these mighty *Prophets* did not augur a single transaction which has occurred . . .'[25] Needless to say, Dawson proved immune to the allegedly contagious phrase of 'protestant ascendancy' in Woodward, though he added an unexpectedly intimate detail in suggesting that 'his Lordship really repents for bestowing his late elaborate Pamphlet on the world.'[26] Dawson's defence of such 'gentlemen Whiteboys' as Sir John Colthurst put him beyond the pale of Irish official attitudes, rendering him vulnerable to suspicions of a foreign or even radical allegiance.

In 1786, however, the major object of concern was still America, and not France. War in the colonies had been waged for close on a decade, with little but humiliation accruing to the imperial power. In Ireland, sympathy for the rebels had been evident, and the military emergency caused by the transfer of troops across the Atlantic had encouraged a Volunteer movement which generated political agendas of its own. Samuel Barber, one of Woodward's sharpest critics, was active in the Volunteers and went on to sustain his radicalism in the succeeding, more testing, decade. (He was jailed in 1798-1800.) Whiteboy disturbances in Munster may have had little real connection with French support for the Americans, but the proximity of Cork to the corridor of naval power linking France to the colonies was keenly registered in the minds of the Irish establishment. Similarly, the assault on tithes may have been not unconnected with certain landowners' secret desire for increased rents, but as such gentry were also suspected of infidelism and even of political radicalism a local explanation citing Whiteboys did not eliminate possible external connections.

One should not of course reduce the debate about the American colonies—now the United States—to a microcosm of some grand conflict between conservatives and progressives. Certain supporters of the colonists—notably Edmund Burke but also, in a different vein, Josiah Tucker—could scarcely be taken as representative of a homogeneous body of opinion. Burke argued about the violated rights of colonists, on English constitutional grounds; Tucker believed that the extension of a vast colonial system was damaging to the metropolitan economy. There was no agreed package of attitudes by which one might distinguish a unified reformist faction. William Paley supported the American cause, but disagreed with his fellow-churchman Tucker on the question of subscription to the Thirty-Nine Articles. Paley, as we have seen, was aware of Ireland's place in the excitements of imperial politics in the 1780s, and evidently sympathised with 'the peculiar wretchedness of the lower Irish' labouring to pay 'injudicious and oppressive' taxes.[27] Yet Richard Whately could later characterise Paley as heartless in his acceptance of the squalor and poverty in which the masses (including the Irish masses) must live.[28] No neat classification of opinions can reduce the period of the paper war to parallel lines of conservative and progressive tendency.

Paley, as Whately noted, worked in the era before Thomas Malthus transformed the entire topic of population and its relation to natural resources and wealth. It might be said of Tucker that he was a precursor of Adam Smith, though scarcely his John the Baptist. Tucker is of peculiar interest in the present context, because he was Richard Woodward's step-father and early sponsor, and because his pamphlets on economic affairs were in circulation in Dublin in 1787. But both Tucker (who died in 1799) and the Paley who wrote the *Principles* were quintessentially pre-revolutionary figures whose ideological positions were (so to speak) destabilised by what still lay ahead. Woodward, though he was to die before either of them, had initiated the pre-history of what was to be a crucial element in anti-revolutionary rhetoric. He was, in a peculiar sense, forward-looking—like the soothsayers of Dawson's dismissive commentary.

The upsurge in Irish conservative propaganda, and subsequently in conservative political activity, which marked the period of the paper war resembles in one striking respect the preliminary stages of the American Revolution itself. That is to say, in each case certain grievances were felt which (considered in isolation or even in simple combination) scarcely amounted to a justification of what followed. However, something like a geometric progression (and not just an arithmetic one) fused these grievances so as to produce an effect far in excess than the sum of its causes. Thereafter, the éffect acquired an energy of its own. For example, American reactions to the Stamp Act had taken the form of detecting sinister hidden meanings in that measure. These did not exist, yet their being suspected required a response from the imperial originators of the measure which in time tended to confirm the existence of such meanings. In Ireland twenty years later, Whiteboy contacts with the French were negligible or non-existent, yet for a variety of reasons a Hiberno-French axis duly emerged.

While the manifest differences between the Church of Ireland's defence of tithes and establishment and the Americans' fight for independence should be noted, more attention to the Irish pamphleteers' awareness of external events is required. Very early in *The Present State*, Woodward noted that 'some of the new American States seem indeed inclined to hazard an experiment, (the first perhaps on record) of separating Civil polity from Religion.'[29] Several respondents took up the point, not only in relation to the recent experience of the United States but also to the earlier establishment of Catholicism in what was now left of British America, that is, in (part of) Canada. The coming together of democracy and separation (as in the States) might be read as sanctioning the establishment of Irish Catholicism in some nightmarish future; yet, with the example of Canada in mind, one did not even have to postulate either political separation or a remote futurist timetable. One of the first contributions to the paper war was *The Anti-tyther*, a protest against the proposal to subsidise Christian instruction in the schools of the state of Virginia. Here one should not be concerned so much with the views of an anonymous author but rather of a local sponsor. As we have noted, *The Anti-tyther*'s Dublin publisher, John Chambers, was a man of decidedly radical views. Even earlier, Arthur O'Leary, the ablest spokesman for the Catholic cause, had contributed to pamphlet controversies on American topics. Yet the significance of Woodward's concern about American experimentation does not fully emerge until one considers the material reserved for his Preface to the London edition of *The Present State*.

We have seen how Woodward engages William Paley here as the principal figure among several instigators or projectors of innovation in church-state relations. He is particularly anxious to expose Paley's 'very North-American plan' according to which, in divided societies, the ministers of several denominations would be publicly supported in proportion to their following among the citizens. Such a notion 'must instantly extinguish the Protestant Religion in Connaught; and in all parts of Munster, and even Leinster, a very few great towns excepted.'[30] So much is grist to the particular mill Woodward was then grinding. But, in fact, Paley's arguments went much further, as the bishop can hardly have failed to observe. Immediately following on his American observations, Paley conceded that

> though some purposes of order and tranquillity may be answered by the establishment of creeds and confessions, yet they are at all times attended with serious inconveniences. They check inquiry; they violate liberty; they ensnare the consciences of the clergy by holding out temptations to prevarication . . . and they often perpetuate the proscription of sects and tenets, from which any danger had long ceased to be apprehended.[31]

Woodward certainly read the last of these sentences as a rebuke to the Irish church establishment, with its obsessive belief in Catholic attachment to the Jacobite cause, and he set out in his London preface to disabuse the archdeacon of Carlisle. Though Carlisle may seem remote from Cloyne, Woodward can hardly have failed to know that Paley's *Principles* had been published at the urging of John Law, then bishop of Clonfert and thus a *confrère* of Woodward's (and fellow-Englishman) on the Irish bench. (Law's father had been a patron of Paley's, and the two younger men remained on close terms.) The Church of Ireland was not waterproofed against ideas of partial or perhaps even complete toleration, as Paley recommended it. Moreover, the archdeacon was of opinion that 'the independent and progressive enquiries of separate individuals' and 'private persons' were more likely to arrive at the truth than any 'species of intolerance which enjoins suppression and silence.' And in the crucial instances of a country where 'different religions be professed' without 'intimidations of law, that religion which is founded in maxims of reason and credibility, will gradually

gain over the other to it.'[32] Paley's illustration of such a situation can scarcely
have reassured conservative Irish churchmen:

> I do not mean that men will formally renounce their ancient religion, but
> that they will adopt into it the more rational doctrines, the improvements
> and discoveries of the neighbouring sect; by which means the worse religion,
> without the ceremony of a reformation, will insensibly asssimilate itself to
> the better. If popery, for instance, and protestantism were permitted to dwell
> quietly together, papists might not become protestants, (for the name is
> commonly the last thing that is changed*) but they would become more
> enlightened and informed; they would by little and little incorporate into
> their creed many of the tenets of protestantism, as well as imbibe a portion of
> its spirit and moderation.[33]

For all the condescension towards Catholicism which this evinces, it still
withers the Church of Ireland for its failure to attract people from the Catholic
population. Prelates like Woodward were quite unwilling to forgo the pleasures
they derived in invoking the separating names of 'protestant' and 'Catholic', and
were hostile also to the notion of a free trade in religious opinions. Nothing could
be further from their attitude than Paley's serene conviction that

> In religion, as in other subjects, truth, if left to itself, will almost always
> obtain the ascendency.[34]

The extent of the archdeacon's commitment to an enlightened ideology can be
registered exactly in his use of 'ascendancy' to connote—not a temporary state of
affairs or conjunction of auspices, but a final and (by implication) irreversible
rightness of thinking. Ascendancy's astrological origins have been left behind,
and reason will ensure that truth prevails in perpetuity. From this all but secular
contextualising of religious belief, we may return then to Woodward and
recognise in his dozen or so exclamations of 'protestant ascendancy' an outraged
reaction. To Paley's discounting the names of rival denominations, he responds
with reiterated invocations of the protestant religion, the protestant government,
the protestant interest, and climactically, the protestant ascendancy. By this last
combination, he seeks to restore a specific confessional identity where Paley
would settle for generalised and universalised 'truth'. But, nervously alert to the
implications of this desired substitution, he incorporates a critical temporariness
into the proposed arrangement by resurrecting 'ascendancy' and attaching it to
the denominational name Paley is prepared to forego. Like Edmund Burke, from
whom he differs on the Catholic question, Woodward rejects the Enlightenment
aspect of British protestantism for an eschatology.

Read in this light, *The Present State* is revealed as addressing itself to two
distinct problems. There is the politico-military crisis of Munster during (or
perhaps after) the Whiteboy disturbances, and there are the politico-philosophical

challenges of Paleyan liberalism. The latter are only acknowledged in the London preface, though the topic was preserved in the 'extract' therefrom included in subsequent Dublin editions. This preface remains a highly problematic document, not least because it is curiously dated 'January 2, 1785' —that is, two years earlier than its publication.[35] As all authors know, printers can make mistakes, and authors themselves can be as remiss in checking their proofs. Yet to type-set a date to a new preface, and to avoid the present by two years, is a mistake difficult to conceive. The legal compendium on tithes, which Woodward cited as one prompt (alongside Paley) to his own publication, dated from as far as back as 1783; we are thereby advised, it seems to me, to contemplate whether *The Present State of the Church of Ireland* did not have its origins in an earlier excitement than that of 1786, in an earlier period when both the American war and the achievement of Legislative Independence in Ireland were fresher in the author's troubled mind. As the occasion of final composition shifted, so too did the substantive issues dealt with. Yet telling traces of the pamphlet's proto-existence remained, or oddly re-emerged, in the London preface of January 1787.

For whatever reasons, 1785 in the date-line to this preface is likely to have been Woodward's detail and not a careless printer's. One reading of it might suggest that the author had combined two separate works, or had been persuaded to adapt an older project to the immediate purposes of the anti-Catholic campaign effectively launched by Duigenan with the *Address to the Nobility and Gentry*. Here, the antagonistic Thomas Dawson's observation that Woodward had come to regret his pamphlet may be recalled, together with Woodward's own insistence in the London preface that he 'took as forward a part in support of the last Bill for giving Relief to the Roman Catholicks, in proportion to [his] abilities, as *any person whatsoever* . . . '[36] The bill in question was Luke Gardiner's of July 1782, reference to which would seem more fluent and natural in a preface written early in 1785 rather than one written two further years later. The insertion of an eight-page 'extract' from the London preface into subsequent Dublin 'editions' (these in some cases made up of earlier unsold sheets, it would seem) begins to look more like a publisher's strategem than an authorial revision or 'up-date'.

Woodward, Tucker, and Paley may strike us now as pre-revolutionary figures whose relative eminence in their day was to be wholly transformed by the events of 1789 and after. None of them has any great claim upon the historian of ideas, yet each in his way illuminates the condition of pre-revolutionary Europe. It is reported of Tucker that he heard from Joseph Butler the observation that nations, and not just individuals, might go mad. Insanity was to prove a popular diagnosis with opponents of the French Revolution. In Paley, Woodward read also a definition of obligation which struck a new note if only in its candour. 'A man is said to be obliged to do something *when he is urged by a violent motive resulting from the command of another*.'[37] This notion was to prove susceptible to a further reductionism when Paley was later thought to teach that one avoided sin solely to avoid eternal punishment. Yet while his own emphasis on violent motive was striking enough, his commentary on the linguistic problems of such philosophising carried even more alarming implications. Distinguishing somewhat between obligation and moral duty, he would not

> undertake to say, that the words *obligation* and *obliged* are used uniformly in this sense, or always with the same distinction; nor is it possible to tie down popular phrases to any constant signification.[38]

Problems of philosophical conceptualisation are complicated by a newly observed volatility in language, and especially in popular discourse. Paley's difficulties will be shared, if not recognised, by the proponents of protestant ascendancy in Ireland. But if the archdeacon of Carlisle struck Woodward as irresponsible or at least naive in his liberalism, there was another side to Paley. Together with a suspicion of language's limited ability to stabilise concepts, his ethics does not lack in risks of its own.[39] By these standards, Woodward was already an outmoded defender of essentially seventeenth-century codes, veteran drummer-boy from the wars of religion, fearfully premature in some regards, and vainly retrospective in others.

If readers are willing briefly to look forward to 1792, when (I shall argue) protestant ascendancy achieves conceptualisation in resistance to Catholic relief, there are British perspectives to be observed also. Not surprisingly, most commentators on the politics of the day point to events in France as the dominant influence on government's attitudes towards Catholics. The protestant ascendancy debates were no different in this regard than any other minor rhetorical skirmish. But recent discussion of this matter has neglected to look at comparable developments in Britain. Concentrating on English material, Harry Dickinson has elaborated a view of *loyalism* as a relatively new and energetic ideology current in the 1790s which was sufficiently pervasive to see off the threat (or allure) of political radicalism. It is a sign of the times that Paley should now feature as a propagandist concentrating on the poorer sections of society, as in his *Reasons for Contentment Addressed to the Labouring Part of the British Public* (1793). Here one observes an effect of Burke's *Reflections*, but the prominence of dissenters (Joseph Priestley, Richard Price and others) in early support of the Revolution had already triggered off a reaction in Established Church circles against any relaxation of the laws concerning religion. Thus, the Dublin addresses of January and February 1792, the Irish House of Commons debate of the same period, and the later September resolutions and county meetings in support of protestant ascendancy need not be read in an exclusively Irish context.[40]

More particularly, however, English loyalism employed the 'address to the king' as a central method of rallying opinion, identifying supporters and isolating covert radicals. After the September Massacres in France, British loyalism intensified its appeal through a Loyalist Association founded in November 1792. The Irish autumn also saw a renewal of loyalist activity, through the series of county meetings to which R. B. McDowell has usefully alluded.[41] A contrast may be drawn between the informality of the Irish variety of this politics and the more systematic approach adopted in Britain: perhaps one could detect in the great denominational ratios of Irish society an implicit base for ideological structuring which reduced the need for associations, banners, badges and the like. (In any case, the Orange Order came into existence in 1795.) Thus, protestant ascendancy can be seen as a part of a wider mobilisation of loyalist ideology in the early 1790s and even as precursor to that movement's formal organisation.

Neglect of this context has resulted in some tautological explanations of a latter-day 'protestant-loyalist bloc' as the successor to the ascendancy.[41] What is mildly confused here is not simply the relationship between the notions of ascendancy and loyalism in 1792, but specification of the referent to which the former term can be applied. If, as will ultimately occur, protestant ascendancy is transformed into a term denominating what amounted to a social class which dominated Ireland throughout the eighteenth century (and perhaps even earlier), then a particular model of society results. In this model, the Church of Ireland is merged into a powerful image which stresses its position at the top (the ascendant point) of a social system, with the other churches (presbyterian and Catholic) obliged to fit in beneath, in the middle and lower orders respectively. Thus, the metaphor of ascendancy powerfully informs a rigidly conceived hierarchical order.

Evidence of what precedes deployment of this metaphor can be gleaned in rich abundance from one particular contribution to the 1792 parliamentary debates on proposals for relaxation of the penal laws. For the moment, we focus solely on the condition of the poor in Ireland, that social constituency which is more mellowly described in British contexts as the labouring part of the public. George Knox's speech will preoccupy us for several reasons, but here he is on the issue of poverty at a time of radical demand:

> Real misery bears its load unheard. It makes no ostentation of grief, no parade of woe. It does not vociferate its clamorous complaint. Where is it to be found?—in the wretched peasantry of this country, Protestant as well as Papist—You will find it in their miserable hovels, and among their naked families—you will find it in their precarious tenures,—in the extravagance of absent landlords, and the extortion of their griping [sic] agents—*there* is real misery, and *there* is a call to the humanity of this house—But the Catholics knock at our door, force into our chambers, and with the arrogance of masters, and the haughtiness of tyrants they tell us, "truly they are our slaves."

The parliamentary performances of late January and February 1792 require fuller consideration in the next chapter. Knox, however, serves here to illustrate the emotive power of an appeal on behalf of the Irish poor, a power dexterously turned against the claims of Catholics generally. It is true these claims were lodged on behalf of a decidedly middle-class and vestigial aristocractic sector of the Catholic community. But it is generally accepted that the bulk of the poor were Catholic also. What Knox's argument demonstrated were two subtly related conditions—a) a resentment of language as such, with unheard and unvociferated suffering to benefit in the place of petitioners; b) the implication of both protestants and Catholics in the category of the poor. Knox will come up with his own resolution of this congestion, with protestant ascendancy playing hide-and-seek among his presuppositions. Meanwhile, the simultaneous emergence of loyalism and ascendancy is suppressed because a sequential relationship will be required of them. The rediscovery of protestant ascendancy as the Irish form or equivalent of 1790s British loyalism jeopardises the belief that the protestant ascendancy ruled the roost from 1690 onwards, but that discovery is also dependent on a recognition of 1792 as the crucial date for the inauguration of this ideological concept just as it marks a profoundly important stage in the advance of relief legislation.

5

THE EVIDENCE OF 1792

I. INTRODUCTORY REMARKS MAINLY ON EDMUND BURKE

The particular starting point for the present reconsideration of the origins of protestant ascendancy was an article which asserted that 'a respectable number of the protestant pamphleteers' of 1786-88 had employed the term in justifying their hard-line position. (This number, under examination, may now be assessed as somewhere in the region of 4.) But the asserter of that doctrine had gone on to dismiss from serious consideration claims made for the year 1792 as the occasion in which protestant ascendancy had achieved conceptualisation. In the course of making this second pronouncement, he had been peculiarly harsh on Edmund Burke.

We were informed that 'Burke observed Irish politics from England, and because of his ancestry and sympathies, was deeply hostile towards the Castle executive.'[1] On the basis of this original observation, Burke's extensive and incise commentary on the protestant ascendancy resolutions of 1792 is dismissed without so much as a glance or a misquotation, as if he were really a figure of no substance whatever. Even more remarkable is the asserter's dismissal of the contention that Burke silent in connection with the pre-history of protestant ascendancy in 1786-7 is a negative witness to its unimportance. It is not surprising, we are told, that Burke 'had nothing to say of Woodward's earlier publication on the same subject: he was so fully involved in the mid-1780s with his impassioned pursuit of Warren Hastings that he gave Irish affairs little or no attention.'[2]

Here is historical argument requiring careful attention. First, it is now claimed that *The Present State of the Church of Ireland* was 'on the same subject' [i.e. protestant ascendancy] as the Dublin Corporation resolutions of four years later. Dr James Kelly's unwillingness to distinguish between the popularity of the pamphlet and the (alleged) subsequent popularity of a phrase occurring within it has now advanced to the point where he claims that the phrase names the topic which the pamphlet deals with. If this were the case, and on the evidence analysed in the previous chapter but one, Woodward would have to be declared among the least successful pamphleteers of the age, for then his topic (and not just a phrase) fails to gain acceptance.

But this is to submit Dr Kelly's writing to a scrutiny for which it is not prepared. His remark was part of a condescending dismissal, not part of a professional exchange. At least, it is only in such terms that one can explain the other remarkable feature of his treatment of Edmund Burke. Burke, we were told, was too involved in the impeachment of Hastings to concern himself with Irish affairs in the mid-80s. We were not told that the circulation of Burke's letter to Viscount Kenmare in 1782 was deemed by many (including Richard Woodward) to have encouraged Irish Catholics in the later pursuit of concessions or, at the very least, to have undermined the security of the *status quo*. In the light of this belatedly recovered detail, Burke might be thought unlikely wholly to ignore events in his native country, even during the Hastings impeachment. It is true that he tended to discount the scale of the Whiteboy troubles in Ireland: we find him in September 1786 declaring that 'The Affairs of Ireland are somewhat deranged and the public peace somewhat disturbed tho' not at all to the degree to which the Irish, in their Exaggerating manner, have represented the disorder to have mounted.'[3] Even to have come to a judgment not endorsed by a latter-day historian, Burke was paying some sort of attention.

There is much more. Far from his attitude's signalling some disengagement from Ireland, it was followed up in October 1786 by Burke's travelling to Dublin with his wife and son, where they stayed for at least three weeks. During this—his last—visit to Ireland, he was in touch with relatives whose family links to Munster, and precisely to the county of Cork, ensured that he heard views of the current situation of the Whiteboys. In *The Great Melody*, Conor Cruise O'Brien lends his authority to the local tradition that Burke was actually born in the Blackwater valley—and was aware of the fact. As the place in question lies within the diocese of Cloyne, it would seem improbable in the extreme that Burke wholly missed the controversy between Woodward and O'Leary who ministered to their sheep and goats in the eccesliastical division of his birth.

The full-blown controversy lay some little time ahead, when the Burkes reached Dublin and met their Cork kin. But already by September 1786, the Whiteboy *Congratulatory Address to his Majesty* had been published in Dublin, followed in October or November by Patrick Duigenan's *Address to the Nobility and Gentry* which in turn answered Luke Godfrey's *Project for a Better Regulation*. The paper war was already under way, even if Woodward's pamphlet (which would indict Burke) still lay some weeks in the future. To suggest that Edmund Burke, whose roots ran deep in the Blackwater valley where so much disturbance had recently occurred, was indifferent to the issue *while actually visiting Ireland and speaking to relatives* is at best naive on Dr Kelly's part. In contrast, to suggest as I have done, that Burke felt no need to comment on protestant ascendancy in 1786-7 because (as the evidence shows) no coherent notion of that name had emerged, is wholly responsible to the facts as they can be ascertained and to the judgments which analysis of the evidence sanctions.

The argument in favour of accepting 1792 as the inaugurating moment of protestant ascendancy as an ideological force was first made in July 1981 in a conference paper later absorbed into *Ascendancy and Tradition in Anglo-Irish Literary History* (1985).[5] The evidence therein advanced was drawn largely but not enclusively from the commentary of Edmund Burke upon events unfolding in the chambers of Dublin Corporation and the Irish House of Commons. Later, in the 1987 volume of *Eighteenth-Century Ireland* extensive quotations from the parliamentary debates of February 1792 were analysed, in order to consolidate the case for 1792 and to rebut objections designed simply to reinsert protestant ascendancy into a generalised eighteenth-century 'context' from which the traumatic events of 1789 and after had been excised.[6] There then followed the more detailed, but now discredited, argument in favour of 1786/7, this prompted by (but unattentive to) publication of the terms of the 1792 resolutions.[7] Having surveyed the evidence advanced in favour of the earlier date, I believe that a drawing together of that bearing upon 1792 is now in order. In addition to the parliamentary record, the Corporation resolutions, and Burke's great melody upon them, we shall be able to add at least one demonstration of Burke's attention to the pamphlets of the mid-1780s from which it has been claimed that Warren Hastings distracted him.

It is childish to think that the bringing an ideological concept into being can be the work of a moment, or of an individual, or even of a single traceable series of events. Claims that John Giffard, Richard Woodward, or Boyle Roche, *invented* the phrase bear only the most tenuous resemblance to the historian's business of sifting through the ever-increasing body of evidence associated not only with the phrase but also with the complex process by which concept emerges from, or otherwise succeeds, phrase. To represent the larger textual and contextual structures in which the debates of 1792 occurred would scarcely be possible within a single volume, yet summary accounts of these structures run a serious risk of distortion. Consequently, the method of linguistic analysis admirably serves to focus upon the particular while also providing evidence of the formal shapes and general contexts of the occasion. In the end, one possesses and retains this evidence over and above any temporary, symbolic, access to the occasion itself.

II. THE DUBLIN COMMON COUNCIL'S ADDRESS TO THE KING, JANUARY
    1792; AND THE CORPORATION'S ADDRESS TO THE CITY'S MPS

The *Calendar of Ancient Records of Dublin* provides the following text for the first of these documents:

> To the king's most excellent majesty.
>
> The humble address of the Lord Mayor, Sheriffs, commons, and citizens of the city of Dublin.
>
> May it please your majesty.
> We, your majesty's most dutiful and loyal subjects, the Lord Mayor, Sheriffs, commons, and citizens of the city of Dublin in common council

assembled, beg leave to approach the throne with the most unshaken sentiments of loyalty and affectionate regards for your majesty's person, family, and government.

Sensibly impressed with the value of our excellent constitution both in church and state, as established at the glorious revolution, we feel ourselves peculiarly called upon to stand forward at the present crisis to pray your majesty to preserve the Protestant ascendancy in Ireland inviolate and to assure your majesty that we are firmly resolved to support it free from innovation and are determined most zealously to oppose any attempt to overturn the same, having a firm reliance on the attachment of your majesty and that of your royal progeny to that constitution, which the house of Brunswick was called forth to defend.

In testimony whereof, we have caused the common seal of the said city to be hereunto affixed this 20th day of January, in the year of our Lord, 1792.[8]

The committee responsible, with the recorder (a paid official), for drawing up this address can be readily identified. They were:

Aldermen: Nathaniel Warren, 1st commissioner of police; William Alexander, merchant; John Exshaw, bookseller; William James, merchant; Henry Howison, merchant; John Carleton, merchant.

Commons: John Giffard (Guild of Apothecaries); Isaac Mander (Bakers); George Twaites (Brewers); George Sall (Smiths); Ambrose Leet (Sheriffs-Peer); Robert Powell (Sheriffs-Peer).[9]

The Chief Secretary, Robert Hobart, acknowledging receipt of the address and its successful transmission to the king, wrote at the beginning of the following month in reply to the Lord Mayor. Hobart, however, made no reference to the notion of protestant ascendancy for the preservation of which the king had been expressly implored by a committee established at the behest of 'certain of the commons', that stratum of the city Corporation known as the common council and made up essentially of representatives from the guilds.[10]

From the same source comes the text of the entire Corporation's address to the city's MPs whom it was pleased to regard as its representatives in parliament:

To the right honourable Lord Henry Fitzgerald and the right honourable Henry Grattan, representatives in parliament for the city of Dublin.
My Lord and Sir,
At times like the present, when we see the public newspapers filled with resolutions of different associations expressive of discontent and urging the necessity of alterations in the happy constitution under which we have lived and prospered. [sic] It is become necessary for us as a Protestant corporation to speak our sentiments to our representatives in parliament, lest our Roman Catholic brethren may be induced to believe, if we remain silent, that we approve of the changes we have seen proposed.

We therefore entreat of you, our representatives, that you will oppose with all your influence and great abilities any alteration that may tend to shake the security of property in this kingdom or subvert the Protestant ascendancy in our happy constitution.[11]

In the *Calendar of Ancient Records*, the text of this address is followed by a summary order:

The Lord Mayor and Board of Aldermen unanimously agree with the Sheriffs and Commons in the above address and that the same do stand as the address of the Lord Mayor, Sheriffs, commons, and citizens of the city of Dublin, be engrossed, and put under the city seal. And that the Lord Mayor and Sheriffs be requested to present said address and that same together with the answer of our representatives be published three times in the Dublin Journal and Dublin Evening Post. And also that said address and answers be printed on post paper, and that the Lord Mayor be requested to send a copy thereof to the chief magistrates of the different cities and towns corporate in the kingdom and to the sheriffs of the several counties.[12]

This is the formal conclusion to the first phase of Corporation activity in connection with protestant ascendancy in 1792: the second will follow in the autumn. In the relation to the question of whose initiative led to the address of 20 January, the *Calendar* specifies 'certain of the commons', i.e. the guild representatives. This factor, together with the fact that the address was drawn up by a committee, consisting in equal number of commons and of aldermen (with the recorder added in his official capacity), rather than by a general Corporation resolution (as with the address to MPs) would suggest 'certain of the commons' were loud in their singing, if not the actual calling, of the tune. It is noteworthy that the Address asked the king to attend to the *preservation* of the protestant ascendancy: this indeed acknowledged something like the prior existence of the term, but signalled also the importance of establishing prior existence as a function of this ideological strategy.

The MPs were exhorted in slightly different terms. Whereas the protestant ascendancy had been centrally placed in the address to George III, it featured only in the concluding moment of the address to Grattan and Fitzgerald where, however, it accompanied a signal reference to 'the security of property in this kingdom'. It might be thought that the former address scarcely constituted much more than a rhetorical exercise remote from the practical politics of defeating concessions in favour of the Catholics. The latter, however, addressed itself to the immediacies of Dublin's representation in the Irish parliament then about to meet, and underlined the threat to property rather than the value of the constitution in church and state. Real estate formed one kind of property, and the rights or disabilities of Catholics in this connection undoubtedly gave rise to real concern among protestant landowners. But protestant monopolies in guilds and boroughs impinged on the issue of property also. If, as may be the unproveable case, the guildsmen on the Common Council were the prime movers in the address to the king, then protestant ascendancy was more prominent in that essentially formal exercise than in the local business with the MPs where it provided little more than a concluding rhetorical florish. One should not underestimate the importance of the phrase's incorporation in both addresses, while also noting the different way it features in each.

Finally, in this phase of the 1792 chronology, one should note the emphasis placed on newspaper publicity as a form of political propaganda. As far as the popularisation of protestant ascendancy is concerned, nothing in 1787 matched the 'published three times' undertaking of the Corporation. Of course, in the intervening five years the press in Dublin had altered in tone and volume. A crucial alteration saw the increased politicisation of the press, not just in terms of partisan expression or allegiance but by means of covert supervision by agents of Dublin Castle. Of the two papers chosen by the Corporation to carry the triple-report of their address, the *Dublin Journal* had been 'independent, non-partisan, conservative, concentrating mainly on advertising until 1788' when a lease was taken by John Giffard with the backing of the Castle; thereafter it castigated opposition of all shades with unabashed enthusiasm.[13] Thus, in January 1792, Giffard sat on the committee drafting one protestant ascendancy address and edited the paper in which the other was publicised. While one secret agent controlled the *Dublin Journal*, another—Francis Higgins, 'The Sham Squire'—had sole charge of *The Freeman's Journal*. In this case subverting of the paper had begun before the paper war, but the extension in 1788 of this policy to the *Dublin Journal* and its implementation through the person of a Common Council guildsman represented a qualitative change in the relationship between journalism and politics between 1787 and 1792.

But more important for the debate (between the two dates as baptismal moment of a concept) was the absence in the earlier instance of a formal endorsing body seeking a complex political co-ordination both within parliament locally and within the higher reaches of royal opinion. Corporation, press, parliament, the throne itself were implicated in the dissemination of two addresses utilising (in their different ways) the term protestant ascendancy. This is not to argue that some such body is a necessary element in the formulation of a concept, rather it is to demonstrate the fully reciprocal and articulated processes which were at work early in 1792; back in 1787, many among Woodward's allies omitted to echo or adopt his reiterated cry.

III. J.L. AUSTIN'S PERFORMATIVE LANGUAGE

Before proceeding to examine evidence from other sources, we should pause to consider that already before us from a linguistic rather than purely historical perspective. It had earlier proved useful to consider Saul Kripke's notion of 'baptism' as a specific though complex moment in the process of naming things, and to extend this consideration by further reference to the work of the late Gareth Evans. What was established on that former occasion, in preparation for an analysis of Woodward's utterances of December 1786, continues to serve here. But the addresses framed by Dublin corporators in 1792 possess distinctive features which make them especially susceptible to examination within terms established by J. L. Austin in the opening stages of the post-war British movement of linguistic philosophy. In 1962 Austin, published a series of Harvard lectures in which he distinguished between performative and constative language. In the performative case, language does simply not state facts or refer to external things, it does or performs these 'facts' or 'things'. Thus the clergyman's 'I pronounce you man and wife' enacts and does not simply report a marriage.

The language used in addressing the king is pervasively performative. 'We feel ourselves called upon to stand forward . . . to pray your majesty . . . and to assure . . . resolved to support it . . . ' The feeling, standing forward, praying, assuring, resolving and supporting is inseparable from the sentences in which these words occur. One may wish to argue that military strength and/or economic power could also support protestant ascendancy; but with reference to the performative language of the address, any such other support would be augmentary to that of the address itself. On the occasion, no such additional support materialised. And it should be noted that protestant ascendancy, even while its preservation is being called for, is essentially being brought into the linguistic game by the performances of those sentences in which it occurs.

Austin had several rules which govern the performative side of language. An utterance, if it is properly performative, cannot be unilateral: there must be what he called 'audience uptake'. The instances discussed by philosophers tend to pass over the case in which the utterer is a collective—a borough corporation, a committee, a parliament or whatever. But if we take the address as something uttered by or from a single source, then the 'uptake' is to be located in Chief Secretary Hobart's transmission of the royal response. Here, once again, the distinction between 'uptake' of the utterance as a whole and of a phrase within the utterance must be made. (Cf. Woodward's success with his pamphlet in 1787 and the contrasting fate of his phrase of protestant ascendancy.) The lack of 'audience uptake' in the king's case is even more striking in the case of Grattan and Fitzgerald's resistance to the corporation pressure upon them to 'oppose . . . any alteration that may tend to . . . subvert the Protestant ascendancy . . . ' Opposing, altering, tending and subverting might also be describing as performative linguistic elements, just as voting in the House of Commons was. As we shall see, the corporators did not lack audience uptake, but they found it among persons other than those they formally addressed. The most supportive will be several, but by no means all, of the speakers in a House of Commons debate. The most significant, perhaps, will be a partial adoption of the phrase protestant ascendancy in a 1792 address from the General Committee of the Roman Catholics. When such an 'uptake' by the opponents of protestant ascendancy was achieved, then the concept could be said to have been fully 'baptised'.

It may be objected by purists that the notion of protestant ascendancy as a *concept* has been smuggled back into an argument conducted along rather different lines. But beyond the distinction between constative and performative language, Austin had made another which has been noted in an earlier chapter—the distinction between illocutionary and perlocutionary force. Here we are concerned with the illocutionary. According to Austin, the same locution (sentence or phrase) can in two different contexts possess very different illocutionary values: for example, 'the court is in session' when spoken in court or when reported in a newspaper. One of the recurring proposals of a certain strand in the protestant ascendancy debates looked forward to the incorporation of the term in an oath (of loyalty or whatever) or in some other contractual context with veritably constitutional implications. No such proposal was ever adopted, and consequently protestant ascendancy never acquired the opportunity to resound with the illocutionary force of a court official's utterance of 'the court is in session' or a generalissimo's 'the rule of law is suspended'.

Yet one major difference between the evidence of 1787 and that of 1792 depends on the vastly increased illocutionary force of protestant ascendancy in the latter instance. Though the parliamentary record will throw up evidence of scepticism and resistance among some members, generally speaking the protestant ascendancy is well on the way to acquiring concentrated unity as a phrase. The possibility of using it (as Woodward did) to refer to Scotland in the seventeenth century and/or Denmark since the Reformation rapidly diminishes. This concentration of its field of application, together with the welding of noun and adjective together, constitutes one necessary but scarcely sufficient condition of its becoming a concept. Added to these factors, however, there is, we can now say, what Austin called illocutionary force, and this manifest at a greater rather than lesser intensity. This third factor, at work with the others, indicates the specifically ideological nature of the concept in this stage of its emergence.[14]

IV. EVIDENCE FROM THE PARLIAMENTARY DEBATES

In *Ascendancy and Tradition* (1985) and more extensively in the 1987 issue of *Eighteenth-Century Ireland*, debates on Sir Hercules Langrishe's Roman Catholic Relief Bill (1792) were presented to show how speakers registered the newness of term protestant ascendancy.[15] Some of that material is inevitably repeated here, but the present argument can be fine-tuned so as to illustrate some of the distinctions between phrase and concept. Before proceeding to that exercise, we can easily establish a link between the addresses masterminded by certain of the commons in the city council and the performance of MPs in the House of Commons two weeks later. Colonel Hutchinson, son of the provost of Trinity College, made an emotional speech deploring any reliance on emotion. In the course of this, he revealed something of the effect created by the corporators' circulating the borough towns and county sheriffs with the texts of their addresses:

> fears have been mentioned in this capital, and in this House, of dangers threatening the Protestant ascendancy; these sentiments have extended themselves to the utmost corners of the island, and have been reverberated back again to us . . . I will hope that this heated collision between the constitutent and the representative body, shall never create a flame which may devour and consume this ill-fated country . . .[16]

That members had been vigorously lobbied by their electorate can hardly be doubted. The role of the Dublin city council in rallying opposition to Langrishe's reform proposals was explicitly acknowledged in debate by the Solicitor General, and emphasised later in the year by no less a commentator than Edmund Burke, whose son Richard attended the House in his capacity as agent for the Irish Catholics. In the *Letter to Richard Burke* (1792), linguistic innovation is stressed, but even a lesser intelligence—Langrishe's—was keenly aware of the importance of language in the struggle symbolised in the issue of concessions to the Catholics. Introducing his bill on 26 January 1792, the baronet avowed that

> If I were engaged in the unfortunate labours of forming a new Constitution, it never would occur to my mind to introduce the words *Protestant* and *Papist* as terms of *political discrimination* . . . it must be our constant *labour*, as it is our dearest *interest*, to *watch* with a pious vigilance, the *excellent one* we have . . . Under that constitution the predominancy is Protestant.[17]

Langrishe's engagement with language here operates on two levels. First, there is the hypothetical problem of wording a constitution, hypothetical because the British Constitution was famously unwritten and impossible to delimit to specific formulations. It is arguable that he had in mind some kind of Irish, as distinct from British, constitution, in which case he might be thought to allude to the enactments of Legislative Independence ten years earlier. There was, however, no proposal to amend these, and so we must conclude that it was the British Constitution which predominantly concerned him. Second, there is the term predominancy itself, resembling ascendancy (of which much would be heard in the coming debate) and following after his judicious phrase about 'our dearest *interest*'. In this latter, Langrishe allowed the idea of material advantage (in our interest) to merge with a half-echo of the protestant interest, and thus recommended his proposals on grounds both of expediency and consistency. As yet there is no sign of protestant ascendancy. The preliminary discussion of the Relief Bill took place prior to the deliberations among Dublin council-members.

But on 18 February—that is, after the Dublin addresses had been circulated— we find George Ogle, an MP for County Wexford who had uttered the words once back in 1786, fully in command of the new rhetoric. He denounced the

tendency of those Catholic claims presented to the House in the wake of
Langrishe's initiative:

> Sir, I do not rise to oppose the introduction of this petition—humble in its
> words, but bold in its tenor; but I rise to say that the claims that are every
> moment making on the Protestant Ascendancy must be met; a line must be
> drawn somewhere, beyond which we must not recede—and I will caution
> gentlemen to be upon their guard. It is my intention when the Bill goes into
> committee, to move to expunge the present preamble, and introduce another
> for the purpose of maintaining the Protestant Interests [sic] of Ireland, and to
> prevent these new claims which every day produces. Every thing which you
> grant in compliance with those claims of the Roman Catholics is just so
> much lost to the Protestants who have sent us here; as one, I am determined
> to maintain their rights; and I think it my duty, even in these critical times,
> to shew that I am not afraid to meet and to repel claims injurious to their
> interest, and destructive to their ascendancy.
>
> Sir, I have said that this is a petition humble in its words, but bold in its
> tenor; and I now add, it means much more than it professses—it is signed by
> certain individuals, but it comes indeed from a Roman *Catholic Convention*
> sitting in Dublin. It is true their claims are not so strongly expressed as when
> they told you "they must have *every thing*, and that they would persevere 'till
> they had totally overthrown your *ascendancy*;" but such as it is, it must be
> met and opposed at any risque.[18]

Ogle, the Wexfordman, was answered by Denis Browne whose County Mayo
constituency was overwhelmingly Catholic in population. Less crudely, which is
to say less consciously, than Ogle he too virtually put the term protestant
ascendancy into papist mouths, for 'he had to say, that in all the conversations he
had ever held with men of that persuasion . . . not one had ever objected to the
principle of Protestant ascendancy . . . '[19] Indeed, 'the wishes of the Roman
Catholics have been misrepresented and misunderstood. They never contended
with the Protestant interest for ascendancy . . . They only desire of you to remove
from them, in days of union and light, those restrictions that were imposed on
them in the days of darkness and division . . . and they do not think your doing
so would be injurious to your ascendancy . . .'[20] Ogle had already responded to
this tacit approval of reform, declaring 'he was convinced it could never be done,
without overturning the Protestant ascendancy in every town in the kingdom.'[21]
The two became further locked in a personal debate all their own, with the term
injurious attaching itself neurotically to the term protestant ascendancy in Ogle's
denunciations and Browne's paraphrasing of these. But in also paraphrasing the
Catholics' position, Browne further insinuated the new phrase into their rhetoric
and into the accompanying summary of late seventeenth-century history:

> reasoning from facts, they tell you, that when they had more of power than

> they now demand by their petition, or have ever any way demanded, your
> ascendancy was preserved . . . They tell you the land is in the hands of the
> Protestants, that a Protestant government and Church, and your connexion
> with England must preserve your ascendancy . . .[22]

This development traces one strand in the weaving of protestant ascendancy as
a concept. While there is little evidence of the Catholics' adopting the new
terminology *ipsissima verba*, Browne (who was no die-hard anti-papist) still found
it possible to associate them with respect for protestant ascendancy. This is not so
much a constitutive element in the conceptualising of ascendancy as it is a
symbolic performance which in time facilitates other, more substantive developments. A lengthy speech by George Knox, friend of Theobald Wolfe Tone and
protegé of Lord Abercorn, has already been cited in connection with the larger
implications of protestant ascendancy's impact on views of Irish history and the
condition of Irish society. Now we can examine two contrasting passages in the
same speech where Knox addresses the question of the new terminology.

Early in his performance Knox sought to establish ground rules for the
discussion:

> It is useful in the investigation of a great subject to lay down certain
> principles, as axioms . . . Now I discover such a principle in the muniments
> of our Constitution, and to that principle I adhere—*connexion with Great-
> Britain.*—And I add another principle, as a corollary to that—*Protestant
> Ascendancy.*—For I say that as long as Great-Britain remains attached to a
> Protestant establishment, and a Protestant Crown, so long must we, being
> Protestants, remain the *ruling power* here, or the connexion is dissolved . . .[23]

The first of these principles has *a priori* status—it is indeed a self-evident
'truth' beyond which no contemporary could conceive of transgressing. But the
second, as Knox inscribes it, is ambiguously placed, for he neither claims the
same ancient authority for it nor does he concede its newness, though he is
speaking only a hour or so after Ogle had re-introduced the term protestant
ascendancy into the parliamentary lexicon. Immediately on hearing the Catholic
petition read aloud, Ogle had seized on protestant ascendancy as the idiom of
resistance, and in his duel with Dennis Browne the term made rapid progress
towards acceptance, usually accompanied by the word injurious. Knox begins by
adhering to the British connection, and by *adding* protestant ascendancy as a
corollary: the euphony is not negligible as a rhetorical effect. But, later in his
speeech, he has altered the relationship between his two principles:

> Now, the Protestant Ascendancy is a vital principle of our constitution,
> interwoven in its whole frame, and essential to its existence.—It is recog-
> nized and established by the most solemn legislative acts, and on the most
> awful and interesting occasions. History, tradition, education, prejudice,

habit and instinct, root it in our minds; and there is as little danger that an
Irish Protestant should disgard it, as that an American savage should discard
the principle of self-defence. I cannot therefore see any necessity for adding
fresh sanctions to this indelible principle . . .[24]

The absence of a written constitution complicates a scrutiny of Knox's
argument, but it is certain that there were no legislative acts in which protestant
ascendancy (as such) was indelibly inscribed. Knox's unexpected analogy of
Amerindian principles of self-defence only makes sense as a reference to a
famously non-literate society, wholly lacking in written documents. Assuming
such a society to be governed by history and/or instinct, he could imply a
similiarly immemorial status for protestant ascendancy in Ireland. While the
agencies which consolidate this condition are impressively invoked—'history,
tradition, education, prejudice, habit, and instinct'—the official agenda of the
speech is to establish protestant ascendancy as having some verifiable constitutional or legislative status. Knox was in effect performing the inscription of
protestant ascendancy into the parliamentary record by claiming its earlier
presence. Having begun by *adding* it as a corollary to the British connection, he
concluded by *adhering* to its venerable constititional authority.

It would be possible to tabulate the MPs who spoke in this debate, according
to—a) the kind of constituency for which he sat; and b) his attitude towards the
new concept. On the first count, a distinction might be drawn between members
sitting for corporative boroughs and those representing counties, with a further
consideration involving a comparison of areas (whether urban, rural, or 'rotten')
as to the proportion of Catholics in the population. While the exercise might
produce intriguing statistics as far as conscious political behaviour is concerned,
the business of a concept's mobilisation goes beyond the narrow bounds of self-
regulated intellectual conduct. For example, in Denis Browne and George Knox
we have two members of parliament who were fundamentally sympathetic to the
Catholic claims yet whose rhetorical performance contributed to the consolidation
of protestant ascendancy as a bulwark against those claims. This is a far more
significant paradox than that of Ogle—a county member—raising fears for the
security of borough towns, though one might add to the list of strange
performances in the Commons of February 1792 the silence or absence of the
member for Old Leighlin, Patrick Duigenan (the Theophilus of 1786), for
virtually the entire debate. The author of *An Address to the Nobility and Gentry of
the Church of Ireland*, to which Richard Woodward had so pointedly referred in
accounting for the publication of *The Present State*, remained unheard until, in
response to Henry Grattan's suggestion that Catholics should be allowed to hold
certain professorships in Trinity College, he vehemently spoke against it. Indeed,
the silence of some members, and the avoidance of the new terminology by others
(including Duigenan!) deserves analysis in itself.[25]

As yet we have not looked at the contribution of Henry Grattan who, in
addition to his celebrity as hero of 1782, was currently under pressure from

Dublin's corporators to resist all attempts to subvert protestant ascendancy. But before looking at this performance at some length, we should consider other members who (like Grattan) expressed some bewilderment at the new terminology. On 22 February, Robert Johnson asked a fellow member if he 'would define what he meant by the Protestant Ascendancy' because 'the first time he [Johnson] had heard the expression was from the mouth of a gentleman [George Ogle] of a vigorous imagination, who emphatically stamped a meaning on the words, which the House felt strongly at the moment.'[26] This came several days after Richard Sheridan had provided a comprehensive and unmistakeable definition, and one detects in Johnson's inquiry the unresolved state of the discussion. General Cunningham, referring on 20 February to Sheridan's performance of the preceding Saturday, had confessed that he 'had never heard the Protestant Ascendancy properly described but once in that Assembly'.[27] The general found the definition 'just' and resisted the Catholic claims. But Sir Thomas Osborne said 'he was descended from an ancient Protestant family, who had been employed in times more critical than the present in the defence of their country, and *that* at a period when many of the ancestors of those who affected such fears for the Protestant Ascendancy would not be found to have been their cotemporaries in Parliament.'[28]

This insinuation of a Catholic pedigree in the family histories of some latter-day protestant zealots may have been aimed at Sheridan—or Duigenan— but the prize for scornful dismissal must surely be awarded elsewhere. John Philpot Curran's own origins were humble enough—his father had been a landlord's agent—and his opening remarks on the new terminology emphasised the degree to which he found its central role in the debate unexpected:

> But another curious topic has been stated again; the Protestant Ascendancy is in danger. What do you mean by that word? Do you mean the right, and property, and dignities of the Church? If you do, you must feel they are safe . . . But if you mean by Ascendancy the power of persecution, I detest and and [sic] abhor it. If you mean the Ascendancy of an English school over an Irish university, I cannot look upon it without aversion. An Ascendancy of that form raises to my mind a little greasy emblem of stall-fed theology, imported from some foreign land, with the graces of a lady's maid, the dignity of a side table, the temperance of a larder, its sobriety the dregs of a patron's bottle, and its wisdom the dregs of a patron's understanding, brought hither to devour, to degrade, and to defame.—Is it to such a thing you would have it thought that you affixed the idea of the Protestant Ascendancy?[29]

From this heady flight of implications, it is possible to deduct a few details over and above the speaker's unfamiliarity with a stable notion of protestant ascendancy. First, the church which Richard Woodward had claimed to be in danger five years earlier was no longer so. Second, the history of persecution was abhorrant to him, and any linking of ascendancy to that history unacceptable. Thereafter, Curran appears to descend into a pool of allusiveness too muddied by the passage of time to allow for clear identifications. Perhaps the reference to the Irish university (i.e. Trinity College Dublin) was intended to implicate Arthur Browne who sat as a College member and who may have occasionally been drunk in the House. However this may have been, nothing connoting established dignity was conceded to protestant ascendancy.

Grattan contributed to the debate on several occasions, his major speech taking up more than fifteen pages of the printed debates on Langrishe's bill.[30] In retrospect, he may seem naive on the non-aggressive intentions of France and unrealistically benign in his lack of sectarian animus. Yet we are concerned not so much with his declared policies and beliefs as with the manner of the declarations. Consequently, lengthy quotation is necessary in order to demonstrate how protestant ascendancy appeared and disappeared at certain junctures:

> Had the English settlers, and the native Irish, been Pagans, they must have united:—Am I to understand that the Christian religion separates and sharpens the natural mildness of barbarous generations, and condemns men, to perpetual degrading casts [sic], so that the errors of the Bramin are the wisdom of Christ [?] Ridiculous!—What then becomes of this argument, founded on the supposition of a peculiar situation? But here another principle is advanced, connected indeed with the argument of situation, the Protestant Ascendancy—I revere it—I wish for ever to preserve it, but in order to preserve it I beg to understand it.
>
> The Protestant Ascendancy I conceive to be two fold, 1st, your superiority in relation to the Catholic; 2nd, your strength, in relation to other objects; to be the superior sect, is a necessary part, but only a part of your situation—To be a Protestant state, powerful and able to guard yourself and your island against those dangers to which all states are obnoxious, is another part of your situation—In the one point of view I consider you as a victorious sect; in the other as the head of a growing nation, and not the first sect in a distracted land, rendered by that division a province and not a nation. It would be my wish to unite the two situations—a strong state, with the Protestant at the head of it; but in order that the head of the state should be secure, its foundations should be broad, [sic] Let us see how far the Protestant Ascendancy in its present condition is competent to defend itself: Can it defend itself against a corrupt Minister? Is the Protestant Ascendancy able to prevent oppressive taxes, controul [sic] the misapplication of public money, obtain any of the constitutional bills we have repeatedly proposed, or repeal any of the obnoxious regulations the country has repeatedly almented [sic]?—There is in this House one man who has more power in Parliament than all the Protestant Ascendancy—I need not tell you, for you know already, as the Protestant parliament is now composed that what you call the Protestant Ascendancy is a name. We are governed by the *Ascendancy of the*

Treasury. Let us try the force of the Protestant Ascendancy in the election of the people. A general election in Ireland is no appeal to a Protestant people, for they don't return the Parliament—The Protestant Ascendancy returns for corporate towns about ten or twelve members . . . The Ascendancy, therefore, in elections, is not the ascendancy of a Protestant people—it is a *Ministerial and an Aristocrate Ascendancy* . . .

I have stated three dangers to which your Ascendancy is exposed; let me suggest a fourth. The intermediate state of political langour whenever the craft of the Minister touches you in your religious decisions. The loss of nerve, the decay of fire, the oblivion of grievances, and the palsy of your virtue, your harp unstrung of its best passions, and responsive only to notes of gratitude for injuries, and grace and thanksgiving for corruption.

From all this what do I conclude?—That the Protestant ascendancy in Ireland requires a new strength, and that you must find that strength in adopting a people, in a progressive adoption of the Catholic body . . .[31]

We have now reached about the two-thirds point in Grattan's peroration, and he will soon add some comments on religious affairs in Canada and the Americas, emphasising that (in a certain view at least) the origins of the demands currently being made by Irish Catholics lay in the American war.[32] This is a recurring theme even in 1792, and had been a pervasive one in 1787. So far, Grattan has— a) noted the advancing of 'another' principle to those previously adequate in such debates, the principle being protestant ascendancy; b) accepted the term for the moment, but also c) required a means of understanding it. As an element in the politics of the day, he finds it ineffective if indeed he finds it anything more than 'a name'. But, shrewdly, he associates the claim for ascendancy with nervous debilitation as well as aggressive resistance. Thus, we find him declaring a few pages later that

I conclude this part of the subject by saying, as broadly and unconditionally as words can import, that the progressive adoption of the Roman Catholics does not surrender, but ascertains the Protestant Ascendancy . . .[33]

Here, as plainly as other words can import, Grattan suggests that 'protestant ascendancy did not exist until it was endangered.'[34] If this formulation has scandalised some commentators, perhaps the moral of the story is that one should attend more precisely to the textual evidence provided by so careful a speaker as Grattan. 'Ascertains' in eighteenth-century parlance does not simply mean 'discovers' but 'makes certain' or 'establishes': Swift used it so, and Grattan knew the Swiftian canon better than his latter-day detractors do.

But the debate was far from over. In its later stages, an impressive number of speakers were reported as making either liturgical invocations of protestant ascendancy or direct acknowledgements of their constituents' opinions—and occasionally the two coincided. For example, all the report provides for the Hon

Mr Loftus is a note to the effect that he 'supported Mr. Ogle. He declared his
own sentiments perfectly coincided with his Right Hon. Colleague, and he knew
he was expressing the wishes of his constituents.'[35] The member styled Lord
Headford said 'he trusted there was no man in that House a more decided, or
stronger friend to the Protestant interest and Ascendancy in Ireland than he
was ... '[36] The printed reports give us the Chancellor of the Exchequer's contribution
verbatim rather than by *oratio obliqua*:

> To my constituents, who sent me here, I owe my first duty—if they should
> say to me—"Give away our ascendancy—give away our elective fran-
> chise!"—I should very reluctantly do it . . . The avowed object of this bill is
> to unite his Majesty's subjects, and to promote concord amongst them,
> preserving at the same time the Protestant Ascendancy . . .[37]

Contrary to Loftus and Headford, and going further than the Chancellor,
G. P. Bushe supported 'this great and original duty of legislation . . . by that
alone, we can preserve the Protestant Ascendancy, for it is by that we can justify
it . . . '[38]

Grattan took note not simply of the substantive attitudes of his fellow
members but also of their general conduct, remarking to them that 'you have in
the course of this night, defended the Protestant Ascendancy, a Protestant King,
a Protestant Church, a Protestant Parliament, and a Protestant constituency.' He
continued, however, to analyse the implications of this position:

> here you draw your lines of circumvallation, but you demolish this work, and
> defy this definition, when you allow that hereafter that constituency, when
> well instructed, may in some proportion be Catholic. The Protestant
> Ascendancy, then, by your admission, don't require a constituency purely
> Protestant, but compounded of such men as are civilized substantial
> freeholders. By the Constitution of this country, land should be represented:
> the land therefore, should be in the hands of a Protestant constituency. If,
> then, your definition is true in its principle, it must be extended, and you
> must say, that the Protestant Ascendancy requires that all the land, as well as
> all the votes, should be Protestant; and this principle will extend to
> commerce; and then you must say, that the Protestant Ascendancy requires
> that all the commerce, as well as all the land and all the votes, should be in
> the possession of Protestants, until at last you sweep the Catholics off the
> face of the island.—The idea of this definition would rest the Protestant state
> on a sect, not on a people; that is, it would make its base narrow, in order to
> make its head secure;—a small foundation and a great superstructure;
> Protestant monopoly, distinct from, and fatal to, Protestant Ascendancy . . .
> We set up the name of Protestant Ascendancy against Protestant power, just
> as we set up the name Revolution against Protestant freedom.[39]

Whatever about the logic of the argument which Grattan attributes to his opponents, his own linguistic performance confirms the imposition of protestant ascendancy within the debate generally. It may be a name, but the work of definition is under way. It may be a euphemism for the exercise of power, but already it has exacted an admission of reverence (however bewildered or tinted with irony) from the most notable supporter of reform. In this fashion one observes the ideological triumph of the emerging concept.

Two aspects of the parliamentary debates remain to be discussed. Grattan's allusion to the business of definition had been precise, for on 18 February 1792, Richard Sheridan had forthrightly provided the House with the following:

> as he knew "Protestant ascendancy", might be used perhaps by some in a very narrow, and by others in a too enlarged sense, he begged leave to submit his idea of Protestant ascendancy to the House:—by Protestant ascendancy he meant, a Protestant King, to whom only being Protestant we owed allegiance—a Protestant House of Peers, composed of Protestant Lords Spiritual in Protestant succession, of Protestant Lords Temporal, with Protestant inheritance, and a Protestant House of Commons, elected and deputed by Protestant constituents—in short, a Protestant Legislative, a Protestant Judicial, and a Protestant Executive, in all and each of their varieties, degrees and gradations.[40]

Politically, this derives immediately from the corporators' earlier activities that month, and the debt will be acknowledged later in the year when the city fathers circulate a similar definition. But, considered at the level of protestant ascendancy's conceptualisation, Sheridan's hard-line attitude is of greater significance. Two days later, as we have seen, General Cunningham referred to Sheridan's definition as the only one he had heard in the House. While Denis Browne of Mayo agreed with the general on the point of definition—'the Protestant Ascendancy was to be preserved by a Protestant King, a Protestant House of Lords . . . ' etc. —he continued by denying that 'the Roman Catholics had solicited any thing contrary to this establishment.'[41]

Though the particular occasion might surprise (and even embarrass) Professor Saul A. Kripke, Sheridan-Cunningham-Browne perfectly demonstrate the link-by-link process described in *Naming and Necessity* as an essential feature of linguistic 'baptism'. The process is repeated elsewhere in the debates, for example when Johnson asked Maxwell to define what he meant by protestant ascendancy as Ogle had emphatically stamped a meaning on the phrase which the House felt strongly at the moment but which (by implication) he, Johnson, resisted.

The propagation of protestant ascendancy by opponents of Catholic relief, together with adoption of the term by some reformers (not, it might be noted, by Langrishe himself), the paraphrasing of Catholic attitudes to include it, the altering practice of a Knox (and even a Grattan) within one speech, the forthright act of definition by Sheridan, and the transmission of definition by several inquiries—all

of these features of the parliament debates point unambiguously to the inauguration
as concept of what had been an infrequent and unfamiliar phrase.

The final stage of this process remains to be investigated, one which indicates
the limits within which the process was confined. Very late in the debate,
Maxwell indicated his intention to add to the proposed oath for Catholics the
following words—'And I do swear that I will not consent to any project to
overturn the Protestant Ascendancy.' It was at this point that Johnson had
required a definition, though the proposer thought that his addendum 'would not
detract from the object of the bill, for he supposed no Roman Catholic would
refuse this oath.' Johnson protested that 'he did not know how, under this clause,
an indictment could be framed, or a man convicted under the general crime of an
attempt to overturn the Protestant Ascendancy.' Maxwell in reply said that,

> if the words conveyed a meaning to the person taking the Oath it was
> sufficient; the oath only related to religious tenets which were equally vague
> and indefinitive; it was restricted to no Court of Law, it was only registered
> in *foro conscientiae* . . .[42]

The House, however, was 'disinclined to the amendment' which was consequently withdrawn. In the effort to inscribe protestant ascendancy into legislation
and into the contractual relation between citizens and the state, Maxwell reached
the end of a link-by-link transmission. It had been possible for the corporators to
have protestant ascendancy strategically introduced into the debates on
Langrishe's bill, after the commencement of the discussion and with measurable
effect upon all sides of the argument. It had been possible to formulate addresses
and circulate resolutions, even to inscribe protestant ascendancy in the prestigious *Register* of parliamentary debate. But it had not proven possible to *legitimise*
the new concept in the strict sense of inscribing it in legislation. Perhaps this
failure later permitted a valorisation of protestant ascendancy, by means of which
it transcended the merely documentary and performative annals of the kingdom
of Ireland and took its place (as Knox anticipated) alongside tradition, prejudice
and instinct.

With that, the story of the parliamentary baptism of protestant ascendancy
should end, for the Irish House of Commons virtually monopolised the identity
of parliament to the exclusion virtually of the Lords. This impression is certainly
conveyed in the printed records, but the volume of debates from which we have
been quoting above concludes with a brief account of proceedings in the upper
house. Two aspects may be economically noted. First, protestant ascendancy
nowhere featured, though Lord Donoughmore (another Hely Hutchinson) came
close to an ironical invocation when he conceded that he was 'ready to sacrifice
somewhat to your [lordships'] prejudices, and much to the pride of your
Ascendancy . . .[43] This was in reply to peers anxious to stress the antiquity of
their titles compared to his. Less strikingly dramatic, and yet at least equally
significant, was the first reported response to the relief bill as it was transmitted

from the Commons. Warmly positive in tone, this was delivered by the bishop of Killala, the same John Law who had assisted in the publication of William Paley's *Principles* nearly a decade earlier and by doing so had unwittingly prompted his fellow-prelate, Woodward, to publish *The Present State of the Church of Ireland* in December 1786.[44]

V. EDMUND BURKE IN MID-1792

As we have seen, Edmund Burke travelled to Ireland at the onset of the paper war, when the preliminary salvos were primed by Duigenan, Godfrey and O'Leary. Whiteboy disturbances were in the news, but he tended to regard accounts of these exaggerated, as was the practice (he wrote) of the Irish. By Irish, Burke meant those in power in Ireland; in other words he meant those who are now called Anglo-Irish. Later, when Richard Burke became a go-between linking the Dublin Catholics and his father in England, he was denounced in the Irish House of Commons as an *English* agent.[45] That Dublin Castle's mogols should be deemed Irish while Richard Burke becomes English may now strike readers as odd—perhaps the result of irony on the part of speakers. Yet each instance underlines the extent to which the late eighteenth century regarded questions of national or cultural identity as determined by the nature of a man's habitual social engagement rather than by his familial or racial ancestry. An attention to language, and especially to new terms of social description, characterised Edmund Burke's response to the events of 1792 in Ireland.

Early in 1792, Richard Burke was based in Dublin and the correspondence between father and son provides a valuable secondary record of the debates taking place on the issues of Catholic relief. Beyond this private reflection of events, we can also look to the text of a lengthy *Letter to Richard Burke* which his father published in pamphlet form in May 1792. As an account of protestant ascendancy it is unrivalled in lengthy, profundity and—it has to be said—anger. Yet if Burke had (as has been claimed) some hereditary disposition against Dublin Castle which coloured his account of internal Irish affairs, this did not diminish his abilities as an analyst of linguistic innovation and ideological insinuation. The *Letter* deserves to be quoted extensively. In order to facilitate the subsequent discussion of its structure and argument, I have divided its lengthy periods into numbered paragraphs, a barbarism of style which (I trust) readers will regard as a temporary lapse:

[Para 1] A word has been lately struck in the mint of the Castle of Dublin; thence it was conveyed to the Tholsel, or city-hall, where, having passed the touch of the corporation, so respectfully stamped and vouched, it soon became current in parliament, and was carried back by the Speaker of the House of Commons in great pomp, as an offering of homage from whence it came. The word is *Ascendency*. It is not absolutely new.

[Para 2] But the sense in which I have hitherto seen it used was to signify an influence obained over the minds of some other great person by love and reverence, or by superior management and dexterity. It had, therefore, to this promotion no more than a moral, nor a civil or political, use. But I admit it is capable of being so applied; and if the Lord Mayor of Dublin, and the Speaker of the Irish parliament, who recommend the preservation of the Protestant ascendency, mean to employ the word in that sense, that is, if they understand by it the preservation of the influence of that description of gentlemen over the Catholics by means of an authority derived from their wisdom and virtue, and from an opinion they raise in that people of a pious regard and affection for their freedom and happiness, it is impossible not to commend their adoption of so apt a term into the family of politics. It may be truly said to enrich the language.

[Para 3] Even if the Lord Mayor and Speaker mean to insinuate that this influence is to be obtained and held by flattering their people, by managing them, by skilfully adapting themselves to the humours and passions of those whom they would govern, he must be a very untoward critic who would cavil even at this use of the word, though such cajoleries would perhaps be more prudently practised than professed. These are all meanings laudable, or at least tolerable.

[Para 4] But when we look a little more narrowly, and compare it with the plan to which it owes its present technical application, I find it has strayed far from its original sense. It goes much further than the privilege allowed by Horace. It is more than *parcè detortum*. This Protestant ascendancy means nothing less than an influence obtained by virtue, by love, or even by artifice and seduction; full as little an influence derived from the means by which ministers have obtained an influence, which might be called, without straining, an *ascendency* in public assemblies in Engand, that is, by a liberal distribution of places and pensions, and other graces of government. This last is wide indeed of the signification of the word.

[Para 5] New *ascendency* is the old mastership. It is neither more nor less than the resolution of one set of people in Ireland to consider themselves as the sole citizens of the commonwealth; and to keep a dominion over the rest by reducing them to absolute slavery under a military power; and, thus fortified in their power, to divide the public estate, which is the result of general contribution, as a military booty solely amongst themselves.

[Para 6] The poor word ascendency, so soft and melodious in its sound, so lenitive and emollient in its first usage, is now employed to cover to the world the most rigid, and perhaps not the most wise, of all plans of policy. The word is large enough in its comprehension. I cannot conceive what mode of oppression in civil life, or what mode of religious persecution, may not come within the methods of preserving an *ascendency*. In plain old English, as they apply it, it signifies *pride and domination* on the one part of the relation, and on the other *subserviency and contempt*—and it signifies nothing else. The old words are as fit to be set to music as the new; but use has long since affixed to them, their true signification, and they sound, as the other will, harshly and odiously to the moral and intelligent ears of mankind. [Para 7] This ascendency, by being a Protestant ascendency, does not better it from the combination of a note or two more in this anti-harmonic scale. If Protestant ascendency means the proscription from citizenship of by far the major part of the people of any country, then Protestant ascendency is a bad thing; and it ought to have no existence.

[Para 8] But there is a deeper evil. By the use that is so frequently made of the term, and the policy which is ingrafted on it, the name Protestant becomes nothing more or better than the name of a persecuting faction, with a relation of some sort of theological hostility to others, but without any sort of ascertained tenets of its own, upon the ground of which it persecutes other men; for the patrons of this Protestant ascendency neither do, nor can, by anything positive, define or describe what they mean by the word Protestant. It is defined, as Cowley defines wit, not by what it is, but by what it is not. It is not the Christian religion as professed in the churches holding communion with Rome, the majority of Christians; that is all which in the latitude of the term is known about its signification.[46]

Shortly, Burke will have a little more to say on the relation of language to politics. But the first (artificially) numbered paragraph here confirms the relation between the city corporation and the Irish parliament which has been deduced from a reading of the debates. In fact, Burke goes further and implicates Dublin Castle in what he clearly believes to have been an orchestrated campaign to impose protestant ascendancy on the Commons. Evidence of the Castle's involvement has been published before, and while it deepens the plot it in no sense jeopardises the account unfolding of an ideological innovation. The baroque complexity of Burke's metaphor—protestant ascendancy is a coin (like Woods' ha'pence, perhaps) minted in secret, ratified by public authority, and then displayed to the people—was perhaps suggested by the ornate architecture of the Tholsel, a seventeenth-century building in which corporation business was effected. It has been proposed also that the conceit of a street-parade, in which the new coinage is carried with pomp and ceremony, derives from (or is assimilable to) new fashions in electioneering.[47]

He is next concerned to show how a word, which was not wholly new but which had no previous application in the political sphere, might be transferred thereto, if its sponsors were committed to conveying moral authority or at least to basing their practice on wisdom and affection. From this high programme, descent is inevitable; but if the sponsors mean to use protestant ascendancy as a means of flattering and managing the people, critics of language might (from their knowledge of political conduct generally) find such a usage permissible. At this point (Para 4), however, Burke shifts back to consider a classical analogy (in Horace) by means of which present behaviour is rendered less acceptable. As the ironical alternations between love and seduction, virtue and artifice intensify, so does the focus of the argument close upon the idea of signification.

Here, we find Burke not only engaged in fine discriminations about the Irish political terminology of the day but also engrossed in meditation upon a fundamental shift in eighteenth-century thought. Janus-like, he looks back to the classics for a model or even a philosophy of linguistic stability according to which a word has a proper signification, around which—to be sure—degrees of looser usage may be tolerated. But Janus-like still, he also looks towards an imminent future in which mobility rather than stability will characterise verbal signification. Once 'ascendancy' has been moved into the sphere of a corrupt politics then there is no limit to the kinds of oppression which might be signified by a word formerly signifying influence. He is haunted by the vestigial notion of 'true signification' in such terms as pride and domination, and even hopes that the new term will come to sound harshly in our ears. But there is little confidence in the argument as it turns to consider the merely negative qualities of 'protestant' and the limited latitude its signification can be allowed.

The fifth paragraph is thus free to indulge in bitter paradox—ascendancy is rent and rendered in turn as mastership, resolution, dominion, slavery, power and booty. But underpinning these asperities lies a simpler essential distinction between new and old. Petty quarrels about Irish slogans are assimilable into the romantic revolution in thought and feeling. Irony follows paradox, the anti-harmonic takes over from soft and melodious tones, melodious is even mockingly echoed in odiously. As an anatomising of language, this is a *tour de force*, however misguided the author's view of Dublin Castle may have been.

A little later in the *Letter to Richard Burke*, the relationship between politics and language is resumed:

> A very great part of the mischief that vex the world arises from words. People soon forget the meaning, but the impression and the passion remain. The word Protestant is the charm that locks up in the dungeon of servitude three millions of your people. It is not amiss to consider this spell of potency, this abracadabra, that is hung about the necks of the unhappy, not to heal, but to communicate disease. We sometimes hear of a Protestant *religion*, frequently of a Protestant *interest*. We hear of the latter the most frequently, because it has a positive meaning. The other has none.[48]

Burke's tendency to play down the differences between Catholicism and protestantism may stem from his own background as well as from a more general regard for the central Christian beliefs common to both. His distaste for any talk of protestantism as a religion in itself is, however, also a distaste for linguistic imprecision. Thus protestant ascendancy offends him on the same grounds that protestant religion does, and he remains exceedingly sparing in his use of the new term even in condemning those associated with it.[49] His image of the concept as a contaminating charm aptly conveys one function of the ideological realm—that of concealing while seeming to reveal.

During the summer of 1792 freeholders in several counties met to express their views on the issue of Catholic relief. In the proceedings and declarations of some of these, the concept of protestant ascendancy played a part in giving pithy expression to a less distinct object of anxiety and animus. As Wolfe Tone noted, 'protestant ascendancy' meetings were matched by meetings of politically active Catholics, and the newspaper columns resembled a chess-board advertising resolution and counter-resolution.[50] The situation, already tense, was further exacerbated by the circulation of a printed letter, signed by a wealthy Dublin merchant but alleged by some to have been composed by Richard Burke; the letter called for the election of a new Catholic Committee to demand the franchise and the right to serve on juries. On 11 September, Dublin Corporation published in reply a lengthy 'Letter to the Protestants of Ireland' which began and ended with invocations of protestant ascendancy. The opening sentence referred to support received 'when we stood forward in defence of the Protestant ascendancy' (i.e. in January and February), and the final paragraph took up Richard Sheridan's parliamentary definition:

> And that no doubt may remain of what we understand by the words Protestant ascendancy, we have further resolved, that we consider the Protestant ascendancy to consist in—a Protestant king of Irreland—a Protestant parliament—a Protestant hierarchy—Protestant electors and government—the benches of justice—the army and the revenue—through all their branches and details Protestant.
>
> And this sytem supported by a connection with the Protestant realm of Britain.[51]

This went somewhat further than Sheridan's definition, and its inclusion of the revenue service might be read as indicating the objective of controlling petty offices and lucrative occasional functions as well as the higher task of protecting the king's coffers from papist hands. The county meetings, now apprized of the exact meaning of protestant ascendancy, did not unanimously adopt the usage. Indeed, if one takes the resolutions of fourteen county meetings reported through advertisements in the August and September issues of *Dublin Evening Post*, only two follow fashion. The Monaghan grand jury expressed its 'firmest confidence that no branch of the Legislature will admit of any alteration that can endanger that Ascendancy which an established Religion and Government MUST maintain' while Carlow condemned 'any measure that will in any wise tend to diminish the Protestant Ascendancy and Influence in this country . . . ' Edward Byrne, merchant and chairman of the Catholic Committee, featured more prominently in the demonology of the resolutions than ascendancy did in the counteractive pious ejaculations. It seems likely that Monaghan, while it had held its county meeting earlier, had scarcely bothered to publicise the results nationally, until after the furore caused by circulation of Byrne's letter, for the notice in the *Evening Post* ends plaintively with an N.B. reading 'The above should have appeared sooner but was mislaid thro' mistake.'[52]

Most of the resolutions were hostile to the Catholic claims and particularly hostile to the Catholic Committee's plans for what the Limerick grand jury called a 'popish congress' or 'popish democracy'. In the opinion of Richard Burke, the Chancellor John Fitzgibbon had personally directed the course of the meeting— 'the declaration from Limerick is supposed to be his.'[53] Westmeath, on the other hand, managed virtually to adopt a neutral position, perhaps because of the long tradition of Catholic nobility in that county. Mayo was only moderately hostile, and even then a dissenting group of grand jurors placed their own resolution in the prints late in September. The Londonderry resolution called forth a lengthy letter in reply which the *Evening Post* published on 14 August. Signed Vindex, it excoriated the grand jurors for bad grammar and linguistic inadequacy at large, and proceeded:

> In your next resolution, you have shewed as much knowledge in etymology, as you have already of other sciences: you talk of "an union between clergy and Laity," insidiously conveying the idea of an *hierarchy*, which is to overthrow the Protestant Ascendancy—AN HIERARCHY OF LAITY!—Good, good Gentlemen! among three and twenty of you, was there not one that had *Greek* enough to keep you out of this gross blunder? It is a figure of speech that would do honour to Mrs. Malaprop herself . . .

Though Vindex went on to pour scorn on the jurors' phrase about 'the freedom of a franchise', he passed over protestant ascendancy without comment. In the eyes of a pedantic philologist, it had evidently passed muster. The Wexford grand jurors also attracted the attentions of a critic, perhaps because their meeting was conducted in some confusion and not without vigorous opposition to the operations of George Ogle, MP for the county and recent hero of the parliamentary debates. An 'Old Whig' wrote to the *Dublin Evening Post* to provide embarrassing details of the affair, plainly calling Ogle a placeman, and yet absorbing protestant ascendancy into his own liberal summary of Irish history and politics:

> a restoration of the ancient right of Elective Franchise to all good subjects, who have a real interest in the State, which right our Ancestors when they established the Protestant Ascendancy at the Revolution, did not fear to leave with the Roman Catholics, and which was wrested from them long after that period—not for the security of the State, but to gratify the resentment of individuals.

The acceptance of the new concept by such liberals as Vindex and the Old Whig is more convincing evidence of its establishment than the isolated utterances of an Ogle or a Boyle Roche. Yet all in all the resolutions are sparing in the adoption of protestant ascendancy. When the mayor of Youghal, County Cork, wrote to his Dublin counterpart on 4 October 1792 congratulating the metropolis on the way in which the city fathers had 'early watched over the Protestant ascendancy in church and state, to keep it pure and undefiled and transmit it unadulterated to posterity', the corporation resolved to publish the text three times in the *Dublin Journal*, then controlled by John Giffard who represented the Apothecaries' guild on the common council.[54] The corporators' propagation of the new concept was intimately linked to subversion of the press by Dublin Castle. The new journalism of 1792 served to forge bonds between borough towns such as Youghal and the grand jurors of Limerick and Monaghan, the constituency activities of MPs and the supervisory roles of political magnates like Fitzgibbon. An ideological sphere, different in its tonalities and dynamics from that in which Woodward and Godfrey had debated tithes, had come into existence. It was to prove no more immutable than any other structure of domination and conflict, but for the moment at least protestant ascendancy was no longer a casual or isolated trope: within that sphere it acquired conceptual power.

VII. WOLFE TONE BEFORE, AND JOHN PHILPOT CURRAN AFTER, 1792

It should come as no surprise to historians concerned with the emergence of ideologically charged concepts that the component terms of protestant ascendancy did undergo changes of usage between the fanfare of December 1786 and the fully orchestrated addresses and resolutions of January and September 1792. The term was in some limited circulation in the late 1780s and very early '90s, but still lacked the beguiling clarity of an ideological slogan, and was far from the kind of definition-in-action provided in 1792. One can detect, however, the imminence of its acceptance (as unrecognised ideology) in the 1792 *Address from the General Committee of Roman Catholics to their Protestant Fellow Subjects* signed by Richard Mc Cormick and printed by Patrick Byrne:

> As to the arguments by which the farsight of suspicion prognosticates our *gradual encroachment* first, and then our *final usurpation*, as to the infringement which our emancipation would make upon *the Protestant interest and ascendancy*; as to the suggested *danger of the Church and of the State, and as to the insecurity of titles, and the resumption of forfeited lands by a repeal of the act of settlement*—to all these chimerical apprehensions, we pledge ourselves to our Protestant fellow-subjects, and to the public in general, *that a clear, full, and satisfactory answer shall be given.* [55]

Two aspects of this passage argue in favour of our detecting the success of protestant ascendancy in 1792. First, there is the adoption by a representative body of the Catholics of the term ascendancy itself. This may in part involve an element of paraphrase, deriving from the protestations of the rival party, but the inclusion of the term is qualitatively different from the mocking echoes of Woodward traceable in the work of his opponents five years earlier. Second, the response to 'the farsight of suspicion' is oddly inconclusive: once again, protestant fears are said to be delusory or 'chimerical', but the final answer to these detailed and repeated apprehensions is merely to insist that a final answer will be provided—some time later. Whatever the immediate tactics of the committeemen responsible for this address, the text as we now have it strongly suggests that the invocation of ascendancy did have a distracting effect upon the Catholic party who (here at least) devised no cogent or specific response to this new ideological factor.

We need to distinguish this incident, occurring in the year of the Corporation's initiatives and the Parliament's debates, from an allusion to be found in Wolfe Tone's now famous *Argument on Behalf of the Catholics of Ireland* written in August of the previous year. Discussing the Jacobite parliament of 1689, and the manner in which it brought a return of opportunity to Irish Catholics, Tone wrote that 'it was a sudden and unhoped-for restoration of power to men, whom it had been the policy of protestant ascendency for 150 years to depress.'[56]

Here, indeed are the *ipsissima verba* of Woodward's *Present State*, but the term adopted is applied by Tone—if we take his figures seriously—to a period commencing in the reign of Henry VIII. Given Tone's complaint the following year that the title, protestant ascendancy, assumed (he stated) by the opponents of the Catholic claim, was 'a very impudent one', we may feel that he did indeed use the term in his *Argument* to denote (with some precision) the post-reformation state of Irish affairs generally. Yet the complaint of mid-1792 is significant precisely because it demonstrates his resistance to the incorporation of this historical term into the nomenclature of contemporary political factions.

Evidence from the mid 1790s is abundant and contradictory, as one would expect in a period of great turmoil, excitement, disappointment, and anxiety. We have seen how resolutely Burke resisted the imposition of protestant ascendancy in the wake of the January/February 1792 initiatives, an attitude he maintained for the five remaining years of his life. In 1795, Burke was addressed in an anonymous printed *Letter . . . on the Present State of Ireland* which is known to be the work of the barrister John Philpot Curran. Like Tone, Curran had much to say about the crisis of 1689 and its resolution in the Williamite settlement following the defeat of James II at 'Derry, Aughrim, Enniskillen, and the Boyne'. Like Tone, Curran admits the term ascendancy but does so initially in a manner consistent with Burke's rejection of protestant ascendancy. The noun, unencumbered by the increasingly adhesive adjective, features in something like its standard mid-eighteenth-century English usage. In addition to this minor piece of philological evidence, Curran's imagery works itself up to a gruesome pitch worthy of novelists such as Charles Robert Maturin and Sheridan Le Fanu:

At that memorable aera, the bigotry, the tyranny, and the folly of the last of the Stuarts, bowed beneath the ascendancy of British genius and British fortune. The simplicity of Ireland, and let it not be forgotten, the simplicity of a too forgiving loyalty, forgot his crimes in his misfortunes, made a desperate effort in his cause, and perished in his ruin. But why do I say perish? She did not perish. She could not expire on the sword; the last gasp that closes and cures the bitterness of death is denied to a nation:—She did not die; but she lived to feel, without exhaustion, all the agony of dissolution; to be the spectatrix of her own funeral, and the conscious inhabitant of her own sepulchre.[57]

As Cruise O'Brien observed years ago, Burke had his 'gothick' side, and may have appreciated the conceit for all that it anticipates *Melmoth the Wanderer* and *Borrhomeo the Astrologer*. Later in the *Letter* Curran turned to a more recent history, and having alluded to the Catholic petition of January 1793 and the Relief Act of the following April, reassured his correspondent on a question of ideological terminology. 'From that hour [ie. 1793] the jargon of Protestant Ascendancy, of the danger of the Protestant Constitution in Church and State, became the subjects of generous indignation, of candid shame, but never once more of serious disputation.'[58]

THE ENDS OF ASCENDANCY

I. PROBLEMS OF GENERAL TERMINOLOGY

On the whole, the history of terms and concepts has been the concern of left-wing inquirers, though indeed the notion of the 'left wing' is now itself in need of clarification. That neither Josiah Wedgewood nor William Blake used the term 'Industrial Revolution' will not surprise historians of the eighteenth century, but one still experiences a slight shock in recalling that 'the Renaissance' (as a concept) dates from the 1840s and has been attributed to the French historian Jules Michelet.[1] The last instance demonstrates vividly how an undeniable historical event or artefact (say, Michelangelo's work on the Sistine Chapel) can be distinguished radically from the largest and least disputed conceptual framework in which it is ordinarily discussed, and demonstrates also how the distinction functions through a word ('renaissance') with a history of use long predating conceptualisation.

Ascendancy and Tradition (1985) sought to establish the hidden connections between the two concepts 'enshrined' in its title. Both of these have been the subject of widespread veneration in the writings of literary critics especially, though it could be argued that historians have been no less respectful in their unquestioning acceptance of ascendancy's credentials. Certainly, in the dual analysis, tradition was subjected to the more thorough interrogation as a concept, perhaps because the author mistakenly assumed that the mass of historical evidence advanced to demonstrate ascendancy's origins in the 1790s would be seriously considered. The etymological ironies of tradition, its earlier function as a term denoting an ecclesiastical crime, and its embarrassing closeness to the term treason, may have ensured that bland acceptance of its positive value could not be sustained.

Two further factors distinguish between the problems confronting the conceptual analyst of ascendancy and tradition. First, tradition has always had a rough ride from critics and historians on the left, who see it as a cultural bulwark of the political *status quo*. To be sure, there is an important strand in left-wing thinking which approves of something which might be called tradition but is, more frequently, named with reference to the customary rights of the poor. Such approval has been reserved, however, for discussion of tradition in the context of social and economic changes whereby these rights and modes are violated by more or less climactic extensions of enclosure, manufacture, industrialisation, and money-based marketing. In 1991, E. P. Thompson reopened this discussion with *Customs in Common*, a collection of essays old and new centred on his notion of 'the moral economy.' While he is sensibly unperturbed by the great Irish debate on ascendancy, his incidental observations on food riots in eighteenth-century Ireland implicitly challenge the popular view that disturbances in that quarter must have related to political grievance (either Jacobite or proto-nationalist) and not to the economic grievances that bother all mankind.[2]

On the other hand, ascendancy has either been seen as a wholly deplorable state-of-affairs-cum-elite, or it has been celebrated for its enlightenment, benevolence, and cultural fertility. Between the two responses to ascendancy there has been no dispute about meaning or etymological nuance; it has been simply a matter of which side the respondent aligns with. W. B. Yeats's double-vision of the protestant ascendancy, as related in the commentary on 'Parnell's Funeral' (1934), possesses a greater degree of insight and originality than his uncritical admirers can admit. The cause of their imperception—an example is given in the 'Afterword' below—is percisely their excision of his references to traumatic modernisation. Ascendancy, in other words, had been reduced to a simple question of for or against, whereas tradition necessarily requires a more complex response.

Herein lies the second factor distinguishing between the two. Responses to ascendancy have been conditioned by the belief that the notion—whether of a social elite or of a quasi-constitutional state of affairs—is exclusively Irish. Certainly, twentieth-century usage has copperfastened such beliefs by the elaboration of a longer piece of nomenclature—the Anglo-Irish Protestant Ascendancy—to which chroniclers of fiction have found it easy to attach a literary tradition.[3] But the evidence of Woodward's *Present State* demonstrates unambiguously that the bishop saw no difficulty in applying the term ascendancy to the relations (at sundry times) between church and state in Italy, Spain, Portugal, Germany, Denmark, Sweden, Hungary and Poland, and in more specifically applying the term protestant ascendancy to conditions in England or Britain.[4]

By some perverse law of historiographical protocol, no further scrutiny of its origins or etymology, its appearances and disappearances, its ironies and sublimities was attempted prior to 1981 when a conference paper rehearsed some of the argument which ended up in *Ascendancy and Tradition*. Foreign researchers assumed that it was part of a local yet professional vocabulary and sought to reproduce the manner in which it was enunciated at home. Native historians were largely content to accept that the binary structure, of being either 'attached' or 'hostile' to the thing, represented (in however crude a form) all the options that were conceivable. This of course involved a semi-conscious editing out of W. E. H. Lecky's comments on the resolutions of 1792, but the deception was mild compared to that perpetrated by selective readers of Yeats. All in all protestant ascendancy was taken to be somehow *sui generis* as a social entity and so beyond any discussion requiring a comparative or critical perspective.

It could be argued that this eventuality was a condition desired (by implication) in the original formulary account of protestant ascendancy. Richard Sheridan had defined the term in relation to a monarch to whom allegiance was owed on the absolute condition of his/her being protestant. This contractarian notion of loyalty has its place in an Irish protestant tradition, with presbyterianism influential in moderating the high church claims of the establishment.[5] The men of 1792 had declared that 'the Protestants of Ireland would not be compelled *by any authority whatever* . . .'[6] Exclusivity in relation to political office and commercial monopoly—which the proponents of ascendancy protected in 1792— is not without a mental structure comparable to that which believes in the uniqueness of some social constituency, a uniqueness which by its own definition is immune to analysis. Yeats's concentrated interest in ascendancy within the 1930s is an aspect of his wider engagement with totalitarianism.

This blurring of distinctions renders the notion of protestant ascendancy still insufficiently prepared for the rigours of a Kripkean analysis. By the same token, however, the terms on which the philosophers of language operate are usually so clinical as to exclude all instances chosen from the fury and the mire of human history. The attempt to apply philosophical methods to specific historical problems is usually justified not so much by solutions as by the clarification of what exactly the problems were in the first place. Such, I believe, has been the case with protestant ascendancy. On the surface, more might be expected from the example of those scholars who have turned to interrogate the linguistic medium of political and social discourse. It is precisely here that one encounters the effects of that belief in the peculiarly Irish character of protestant ascendancy. While the work of scholars outside Ireland is often deeply suggestive, it is often also irritatingly remote from the precise focus one has envisaged.[7]

Two contributors to a collection of essays edited by Penelope Corfield provide valuable observations of a general nature. Writing of 'the eighteenth-century ferment in social terminology', Corfield herself instances a curious proposal, sponsored by the *Gentleman's Magazine* in 1788, that some individual or committee should be appointed 'to ascertain all such words as are wanting in our language, to convey clearly and precisely such ideas as naturally arise in the mind of every man.'[8] It is tempting to diagnose Richard Woodward as having nurtured ideas without adequate words when he reiterated his phrases of protestant ascendancy, and indeed Edward Sheridan's response to *The Present State*'s use of language might be taken as illustrating the magazine's complaint. But the proposal is essentially absurd, based as it is on the assumption that ideas can be examined outside language.

Though dealing with a later period, Geoffrey Crossick substantiates a view of language engaged in social events when he writes that 'the words used by Victorians to describe their society were no mere reflection of external reality, but an intervention within it.' In theory at least this allows for occasions when no such intervention is taking place, and so it is insufficient simply to conclude that when Lord Brougham announced in 1831 that 'by the people . . . I mean the middle classes, the wealth and intelligence of the country, the glory of the British name, or when Cobden asked Peel, 'Do you shrink from the post of governing through the *bona fide* representatives of the middle class?' *they were more concerned with political rhetoric than with identifying a social group.*[9]

All language use is at some level an exercise in rhetoric; that is to say, even a plain unadorned style is still a style. Rhetoric is now thought of as an outmoded set of exercises or rules more efficicious in the days of the emergent bourgeois individual (or earlier) than in an age of mass communications and generalised modes of writing. Fredric Jameson has pointed to the significance of the shift from rhetoric to style, and one can perhaps suggest romantic individualism as the problematic storm-centre of that transaction.[10] One can approve Crossick's emphasis on language as an active 'intervention' rather than a passive 'reflection', and yet wish for some less mechanistic terminology to describe what is properly to be called a dialectic. Crossick draws attention to a suggestive model in John Gray's account of the language of Victorian reforms of factory legislation and conditions: there language itself was a crucial field of political action.[11] It is not enough then to say that Woodward began the practice of naming as 'the protestant ascendancy' what had been previously called 'the protestant interest'. He—or rather—*the prose* was registering a movement within the field of political, social, and economic action, a movement occurring beyond his control, even beyond his observation.

II. REINHART KOSELLECK AND *BEGRIFFSGESCHICHTE*

To advance beyond the mechanistic residuum in the arguments of Crossick and others may involve engagement with a very different philosophical difficulty. Yet advantages of an external mode of analysis outweigh any danger of a reversion into residual idealism. The second of Reinhart Koselleck's three lengthy essays in *Futures Past* opens with a discussion of the relationship between '[concept-history] and Social History'. While one will have reservations about certain aspects of Koselleck's project, these essays provide a valuably concentrated set of criteria by which phrase and concept may be distinguished.

Initially, Koselleck confirms for Germany what we have seen Corfield declare in relation to England. 'From 1770 onward . . . both new meanings for old words and neologisms proliferate, altering with the linguistic arsenal of the political and social space of experience, and establishing new horizons of expectation.'[12] He stresses the impact of the French Revolution which made linguistic rules and conceptual distinctions the everyday business of politicians. The reformist work of the Prussian statesman, Karl August Hardenberg, involved the introduction of new concepts in law and administration. Increasingly, concepts oriented on the future were created; positions to be captured (so to speak) had first to be formulated linguistically before it was possible to occupy them. The substance of many concepts was thus reduced in terms of actual experience, while their aspirative quality increased proportionally. (Here one might break off to recall the astrologically predictive residue in ascendancy, its inbuilt energy of crisis, and the mockery of some commentators on the topic of prophecy and soothsaying.)

The basic advantage of the method of *Begriffsgeschichte* (or 'concept-history') is that it escapes from the primitive circular movement from word to object, language to reality, and back. Between concept and materiality there is a tension which is now overcome, now reactivated, now apparently irresolvable. The transformations of meaning and of things, changes of objective condition and the urge to innovate in language, correspond *diversely* with each other. Though words can in careful usage be rendered unambiguous, concepts are necessarily ambiguous. The concept is bound to a word or a phrase, but it is at the same more than that. A word/phrase becomes a concept when the plenitude of a politico-social context of meaning and experience, in and for which the word/phrase is used, can be condensed into that one word/phrase alone. Concepts are the concentrate of several substantial meanings. A concept is not simply indicative of the relations which it covers; it is also a factor within them. Each concept establishes a particular horizon for potential experience and theoretical inquiry, and thus sets limits. The history of concepts is therefore able to provide knowledge unobtainable from empirical research.

There are already one or two problems breaking the surface of Koselleck's profundity, particularly in connection with what is termed here 'ambiguity'. He is of course reticent on the question of ideology, and debts to figures as various in their remoteness to historical work as Saussure and Heidegger are discernible. One accepts gratefully some fine observations on the 'relation of the language of original source and the language of analysis' and, consequently, also on 'the difference prevailing between past and present conceptualization'. While one notes the particular historical condition of inquiries concerning the German *Stadt*, one declines however to endorse promptly 'talk of a "state" in the High Middle Ages' and any general 'extension of later concepts to cover earlier periods'.[13] Here the issue invisibly revolves round the context, motivation, and historical placement of historians themselves.

Nevertheless, Koselleck's project of a multi-volume lexicon of historical concepts can only excite envy in less philosophically energetic communities of scholarship. Summarising a 1967 outline of the project, his translator has drawn up a provocative series of questions:

> Is the concept in common use? Is its meaning disputed? What is the social range of its usage? In what contexts does the term appear? Is the term articulated in terms of a concept with which it is paired, either in a complementary or adversary sense. Who uses the term . . . and to address whom? etc.[14]

These guidelines, together with the account of the exponential growth of concepts in the age of the French Revolution, can do much to clarify further the difference between Woodward's invocations of protestant ascendancy in 1786 and the Dublin Corporation's resolutions of five to six years later. Empirical data, resulting from a close reading of the pamphlets which constituted the paper war, cannot establish the existence of a concept of protestant ascendancy. This failure stems not simply from the miniscule proportion of combatants who utilise the phrase but from the inchoate relations then still pertaining between the highly complex politico-social field of meaning and experience, in which the term was used, and the new term itself. It may be true that Woodward, deliberately or otherwise, was engaged in the propagation of a notion—the ascendancy of protestantism within the state—with reference to Ireland, but also with reference to Britain and (with modifications) in other countries also. The unsustained application of the term to Britain etc. manifestly demonstrates the non-establish-ment of a concept, of which (had things worked out differently) Ireland would have furnished one instance (of several).

There is a fundamental difference between the general terms dealt with by Koselleck and other practitioners of *Begriffsgeschichte* and the Irish notion of protestant ascendancy. In the case of 'state', 'revolution' etc. it is possible to compare a relatively large number of instances of each concept. The state can be examined in its British, French, and Danish forms. Revolution may be conceptu-ally sheet-anchored to the French events of 1789 and after, but the Glorious, the American, and the Bolshevik revolutions continue to demand attention. The concepts of state and revolution are not simply the common-denominators of these instances or of all 'similar' instances, because the words state and revolution have independent histories of their own, with extensive non-conceptual usages. Therein lies the 'ambiguity' of concepts.

With protestant ascendancy we confront the peculiar problem of a category of which there is only one instance, employing a noun with a very restricted usage beyond that instance. To be sure, insecure nineteenth-century activists will speak darkly of 'a papist ascendancy' or brightly of a gospel one. These are purely aspirative, in the negative or positive sense of that term. But they illustrate indirectly the limits set by the concept of protestant ascendancy for itself. Koselleck defines his 'horizons of expectation' in terms of the future made present, the not-yet, the nonexperienced, that which is to be revealed. 'Hope and fear, wishes and desires, cares and rational analysis, receptive display and curiosity: all enter into expectation and constitute it.'[15] At this general level, horizons of expectation are part and parcel of every historical situation. But in the particular case of ascendancy in the nineteenth century we will note that, not only does protestant ascendancy generate anxious and desirous mirror-images (the papist, the gospel, ascendancies) which are indicative of its own horizons, protestant ascendancy itself is an expression of expectation as well as experience, is an expression of expectation over and above experience. This point has been made before, in terms which apparently gave offence to level-headed historians, and it can be repeated now perhaps with more justification. 'Protestant ascend-ancy did not exist until it was endangered.'[16]

Perhaps the point was made as early as 1786. Woodward's declaration, 'The Ascendancy of the Established church, and the Protestant interest, is secure in England,' together with the non-adoption of the term ascendancy in the discussion of English church-state relations, makes an admission *vis à vis* Ireland.[17] Ireland does not experience the same security, and the term ascendancy may be used to distinguish the two cases. So far, the argument is unaffected by the particular choice of noun to distinguish the Irish condition of lesser security. Woodward could have employed dominion, supremacy, even hegemony, but the actual use of the term ascendancy underlines the experience of insecurity by invoking its former contexts of astrological determination and the crucial importance of specific conjunctions of powers at inaugurating moments. Expectation, in the specific form of longing, informs the choice of term, rather than experience which might implicate confidence.

Nevertheless, the state of the Church of Ireland in 1786 was not as parlous as these melancholoy reflections might suggest. As James Kelly has emphasised, parliament backed the conservative rather than reformist programme in the spring of 1787. Tithes were safe; disestablishment, whether by Capuchins or presbyterians, was strictly unthinkable. Here too one finds confirmation of the non-conceptual status of protestant ascendancy at that time. No crisis came to a head. No politico-social context in which and for which the phrase was ventured reached the pitch wherein the meaning and experience of protestant ascendancy could be condensed into that one word/phrase alone.

By 1792, however, things were very different. Writing nearly a hundred later, W. E. H. Lecky quoted carefully from the statement of definition agreed by the supporters of protestant ascendancy, and then proceeded in two sentences to etch the situation with reference to Catholic relief. First there are some measured phrases—'It is, I think, undoubtedly true, that a wave of genuine alarm and opposition to concession at this time passed over a great part of Protestant Ireland.' And then, following immediately, this catalogue of circumstances:

> The democratic character the Catholic question had assumed; the attempts of the northern Dissenters to unite with the Catholics on the principles of the French Revolution; the well-founded belief that some of the new Catholic leaders were in sympathy and correspondence with the democratic leaders; the incendiary newspapers and broadsides which were widely circulated, urging the Catholics to rest content with nothing short of the possession of the State; the outrages of the Defenders to which a more or less political significance was attached, and finally the great dread of innovation which the French Revolution had everywhere produced in the possessors of power, influenced many minds.[18]

Here indeed is a 'plenitude' of meaning and experience, qualitatively different from the situation of six years earlier. The occurrence of the French Revolution, ramifying in the growth of universal doctrines of political change (democracy), and propagated by an energised newspaper press, had no precedent. In so far as the Defenders of 1792 repeated the outrages of Whiteboys in the mid 1780s, there is continuity. But when Woodward sounded the war-cry late in 1786, General Luttrell had already pacified Munster: the bishop's proffered rallying slogan of protestant ascendancy was not widely adopted, and within a few weeks parliament and the lord lieutenant obliged with addresses and measures which Woodward later acknowledged as satisfactory.[19] If we see the plenitude of alarms in 1792 coalescing into a new concept, we must emphasise the inverted relation between experience and conceptualisation. Protestant ascendancy is to answer against the politico-social context in (and *not* for) which the phrase is used. Meaning and experience as it were diverge as they also are condensed into the phrase-becoming-concept. In this divergence we detect the ideological nature of protestant ascendancy as a concept in the revolutionary decade of the 1790s.

William Paley's benign observations of 1785 remain relevant, though in an ironic fashion. *The Principles of Moral and Political Phiosophy* had gone a long way towards arguing that religious establishment should relate directly to the allegiance of the people, and done so in a way which implicated notions of *majority* opinion. This free trade in religious opinion amounted virtually to an anticipation of democracy. Majority, however, necessarily implicates minority. Ascendancy, if it is not a notional 'ascendancy of truth', requires one party to be in the ascendant position and another to be subordinate to that party. Protestant ascendancy consequently not only is anti-democratic in its political orientation, but it concedes the terms of democratic pluralism and so tacitly admits a horizon or limit to its own viability. Woodward had protested at the relativism of Paley's willingness to allow 'chance' determine whether the civil authority in any given society should be right or wrong in its choice of this religion or that.[20]

The particular formulation which, in response to Paley, Woodward helped to launch into the vocabulary of reactive politics ironically conceded a related limit—that of temporary duration. To be in the ascendant implicates a future in which one will not be in the ascendant. One might see in this paradox a local Irish version of the discovery of historical time for which the late eighteenth century has been celebrated from Hegel onwards. There is something of the pre-emptive strike—against the 'spirit of the age', against romanticism whether liberal or revolutionary—in the Woodwardian campaign during the paper war. It is too soon, too late. The anti-revolutionary position is shot through with the imagery of revolutions, reversals and terminations.

If for a moment we link the logical term 'ends' (as in means and ends) provocatively with the more common-place term 'end' or 'ending' (as in termination), then a paradoxical statement can be ventured. It is this—The ends of protestant ascendancy were to be its ending. Certainly, empirical data gleaned from nineteenth-century sources ranging from Daniel O'Connell's correspondence to the records of the Irish Metropolitan Conservative Association would suggest a remarkable submergence of the concept in the first half of the century. Yet we know also that the protestant ascendancy later re-emerged, most notably in Yeats's oft-quoted tributes but also in the casual description of an Irish landed class of uncertain historical provenance. The implication of an imminent end to protestant ascendancy—always in the future—was balanced by a gradual colonisation of the past. This process is linked to an elevation of protestant ascendancy as a class on the social scale. Linked in the 1790s to the politics of urban corporations and merchant guilds— what Lecky called 'bodies . . . constituted on the narrowest principles . . . notorious for their jobbing and for most of the vices that spring from monopoly'—protestant ascendancy as a concept acquired estates, dignities, and titles a century later, at the moment when the Land War was problematising all such attributes.[21]

On first inspection, this is not a development for which Koselleck and his begriffstricken colleagues are unprepared. The methodology of concept-history allows for an analysis in which 'singular findings ... do not prevent historical discourse from scientifically defining established historical concepts and deploying them in different periods and domains.'[22] However singular Koselleck's instance (in connection with the emergence of Prussia first as a bourgeois constitutional state in 1848) may be, it is far from being unique in the concepts involved: other bourgeois states emerged at different times, and other forms of statehood are available for comparative study. Yet the risk implicit in his comments is immediately highlighted if they are transferred to the discussion of a *sui generis* instance. If historians were to argue for a continuity of the German state from pre-Reformation times through to the era of Bismarck or Hitler, it would be relatively easy to reveal the discontinuities at work simply by engaging in multiple exercises of comparative study—the French and German state in 1450, the English and German in 1700, and so forth. Not only would a great diversity of political and institutional material indicate massive areas of difference from the German state of this century, but the proliferation of lexical material (the word-as-not-concept) would also complicate any identification of a single line of submerged 'tradition'.

With protestant ascendancy, no external non-Irish parallel can be invoked. Woodward's ascendancies in Lutheran Denmark, Calvinist Scotland, and Catholic Portugal came to nothing on the very pages he wrote on: the word never got beyond itself, never became the concentrate of several substantive meanings. But if anyone is tempted therefore simply to refer to whatever social elite ruled the Irish roost in 1700 or 1740 by means of that resonant term coined fifty or ninety years later, then the complex substantive meanings of insecurity, of newly discovered historical temporality, of imminent and insidious democracy, of universalising 'truth' are to be transferred also into the era of Jonathan Swift. In the absence of controls through instances of the same concept studied in contemporaneous external contexts, protestant ascendancy acquires untrammelled mobility throughout dehistoricised 'time', on the basis of unverifiable and (thus) irrefutable 'evidence'. *Begriffsgeschichte* may justifiably claim to provide knowledge unavailable through empirical research. But it has never (as far as I know) sought to augment the spectral and the speculative.

More substantial problems arise, however, from the character of protestant ascendancy's being the sole instance of the concept-category to which it belongs. The concepts which preoccupy historians and social scientists are for the most part general—state, empire, revolution, etc. It is true that class is regarded by some commentators as being general in the same sense—there is/was a working class, middle class, upper class etc. But others would regard class as a quite different kind of concept, not general in the sense that one can particularise various instances of it, but pervasive in that the relations which constitute class are active in all but the most primitive modern societies. Now we must pose the question—of what concept-category is protestant ascendancy the sole instance? If that were answerable in a full and satisfactory manner, the avenue back to the early or mid eighteenth century would be blocked for those (historian or partisan) engaged in its colonisation on behalf of the protestant ascendancy.

The question posed really requires in response a comprehensive dissertation on theories of class as they appertain to Ireland over the last two centuries. Doubtless some would want to answer promptly that the protestant ascendancy was a class or sub-class; much execration and self-praise has flowed from this belief. But is this class considered as a system of relations in the Marxist sense, or class of which 'upper', 'upper middle', 'middle' are the several instances of a general concept? Instead of seeking answers to proloferating questions of this kind, it may be more profitable to make a final distinction of a technical kind. Protestant ascendancy names the sole instance of a concept-category which remains itself nameless.

A REPLY TO SOME COLLEAGUES

The present collage of essays has attempted to combine different kinds of approach to a problem in Irish cultural history preoccupying commentators for some years. Broadly speaking, one could define it as an exercise in the history of ideas, specifically located on the fault-line of sectarian difference, and (as a consequence?) in an area where the specification of differentiating ideas is left unspoken. Some circumstances of its appearance should be noted.

These relate to practical difficulties attending the exchange of scholarly opinion, as instanced in the question of Edmund Burke's alleged inattention to Ireland in the autumn of 1786 (see p. 110 above). Publication of individual articles in *Eighteenth Century Ireland / Iris an Dá Chultúr* has been rendered less than pointed by the infrequency of its appearance. Thomas Bartlett's survey of these exchanges drew attention to their substance without, perhaps, indicating their significance in methodological terms. Indeed, he was uncharacteristically sloppy in distinguishing between one contributor and another.[1] For these reasons, book publication is preferable to intermittent (and too often) isolated articles.

The most extensive recent treatment of Catholic relief as a project has been Bartlett's *The Fall and Rise of the Irish Nation*, the very title of which points to a new concept, defined neither by class nor ethnicity, nor even by confessional allegiance. This 'nation' was not to find itself for many decades after the events discussed here had ceased to ring in the world's ear. Perhaps for this reason, Bartlett's coverage of the period under scrutiny here is encapsulated in one of his shorter chapters, 'The Catholic Question and Parliamentary Reform, 1780-90'. Oddly enough, he censures Thomas Wyse for neglecting this decade in the *Historical Sketch of the Late Catholic Association of Ireland* (1829), while he himself simultaneously declines to comment on the vast bulk of printed material published in Dublin in 1786-1788. Nevertheless, it is striking how Bartlett opens the chapter in question with a bold if implicit re-locating of the emergent ideology in the post-revolutionary decade—'by 1793 the banner of "Protestant Ascendancy" had been unfurled and a last ditch found for it to flutter over.'[2] His tacit endorsement of the argument that ascendancy is a retrospective must carry weight with those who felt conceptual considerations to be mere tactics designed to discredit the old view of an Augustan elite.

The focal event or episode—the paper war set in the context of Whiteboy disturbances in Munster and the resulting debate about tithes and rents—has not itself been neglected. But the emergence of a concept of protestant ascendancy has been a persistent underlying object of examination here—with the emphasis falling on the word *concept*. Unclarity on this latter point has tended to effect an amalgamation of the two concerns, the pamphlet war and the emergence of the concept. For example, in the fifth (1990) volume of *Eighteenth Century Ireland*, James Kelly responded to an earlier article of mine, 'Eighteenth-Century Ascendancy: Yeats and the Historians'. The reply was aptly subtitled 'A Commentary', for it provided no additional evidence, and little illumination, by which the origins of protestant ascendancy might be further considered. It is my view that the difference between us essentially relates to *concepts*, what they are, how they come about, and how they are used. The difference is therefore one of fundamentals, at least for those who believe in the existence or possibility of concepts. It is for this reason that a linguistic analysis has proved a necessary extension of the bibliographical evidence, so as to avoid philosophical confusion. Dr Kelly, on the other hand, was good enough to observe that he did not think our respective positions 'as dissonant' as I had allegedly maintained. Though the tone of his 'Commentary' belies the suggestion of rapprochement, I hope I have combined argument with affability in taking the subject a little further. It may be helpful to regard our past exchanges, not as a dispute or argument, but—in Richard Rorty's phrase—'a non-encounter'.

This was the immediate disputational context. For brevity's sake, let us place Dr Kelly's version of a contested point beside my own:

MC CORMACK	KELLY
It might be more accurate, if also more pedantic, to argue that protestant ascendancy was not the issue in the paper war of 1786-88, but rather that the concept of protestant ascendancy later issued from that debate as it did from other determinants also.[3]	[Mc Cormack] has not given due attention to the eighteenth-century context out of which the formulation 'Protestant ascendancy' derives. If he had done so, I do not see how he could argue 'that Protestant ascendancy was not the issue in the paper-war of 1786-88.'[4]

What had been a contrastive judgment (not the issue in, but the issue of . . . etc.) is boiled down in the mistranscription to a bald assertion. At the heart of this latter lies a refusal to accept any distinction between phrase and concept, for bishop Woodward's eleven invocations of ascendancy (five of them unpartnered by the adjective 'protestant' and three of them referring to non-Irish affairs) are quite sufficient for my opponent's notion of an ideological concept. It is then but a further step backwards to conclude that some such concept was in play even before late 1786 (a single utterance of Boyle Roche in 1782, George Ogle's two sentences in February 1786?), and to downgrade the far more extensive evidence dating from 1792.

This sleight-of-foot allows it to be concluded that I was 'correct in claiming that the concept of "Protestant ascendancy" became more popular in the early 1790s. It would be surprising if it had not, given its elaboration in the 1780s and the fact that the century-long political domination enjoyed by Irish Protestants experienced its most severe challenge at that time.'[5] But I never claimed that the concept became 'more popular' in the early 1790s', for the good reasons that   —a) I do not hold even the *phrase* to have been popular in the 80s, and the evidence signalled in the marginal annotation (PA, NPA, A etc.) to the checklist at the heart of the present publication is surely eloquent in demonstrating the very occasional and uncertain appearance of the phrase in the paper war, and that   —b) I hold that it was only in 1792 that such a *concept* was elaborated from the earlier, infrequent, casual, and largely neglected utterances of the phrase. One notes, however, how this misrepresentation of my position, and an utter confusion of phrase and concept, facilitates the reintroduction of 'the century-long political domination enjoyed by Irish Protestants' as a veritable definition of the term under discussion. It is as if the debate on 1786 vs. 1792 had been decided in favour of 1690.

In the reply to 'Yeats and the Historians', a number of scholarly misdemeanours were laid at my door. I pleaded not guilty to these charges, not simply on the grounds that I may be right and someone else wrong, but on the more fundamental ground that the act deemed an offence was, in most instances, never committed. For example, it was claimed that I 'assess whether *The Present State* was as popular as its many editions indicate' and immediately it is further claimed 'this too is unconvincing.' Perhaps the attention paid to commercial sources (and their own vested interest) in the preceding pages ploddingly proves a point which might have been accepted from the beginning on logical grounds. But the kind of elementary distinction—between popularity of the pamphlet and acceptance of one (repeated) detail within it—is no less important than that between phrase and concept.

In this latter connection, Irish historiography and such exercises in literary theory as have been attempted in Ireland do not have many case-studies to offer by way of example or guidance in the present inquiry. Yet what is intended under the heading *Begriffsgeschichte* or 'history of concepts' is, as recent comment on Koselleck has emphasised, 'more a procedure than a definite method.' It is pursued not as an end in itelf but rather 'as a means of emphasizing the importance of linguistic and semantic analysis for the practice of social and economic history.'[6] Unremarkable as this may appear, one can only lament the contrast evident in the reply to 'Yeats and the Historians'.

On that occasion my critic described his approach as 'a contextual historical analysis of the arguments and language of . . . Woodward's tract', but nowhere got down to analysing the language as it is particularly realised in specific sentences. He argued that I omit 'to mention that Woodward identified Protestant ascendancy with Protestant control of land, dominance in the constitution, the security of the Church of Ireland and the maintenance of the British connection.'[7] Having quoted verbatim and in full all but three of the sentences in which Woodward uses the term, I deplore this allegation.

It is clear that attention to the actual use of language is at the heart of our non-encounter, and it might be conceded in Dr Kelly's defence that he uses the verb 'to identify' in a casual but unobjectionable way. (Cf. 'Oxbridge is identified with privilege in education.') However, Kelly himself summarises our differences in terms of a larger inadequacy. On the topic of Dublin Corporation in 1792, my analysis 'is also open to correction in some particulars.'[8] No doubt this is true, and constructive criticism is always welcome. Drawing on an article by Jacqueline Hill, Dr Kelly concludes that 'by the early 1790s the Corporation was not as popular a body as [Mc Cormack] believes, and had virtually abandoned the tradition of popular opposition which had produced Charles Lucas in the 1740s.' Once again, I am found guilty of an uncommitted crime. I nowhere compared the Corporation of 1792 to that of Lucas's day, I never mentioned Lucas, and far from utilising 'popular' in the (now) colloquial sense used by Drs Kelly and Hill, I wrote specifically that I was 'always, by "popular", referring to the enfranchised people'.[9]

In several admirable and lengthy contributions to the historical examination of Ireland in the 1780s, Dr Kelly has provided much evidence for our consideration in connection with the development of political ideas. However, as the instances just cited, together with the unfortunate business of Burke's inattention to Ireland while in fact visiting the place, have shown, he is not always comprehensive in his presentation of an argument nor in his summary of a dissenting opinion. We have, in these pages, more than adequately considered the limited occurrence of protestant ascendancy in the exchanges constituting the paper war. Dr Kelly has contributed in no small way to the marshalling of this evidence. But, in addition to the cumulative and positivistic side of the exercise, we should pose some negative questions. What proportion of the literature *omits* the term? And is it not odd that Woodward himself seems to have avoided the 'concept' he is said to have popularised, when he came to reflect on his activities of 1786-7?[10]

A questionable selectivity in presenting evidence also characterises Edna Longley's more recent intervention into the protestant ascendancy discussion. Her chief concern is the reputation of W. B. Yeats, and her contribution usefully demonstrates how misunderstandings about the origins of protestant ascendancy vitiate arguments about Yeats's dual commitment to poetry and politics. Furthermore, and notwithstanding an ever vigilant and most motherly protection of Yeats, Longley is officially engaged in the examination of certain 'protestant writers' at work in the aftermath of Irish Independence. As her principal heroes are Hubert Butler and John Hewitt, there is something distasteful in her relentless application of the denominational adjective—neither could be regarded as a conventional believer. What requires a little more attention here is the manner in which Yeats is obliged to serve as huckster in the transmission of her ideological reconstructions.

Let us look at the passage in question, *verbatim*. She has been quoting Butler's essay 'Portrait of a Minority' with its citation of Swift, Edward Fitzgerald, Parnell etc. as the real leaders of Irish protestant opinion (as against 'the Ulster Protestant, a more fanatical and bitter champion of the Reformation'.) And she continues:

> That the eminently reasonable Butler should echo Yeatsian pedigrees leads me to question some readings of Yeats's relation to 'Protestant Ascendancy' in W. J. Mc Cormack's *Ascendancy and Tradition* and Seamus Deane's *Celtic Revivals*. I put the term in quotation-marks because the historical geographer Kevin Whelan recently objected to its being used in social and cultural contexts, whereas it strictly signified constitutional and political discrimination in favour of Anglicans after 1690.[11]

No-one familiar with the non-convergence of historical and literary critical proceedures in recent Irish debate will be surprised to find that this questioning tackles none of the evidence adduced in *Ascendancy and Tradition* on the emergence of the phrase and concept under discussion. Instead Longley prefers an unpublished comment by a geographer. This method certainly sets the tone for her approach to Yeats. She is quick to observe that Yeats relates protestant ascendancy 'with an eighteenth-century Protestant "sense of responsibility"'.[12] In itself, this detail helps to present the poet as accepting a conventional view of 'the protestant ascendancy' as men of culture. But she fails to report that, earlier in the same passage, he had written of 'the establishment of a Protestant Ascendancy which was to impose upon Catholic Ireland, an oppression copied in all details from that imposed upon the French Protestants'. Moreover, this regime was destined—in Yeats's words—'to modernise the social structure, with great cruelty but effectively'.[13] Suppressing the cruelty, she robs Yeats of one principle in his 'historical dialectic'—his own phrase in this connection—to present a whig more whiggish than the phantom conjured up in Elizabeth Cullingford's *Yeats, Ireland, and Fascism* (1981).

I hope that these chapters exemplify larger investigations preoccupying American philosophers and Irish historians alike. It is to be hoped also that other familiar terms of debate—emancipation, union, repeal, home rule, parnellism, free state etc.—might in time be examined at some length. Nor should the list be restricted to the arena of political action. There are more general terms—Gaelic, Irish, Anglo-Irish, Ulster-Scot—which weave a spell still vulnerable to critical reflection. For the moment, one may conclude that Catholic relief succeeded in 1792/3 because no ideologically complex, nor economically viable, opposition was in the field. Protestant ascendancy gave notice of intention, nothing more. Only in the nineteenth century did the implications of ascendancy and emancipation find the means of recruiting the new dynamics of nationhood. As in *Hamlet*, relief is experienced at the beginning of the tragic action.

NOTES

ABBREVIATIONS

Some publications to which frequent reference is made, or which have confusingly similar titles, are indicated as follows:

Hill (1989)
Jacqueline Hill, 'The Meaning and Significance of "Protestant Ascendancy", 1787-1840', in *Ireland after the Union; Proceedings of the Second Joint Meeting of the Royal Irish Academy and the British Academy, London, 1986* Oxford: Oxford University Press, for the British Academy, 1989. pp. 1-22.

Kelly (1988 a)
James Kelly, 'Inter-Denominational Relations and Religious Toleration in Late Eighteenth-Century Ireland: the 'Paper War' of 1786-1788. *Eighteenth-Century Ireland / Iris an Dá Chultúir* no. 3 (1988) pp. 39-67

Kelly (1988 b)
James Kelly, 'Relations between the Church of Ireland and the Presbyterian Church in late Eighteenth-Century Ireland' *Eire-Ireland* no. 23 (1988) pp. 38-56.

Kelly (1989)
James Kelly, 'The Genesis of "Protestant Ascendancy"; the Rightboy Disturbances of the 1780s and their Impact upon Protestant Opinion' in Gerard O'Brien (ed.) *Parliament, Politics, and People; Essays in Eighteenth-Century Irish History* Dublin: Irish Academic Press, 1989. pp. 93-127.

Kelly (1990)
James Kelly, 'Eighteenth-Century Ascendancy: A Commentary' *Eighteenth-Century Ireland / Iris an Dá Chultúir* no. 5 (1990) pp. 173-187.

Mc Cormack (1982)
W. J. Mc Cormack, 'The Genesis of Protestant Ascendancy' in Francis Barker (et al. edd.) *1789 Reading Writing Revolution; Proceedings of the Essex Conference on the Sociology of Literature July 1981* Chelmsford: University of Essex, 1982. pp. 302-323.

Mc Cormack (1985)
W. J. Mc Cormack, *Ascendancy and Tradition in Anglo-Irish Literary History from 1789 to 1939* Oxford: Clarendon Press, 1985. 424pp.

Mc Cormack (1987)
W. J. Mc Cormack, 'Vision and Revision in the Study of Eighteenth-Century Irish Parliamentary Rhetoric' *Eighteenth-Century Ireland / Iris an Dá Chultúir* no. 2 (1987) pp. 7-35.

Mc Cormack (1989) W. J. Mc Cormack, 'Eighteenth-Century Ascendancy: Yeats and the Historians' *Eighteenth-Century Ireland / Iris an Dá Chultúir* no 4 (1989) pp. 150-180.

INTRODUCTION

1. See Terence Ball, James Farr and Russell L. Hanson (edd.) *Political Innovation and Conceptual Change* Cambridge: Cambridge University Press, 1989. Also Eckhart Hellmuth (ed.) *The Transformation of Political Culture: England and Germany in the Late Eighteenth Century* London: German Historical Institute; Oxford: Oxford University Press, 1990.
2. Richard Rorty *Philosophy and the Mirror of Nature* Oxford: Blackwell, 1980. p. 360.
3. Ernst Bloch 'The Artistic Illusion as the Visible Anticipatory Illumination' (1959) in *The Utopian Function of Art and Literature: Selected Essays* (trans. Jack Zipes and Frank Mecklenburg) Cambridge (Mass.): MIT Press, 1988. p. 143.
4. Theodor W. Adorno *Aesthetic Theory* (trans. C. Lenhardt) London: Routledge, 1984. See also 'Trying to Understand *Endgame*' in Adorno *Notes to Literature I* New York: Columbia University Press, 1991. pp. 241-75. See W. J. Mc Cormack 'Seeing Darkly: Notes on T. W. Adorno and Samuel Beckett' *Hermathena* No. 141 (1986) pp. 22-44. For a defence of Adorno on the truth-content of art see Fredric Jameson *Late Marxism; Adorno, or, the Persistence of the Dialectic* London: Verso, 1990.
5. The central texts of Yeats are those initially gathered in two Cuala Press volumes—*The Words Upon the Window-pane* and *The King of the Great Clock Tower; Commentaries and Poems* (both 1934). The journal *Irish Historical Studies* first appeared in 1938.
6. J. A. W. Gunn *Beyond Liberty and Property; the Process of Self-Recognition in Eighteenth-Century Political Thought* Kingston and Montreal: McGill-Queen's University Press, 1983 p. 262n.
7. See O. Brunner, W. Conze and R. Koselleck (edds.) *Geschichtliche Grundbegriffe* Stuttgart: Klett-Cotta, 1975 onwards.
8. A prime mover in the dictionary project was Richard Chenevix Trench, later archbishop of Dublin. One should not forget the Smith brothers of Cavan who had worked on words beginning Pa. See K.M.E. Murray *Caught in a Web of Words* New Haven, London: Yale University Press, 1977.

9. See Glenn Pearce and Patrick Maynard (edds.) *Conceptual Change* Dordrecht: Reidel, 1973. See also the forthcoming 2nd ed. of Mc Cormack (1985).
10. Readers who have been following earlier discussions of protestant ascendancy will be aware of the present writer's exchanges with James Kelly; see the 'Afterword' (pp. 146-50 above).
11. Thomas Mann 'Foreword' in *Joseph and His Brothers* (trans. H. T. Lowe-Porter) New York: Knopf, 1981. p. vii. The Hungarian poem quoted as the epigraph to the present chapter is Agnes Nemes Nagy's 'Akhenaton' translated by Hugh Maxton.

CHAPTER I

1. The problems of conceptualisation (for historians and others) were raised as early as 1903 in Max Weber's methodological essays: see Thomas Burger *Max Weber's Theory of Concept Formation; History, Laws, and ideal Types* Durham, N. C.: Duke University Press, 1976.
2. Friedrich Nietzsche 'All that is small and limited, moldy and obsolete, gains a worth and inviolability of its own from the conservative and reverent soul of the antiquary migrating into it and building a secret nest there.' *The Use and Abuse of History* (trans. Adrian Collins) Indianapolis: Bobbs-Merrill, 1957. p. 18. For the Burke quotation, see Mc Cormack (1985) pp. 79-80; for Curran, see Mc Cormack (1987) esp. p. 26.
3. 'Introduction' in Ciaran Brady (ed.) *Ideology and the Historians*. Dublin: Lilliput Press, 1991. p. 7.
4. Idem.
5. Richard Rorty *Objectivity, Relativism, and Truth; Philosophical Papers Volume I* Cambridge: Cambridge University Press, 1991. p.
5. Other sources include Gareth Evans *The Varieties of Reference* (Oxford: Clarendon Press, 1982); Saul A. Kripke *Naming and Necessity* (Oxford: Blackwell, 1980); John R. Searle *Speech Acts; an Essay in the Philosophy of Language* (Cambridge: Cambridge University Press, 1969). I claim no competence in philosophy itself, being concerned simply to clarify certain aspects of historians' use of language.

6. See W. J. Mc Cormack 'Setting and Ideology, With Reference to the Fiction of Maria Edgeworth' in Otto Rauchbauer (ed.) *Ancestral Voices; The Big House in Anglo-Irish Literature* Hildesheim: Georg Olms, 1992. pp. 33-60.

7. Here 'class' does not have to be taken in any strict socio-economic sense.

8. Kripke op. cit. p. 48.

9. Mc Cormack (1987) pp. 34-35.

10. Ibid. p. 35.

11. *Parliamentary Register* (1782) p. 261. An alternative reading is 'the Protestants' ascendency', to which the actual printed matter approximates with no greater degree of typographical error. The *Freeman's Journal* of 26-28/2/1782, the promptest report, had 'the Protestant ascendency', but as the *Register* appeared after the lapse of many months, its reading could be interpreted as incorporating a correction (albeit one lacking the inverted-comma apostrophe.) Neither the *Dublin Journal* nor the *Hibernian Journal* quote Roche in their coverage of the 20/2/1782 debate.

13. Kripke op. cit. p. 96.

14. Mc Cormack (1989) pp. 168-9.

15. [Richard Woodward] *The Present State of the Church of Ireland* Dublin: Sleater, 1787 [i.e. 1786]. pp. 20, 56. Unless otherwise specified, quotations are from the first 'edition' of December 1786, cited below as *Present State*. The identifying letters derive from the source cited in n14.

16. Kripke op. cit. pp. 96-7. Parentheses removed.

17. Kelly (1989) p. 116.

CHAPTER 2

1. In order to minimise the proliferation of numbers in this chapter, footnotes and footnote-figures have been avoided, with references to newspapers etc supplied in parentheses. For transcriptions of title-pages and the titles of works generally *within the checklist*, the bibliographer's practice of avoiding capital initial letters has also been adopted. Thus, within a pamphlet title transcription the appearance of an initial capital signals—where it does not relate to a proper noun—the first word of an earlier pamphlet-title which has been incorporated into the later. In keeping with modern practice, I have given page-counts by indicating the last page-number for the principal sequence: thus, a pamphlet may be longer than the 48pp. indicated here, by

virtue of a preliminary sequence given (or implicit) in small roman.

2. Nat. Libr. Ire. P. 161/8.

CHAPTER 3

1. See *The Present State* p. 4.

2. See also *The Present State* (9th 'edition) pp. 10-11.

3. Kelly (1989) p. 117.

4. Kelly (1990) p. 178.

5. Ibid. p. 182.

6. Kelly (1988.b) p. 50 and passim.

7. There is a further pamphlet ascribed to Duigenan—*A Letter to Amyas Griffith*, presented on its title-page as the work of 'Theophilus', the name with which he had signed off the *Address*. Appearing c. 9 April, it was promptly denied by Duigenan's first publisher as not being his author's work. Though it manifests a spleen as vile as anything in Duigenan, I am not convinced it is by the same hand. For one thing, it engages in rudimentary playfulness (calling Griffith 'Amy'); for another, it is published by a bookseller who otherwise does not feature in the paper war.

8. See advertisements in the *Freeman's Journal* 3-6/3/1787 p. 1, and 8-10/3/1787 p. 1.

9. *Inter alia*, Ryan also wrote *The History of the Effects of Religion on Mankind* London: Rivington, 1788. 2 vols.

10. Robert Burrowes, *A Letter to the Rev Samuel Barber* Dublin: Grierson, 1787. pp. 20-21, 29, 38, 46.

11. The ad is repeated on 10, 13, 15, 17, 20, but not on 22 and 24 February.

12. Matter quoted appears (1 March) as an addendum to the text of the ad..

13. Kelly (1989) p. 124.

14. William Hales *A Survey of the Modern State of the Church of Rome* Dublin: M'Kenzie, 1788. p. 142.

15. Joseph Stock *A Reply to the Rev Dr Campbell* Dublin: Exshaw, 1787. pp. 8-9. See *Present State* p. 17.

16. Stock p. 14.

17. Maurice Bric 'Priests, Parsons and Politics: the Rightboy Protest in County Cork, 1785-1788' in C. H. E. Philbin (ed.) *Nationalism and Popular Protest in Ireland* Cambridge: Cambridge University Press, 1987. p. 186.

18. For an account of these editions, see p. 36 above.

19. [Thomas Elrington] *Observations on the Indecent and Illiberal Strictures against the Lord*

Bishop of Cloyne Dublin: Sleater, 1787. pp. 4, 6, 7, 15, 32. Also *To the Committtee for Conducting the Free-Press* [n. t. p.] p. 6.

20. Samuel Barber *Remarks on a Pamphlet entitled The Present State of the Church of Ireland*. Dublin: Byrne, 1787. pp. 9, 14, 6,46, 51-52, 37.

21. Samuel Barber *Reply to . . . Burrowes's and . . . Ryan's Remarks* Dublin: Byrne, 24pp.

22. M. Pollard *Dublin's Trade in Books 1550-1800* Oxford: Clarendon Press, 1989. p. 21.

23. Amyas Griffith *Observations on the Bishop of Cloyne's Pamphlet* Dublin: T Byrne, 1787. p. 35.

24. William Campbell *A Vindication of the Principles and Character of the Presbyterians of Ireland* Dublin: Byrne, 1787. p. 34. The point is repeated almost verbatim later in the work—'Now as Presbyterians would maintain the Protestant ascendancy, and as they out number your church so very far, they ought to form the ecclesiastical establishment . . . ' (p. 68).

25. William Campbell *An Examination of the Bishop of Cloyne's Defence* Dublin: Byrne, 1788 p. 8.

26. Ibid. pp. 24-5, 33, 96.

27. See passage quoted in n24 above, and reference.

28. Campbell *An Examination* p. 100.

29. Kelly (1989) p. 120.

30. [Patrick Duigenan] *An Address to the Nobility and Gentry* Dublin: Watts, 1786. p. 17.

31. John Barter Bennett's copy is N.L.I. P.161/1.

32. Arthur O'Leary *Mr O'Leary's Defence* Dublin: Byrne, 1787. p. [11].

33. Ibid. pp. 29, 120.

34. Ibid. p. 53.

35. Ibid. p. 93.

36. *The Rev Mr O'Leary's Address* Dublin: Cooney, 1786. p. 13.

37. *Mr O'Leary's Defence* p. [iii].

38. *The Rev Mr O'Leary's Address* p. 24; *Mr O'Leary's Defence* p. 79.

39. *Mr O'Leary's Defence* p. 26. The whole question of passion as a debating point between protestants and Catholics was highly vexed, and nowhere more markedly than in this exchange. In *The Controversiad* (1788) O'Leary was lampooned for his concern with an American Catholic priest who had abandoned his orders and married; in *The Prelateiad*, loose living in at least one episcopal palace is charged against the Church of Ireland.

40. See George Butler 'Butler Archbishops of Cashel' *Journal of the Butler Society* no 8 (1978/9) p. 629.

41. James Butler *A Justification of the Tenets of the Roman Catholic Religion* Dublin: Byrne, 1787. p. v. See matter incorporated in n10 to the Afterword below on the rival terms for the titles held by Catholic prelates.

42. N.L.I. Ms 625; see letters of 8/2/1787 and 22/2/1787.

43. It is also an *incomplete* survey of publications issued *during the period* of the paper war. Any reader wishing to make a categorical statement in the form of NPA, PA, QPA etc. in relation to pamphlets not surveyed here should communicate their findings to the author of the present essay.

44. Arthur Browne *A Brief Review of the Question, Whether the Articles of Limerick have been Violated* Dublin: M'Kenzie, 1788. pp. 62-3.

45. *A Letter to the Bishop of Cloyne* [n.p.], 1787. pp. [3], 6.

46. *A Review of Dr Butler's Pamphlet* Dublin: Grierson, 1787. pp. 7, 14-15.

47. George Grace *A Short Plea for Human Nature and Common Sense* Dublin: Byrne, 1787. pp. 29n, 30, 45, 48.

48. *Temperate, Unborrowed Animadversions on the Pamphlet lately Published by Richard, Bishop of Cloyne* Dublin: Davis, 1787. pp. 7, 28. It seems likely that the author is the same who signed himself elsewhere as 'The Utilist'.

49. Browne op. cit. p. 62.

CHAPTER 4

1. For an attribution to Charles Brennan see R. R. Madden's *Irish Periodical Literature* vol 2 p. 323; for Sheridan's authorship (which I accept) see *Archivium Hibernicum* vol 8 (1941) p. 231.

2. M. Pollard *Dublin's Trade in Books 1550-1800* Oxford: Clarendon Press, 1989. pp. 203-9.

3. [Edward Sheridan] *A Critical Review of the B. of Cloyne's Publication*. Dublin: Chambers, 1787. p. 35. Later, still on the same subject, he writes:
'Trinity College is the most amply endowed of any other College in Europe. The Muses wanted no inducement to visit our clime: and yet Ireland has gained the opprobrious name of Boetia. Our good neighbours tell the world that we naturally want intellect as well as courage, but the *persecuted* and exiled Irish

have constantly supported, under vast difficulties, a literary as well as military fame on the most conspicuous stages in Europe.' (p. 54) In *The Question Considered* (1788), Sheridan modified his view of Trinity's role in the paper war. (See p. 20 therein.)

4. *A Critical Review* p. 35.

5. See ibid. p. 33.

6. Ibid. pp. 92-3.

7. Ibid p. 31.

8. Ibid. p. 43.

9. Ibid. p. 50.

10. Ibid. p. 85.

11. [Edward Sheridan] *The Question Considered*. Dublin: Chambers, 1788. pp. 3-4.

12. Ibid. pp. 26, 31-2.

13. *The Present State* pp. 53, 90-91.

14. Daniel Thomas *Observations on the Pamphlets by the Bishop of Cloyne, Mr Trant . . .* Dublin: printed for the author, 1787. pp. 23-5, 33; see p. 23.

15. [George Fleury?] *A Few Serious and Seasonable Observations* Dublin: Smith, 1787. pp. 68-69.

16. Ibid. p. 52.

17. See R. B. McDowell and D.A. Webb *Trinity College Dublin 1592-1952; an Academic History* Cambridge: Cambridge University Press, 1982. pp. 66-68.

18. See below.

19. McDowell and Webb p. 68.

20. Thomas Blount *Glossographia; Or a Dictionary Interpreting the Hard Words of Whatever Language now Used in our Refined English Tongue*. London: Newcomb, 1681. p. 54.

21. Michel Foucault *The Order of Things* New York: Vintage, 1973. p. 51 etc.

22. William Paley *The Principles of Moral and Political Philosophy* Dublin: Exshaw, White etc., 1785 vol 1 p. xviii-xix.

23. Amyas Griffith *Observations on the Bishop of Cloyne's Pamphlet* Dublin: T Byrne, 1787. p. 35.

24. *Present State* pp. 6, 13.

25. [Thomas Dawson] *The Mirror*, by Publicola. Dublin: Cooney, 1787. pp. 5, 57.

26. Ibid. p. 4.

27. G. W. Meadley *Memoirs of William Paley* Sunderland: Graham, 1809. p. 70.

28. Richard Whately *Dr Paley's Works* London: Parker, 1859; also Henry Christmas *Christian Politics* London: Hope, 1855.

29. *Present State* p. 5.

30. *Present State* London: Cadell, 1787. p. ix.

31. Paley op. cit. vol 2 pp. 341-342.

32. Ibid. p. 357.

33. Idem. The * signals Paley's footnote, which reads: 'Would we let the name stand, we might often attract men, without their perceiving it, much nearer to ourselves, than, if they did perceive it, they would be willing to come.'

34. Idem. The anonymous *Strictures on the Bishop of Cloyne's Present State of the Church of Ireland* (London: Dilly; Dublin: Byrne, 1787) was one of the very few pamphlets in the paper war to spot Paley as a precursor (see pp. 7, 43 etc.). Anonymous (for so it was signed) even played with Paley's discounting of denominational labels and preference for 'truth' in a preface addressed to Woodward.

35. *Present State* London: Cadell, 1787. p. xv.

36. Ibid. p. xi.

37. Paley op. cit. vol 1 p. 66.

38. Ibid. p. 67.

39. Cf. from an earlier work, 'The gospel maxims of *loving our neighbour as ourselves*, and *doing as we would be done by*, are much superior rules of life to the TO PREPON of the Greek, or the *honestum* of the *Latin* moralists, in forming ideas of which, people put in or left out just what they pleased; and better than the *utile*, or *general expediency* of the modern which few can estimate.—As motives likewise, or principles of action, they are much safer than either *the love of our country*, which has oft times been destructive to the rest of the world; or *friendship*, the almost constant source of partiality and injustice.' (1776)

40. Harry T. Dickinson 'Popular Loyalism in Britain in the 1790s' in Eckhart Hellmuth (ed.) *The Transformation of Political Culture; England and Germany in the Late Eighteenth Century* London: German Historical Institute; Oxford: Oxford University Press, 1990. pp. 503-533.

41. I have in mind John Fulton *The Tragedy of Belief; Division, Politics and Religion in Ireland* Oxford: Clarendon Press, 1991.

CHAPTER 5

1. Kelly (1990) p. 185.

2. Ibid. p. 186.

3. Holden Furber (ed.) *The Correspondence of Edmund Burke volume V July 1782—June 1789* Cambridge: Cambridge University Press, 1965. p. 282.

4. See ibid. pp. 284-90. Kelly refers to this volume of correspondence but omits to mention that Burke was in Dublin. For the tradi-

tional belief in Burke's Cork birth-place, see Conor Cruise O'Brien *The Great Melody; A Thematic Biography and Commented Anthology of Edmund Burke* London: Sinclair-Stevenson, 1992. pp. 14-15. Among notable members of the Church of England, Burke was not the only traveller in Ireland during the Paper War. John Welsey, a regular visitor who had crossed quills with Fr Arthur O'Leary in the 1770s, was in Ireland in the late spring of 1787. From his *Journal* entry for 12 May 1787, we learn that he breakfasted amicably with his old adversary; no reference to Protestant Ascendancy, or indeed to any other alleged aspect of the current controversy is recorded. Five days later in the *Dublin Evening Post* (17/5/87), we find the following comment on the War, 'So little information can be procured from the generality of pamphlets published, it is no wonder they should be so seldom attended to . . .'

5. Mc Cormack (1982) and (1985).

6. Mc Cormack (1987).

7. Mc Cormack (1989) esp. pp. 173-176.

8. *Calendar of Ancient Records of Dublin* vol 14 Dublin: Dollard, 1909. pp. 241-242.

9. For the names see *Calendar* loc. cit.; the occupations, taken from the almanacs etc. of the day, were previously given in Mc Cormack (1989) pp. 159-81. James Kelly dilates on their significance in Kelly (1990) p. 184.

10. *Calendar* loc. cit. p. 241.

11. Ibid. p. 242.

12. Ibid. pp. 243-4.

13. Brian Inglis *The Freedom of the Press in Ireland 1784-1841* London: Faber, 1954. p. 240.

14. Austin's lectures were delivered in 1955 and published seven years later, *How to Do Things with Words* Cambridge (Mass.): Harvard University Press, 1962. For an application of his ideas to the question of textual evidence see Sandy Petrey *Speech Acts and Literary Theory* London: Routledge, 1990.

15. Mc Cormack (1985) pp. 70, 75, 81-85; and (1987) pp. 23-27.

16. *A Report of the Debates in Both Houses of Parliament on the Roman Catholic Bill.* Dublin: Fitzpatrick, 1792. pp. 65-66. It would have been possible to substitute for this single volume account of the Langrishe debates the *Parliamentary Register*'s coverage of the same days. Indeed, several other texts also suggests themselves. However, the text chosen for quotation here appears to be both

fuller than some rivals, and closer in time of publication to the events than the annual volume of the *Parliamentary Register*.

17. Ibid. p. 12.

18. Ibid. pp. 45-46.

19. Ibid. p. 47.

20. Ibid. pp. 50-51.

21. Ibid. p. 47.

22. Ibid. p. 51.

23. Ibid. p. 78.

24. Ibid. pp. 90-91.

25. Ibid. p. 237.

26. Ibid. p. 226.

27. Ibid. p. 139.

28. Ibid. p. 148.

29. Ibid. pp. 129-30.

30. None of the available records of parliamentary debates for this period can be relied on to indicate accurately the relative length of the different contributions; on this topic see Mc Cormack (1987).

31. *A Report of the Debates* pp. 113-116.

32. Ibid. pp. 118, 122.

33. Ibid. p. 123.

34. Mc Cormack (1987) p. 33.

35. *A Report of the Debates* p. 151.

36. Ibid. p. 159.

37. Ibid. p. 136.

38. Ibid. p. 161.

39. Ibid. p. 216.

40. Ibid. p. 59.

41. Ibid. p. 142.

42. Ibid. p. 225-6.

43. Ibid. p. 252.

44. Ibid. p. 241.

45. Ibid. p. 16.

46. 'Letter to Richard Burke' Edmund Burke *Works* London: Bohn, 1855, vol 6 pp. 64-66.

47. See Mc Cormack (1989) pp. 175-176 n46 for David Dickson on this point.

48. Burke loc. cit. p. 69.

49. See for example, Burke to R. Burke c. 18 November 1792, P. J. Marshall and John A. Woods (eds.) *The Correspondence of Edmund Burke volume vii January 1792—August 1794* Cambridge: Cambridge University Press, 1968. p. 260.

50. See Mc Cormack (1985) p. 71.

51. See *Calendar* pp. 284-287 for the full text in which a survey of protestant/Catholic relations over the previous century does not admit the term, protestant ascendancy, until it deal with the events of 1792.

52. For the county meetings see notices in the *Dublin Evening Post* for 14/8/92 (Wexford), 23/8/92 (Tyrone), 25 /8/92 (Limerick), 28/

8/92 (Fermanagh, Armagh), 30/8/92 (Roscommon), 1/9/92 (Westmeath, Leitrim), 4/9/92 (Sligo), 8/9/92 (Kerry, Mayo, Monaghan), 11/9/92 (Louth), 15/9/92 (Carlow, Cork) etc. For Vindex on the Mayo resolutions, see 20/9/92.

53. Richard Burke to Edmund Burke, c. 8 September 1792, *Correspondence ... vii* p. 201.

54. *Calendar* p. 290. This reference to the 1792 debates and the manner in which the city fathers 'thus early watched over the Protestant ascendancy in church and state' is hardly compatible with the view that the concept had entered the public domain ten years earlier.

55. *An Address from the General Committee of Roman Catholics to their Protestant Fellow Subjects, and to the Public in General.* Dublin: Byrne, 1792. pp. 30-31.

56. [Theobald Wolfe Tone] *An Argument on Behalf of the Catholics of Ireland.* Dublin: Byrne, 1791. p. 41.

57. *A Letter to . . . Edmund Burke on the Present State of Ireland.* Dublin: Chambers, 1795. p. 5.

58. Discussion of the subsequent career of protestant ascendancy as a political concept can be traced through [William Ogilvie] *Protestant Ascendancy and Catholic Emancipation Reconciled in a Legislative Union* (London: Wright, 1800), [James Mason] *Thoughts on the Protestant Ascendancy. With an Appendix* (London: Harding; Dublin: Archer, 1805) etc.

CHAPTER 6

1. See Asa Briggs 'The Language of "Class" in Early Nineteenth-Century Britain' in Asa Briggs and John Saville (edds.) *Essays in Labour History: In Memory of G.D.H. Cole* London: Macmillan 1960. pp. 43-73. Also A. Bezanson 'The Early Use of the Term Industrial Revolution' *Quarterly Journal of Economics* vol 36 (1922) pp. 343-349. For Michelet and the renaissance see Lucien Febvre and Henri-Jean Martin *The Coming of the Book; the Impact of Printing 1450-1800* (trans. David Gerard) London: Verso, 1990. p. 11.

2. E. P. Thompson *Customs in Common* London: Merlin Press, 1991. pp. 295-6.

3. One chronicler of the nineteenth-century Irish novel has expressed the view that 'the work of the native novelists gives us glimpses of the lives of those who existed outside the Ascendancy laager.' Some clarification of the term 'native' would be healthy.

4. *The Present State* pp. 12, 58-59, 84.

5. For a discussion of this and related matters see Marianne Elliott *Watchmen in Sion; the Protestant Idea of Liberty* Derry: Field Day, 1985.

6. W. E. H. Lecky *A History of Ireland in the Eighteenth Century* London: Longmans, 1898. vol 3 p. 64. What is remarkable in Lecky is not so much his treatment of the debates of 1792 but his scrupulous avoidance of protestant ascendancy as a description of earlier circumstances.

7. See in particular J. T. Boulton *The Language of Politics in the Age of Wilkes and Burke* (London: Routledge, 1963), John Barrell *English Literature in History 1730-1780* (London: Hutchinson, 1983), Olive Smith *The Politics of Language 1791-1815* (Oxford: Clarendon Press, 1984), and Penelope J. Corfield (ed.) *Language, History and Class* (Oxford: Blackwell, 1991.)

8. Penelope J. Corfield 'Class by Name and Number in Eighteenth-Century Britain' in Corfield (ed.) p. 102.

9. Geoffrey Crossick 'From Gentlemen to the Residuum; Languages of Social Description in Victorian Britain' in Corfield (ed.) pp. 152, 156. The emphasis in *'they were more . . .* has been added by the present writer.

10. Fredric Jameson *Marxism and Form.* Princeton: Princeton University Press, 1971. pp. 333-4.

11. Crossick p. 152 n13.

12. Reinhart Koselleck *Futures Past; On the Semantics of Historical Time* (trans. Keith Tribe) Cambridge: MIT Press, 1985. p. 77. Hereafter I paraphrase Koselleck for the sake of economy, returning to his *ipsissima verba* when I wish to argue against some of his conclusions.

13. Ibid. p. 91.

14. Ibid. p. xii.

15. Ibid. p. 272.

16. Mc Cormack (1987) p. 33.

17. *The Present State* p. 84.

18. Lecky pp. 64-65.

19. *Present State* (9th 'edition') pp. 4-5.

20. *Present State* London: Cadell, 1787. p. viii.

21. Lecky p. 65.

22. Koselleck p. 91.

AFTERWORD

1. See the articles listed at the head of these notes; see also Thomas Bartlett's review of the controversy, *Irish Historical Studies* vol 28 no.

109 (May 1992) pp. 101-2 in which he writes: 'Mc Cormack remains firm in his belief that the origins of the term [sic] must be dated to 1792, and essentially to the deliberations of the socially inferior members of Dublin Corporation. Kelly's evidence that the term was in use as early as 1782, and that the phrase is to be found scattered throughout Woodward's pamphlet of 1786 is dismissed as 'casual, accidental and without consequence' or 'occasional, inconsistent or isolated', and the whole of Kelly's thesis brushed aside as 'the prehistory of protestant ascendancy' when the term itself was 'lacking in conceptual form and popular usage'. Nor surprisingly, Kelly makes a robust and, be it said, convincing reply to this criticism, and it seems clear that the origins of the term are to be located within the eighteenth-century penumbra of Protestant anxiety rather than within a specific class and that the term itself cannot be dated to a single year, let alone to a single day.'

The allusion to 'Kelly's evidence that the term was in use as early as 1782' neatly ignores the fact that this evidence was embodied two years earlier in Mc Cormack (1987). Moreover, the first sentence of Bartlett's review ignores my comments on the occurrence of the term, protestant ascendancy, in Woodward's 1786 pamphlet, comments available in *The Battle of the Books* (Gigginstown: Lilliput Press, 1986), several years before Kelly's evidence publicly stirred the surface of an inkwell. As for the determined claim that I continue to believe 'the origins of the term [sic] must be dated to 1792', I can only refer to an even earlier source (1985) where I write (with, I thought, a discernible nuance of caution) that *'as a potent collocation* [emphasis now added], Protestant Ascendancy may be dated with some certainty to the early weeks of 1792.' (*Ascendancy and Tradition in Anglo-Irish Literary History from 1789 to 1939* Oxford: Clarendon Press, 1985. p. 68).

It is perhaps pointless to advise detractors of this argument to attempt some elementary distinction between term and concept, or at least to acknowledge that their antagonist posits such a distinction.

2. Thomas Bartlett *The Fall and Rise of the Irish Nation; The Catholic Question 1690–1830* Dublin: Gill & Macmillan, 1992. p. 103. James Kelly's *Prelude to Union: Anglo-Irish Politics in the 1780s* (Cork: Cork University Press, 1992) had not appeared in time for

incorporation into the secondary literature analysed here, but see p. 244 thereof for his brief allusion to the 'outbreak of agrarian disorder in Munster in 1785' on which occasion victory 'went to the conservatives', who (it is claimed) 'developed and popularised the ideological concept of "Protestant Ascendancy" . . .'

3. Mc Cormack (1989) p. 163.
4. Kelly (1990) p. 178.
5. Ibid. p. 186.
6. See Reinhart Koselleck *Futures Past: On the Semantics of Historical Time* (trans. Keith Tribe) Cambridge, Mass.: MIT Press, 1985. p. xiii.
7. Kelly (1990) pp. 180, 181.
8. Ibid p. 184.
9. Mc Cormack (1989) p. 175. I also stand accused of wrongly charging my opponent with 'neglect of the non-conformist response' to Woodward, and an article (Kelly 1988b) is cited in evidence. Again the accusation flies wide of the mark. In replying to two specified articles, I am not psychically empowered to anticipate the contents of a third, still forthcoming when I was writing.
10. The Cambridge University Library's copy of Richard Woodward's *Charge* (1793) contains extensive though anonymous annotations (see pp. 8, 10, 11, 12, 24, 28, 29, 30, 31, 32, 36, 41.) Two are of particular interest: –
i) 'This is the first instance of a Protestant Bishop's giving the Title R. Cath Archbishop & Bishop to the Roman Catholic Prelates, who were always hitherto affectedly stiled *Titular Bishops.*' (p. 11)
ii) 'There are some excellent Remarks in this Charge on the misapplication of *liberality*, on the Consequences of mistaken Philosophy.' (p. 41)

Though these indicate that the annotator was respectful of Woodward's abilities, there is no doubt that he was sympathetic to the Catholic position—if not a Catholic himself. Woodward is described (p. 28) as 'the chief controversial protestant in Ireland'.

11. Edna Longley ' "Defending Ireland's Soul": Protestant Writers and Irish Nationalism after Independence' in Vincent Newey and Ann Thompson (edd.) *Literature and Nationalism* Liverpool: Liverpool University Press, 1991. pp. 198-224. Longley never questions whether these lists of protestant liberals might not be sentimental exercises in pedigree-peddling, nor inquires if some of the heroes (Smith-O'Brien, for example) might

look less liberal if one examined attitudes towards the colonisation of Australia. Such is the power of Yeats to deprive his admirers of the critical faculty.

12. Longley loc. cit. p. 201.

13. W. B. Yeats 'Commentary on "A Parnellite at Parnell's Funeral"', *The King of the Great Clock Tower, Commentaries and Poems* Dublin: Cuala Press, 1934. p. 23.

INDEX

Certain pervasive items (indicated by *) are indexed selectively; material in the bibliographical list (pp. 33–50) and the end-notes is treated similarly.